Searching for Solace

Searching for Solace

A BIOGRAPHY OF
ABDULLAH YUSUF ALI
INTERPRETER OF THE QUR'AN

by
M A Sherif

Islamic Book Trust, Kuala Lumpur

First published in
Kuala Lumpur 1994
by
Islamic Book Trust
3 Lorong 1A/71G,
Jalan Carey
46000 Petaling Jaya,
Malaysia

ISBN 983 9154 00 1

COVER
Of Beliefs, Emotions and Sensations.
Suleymaniah Mosque, Istanbul
Photograph by Gulzar Haider

BOOK AND COVER DESIGN
Zafar Abbas Malik
Imtiaze Ahmed Manjra

PRINTED BY
Percetakan Zafar Sdn. Bhd
Kuala Lumpur

Contents

I would like to record my sincere appreciation to the following for their assistance: Fayazuddin Ahmed, Manazir Ahsan, Iqbal Asaria, Mrs Jasmine Ansari, Abdul Kadir Barkatullah, Fakhri Davids, Maryam Davies, AbdulWahid Hamid, Professor Hamidullah, Inam-ul-Haq Sahib, Zill-e-Hasnain, Maqsood Ali Kazmi, Parvez Manzoor, Ismail Ahmed Meenai, Sharif Al-Mujahid, Yusuf Omar, Khwaja Qamaruddin, Raisuddin Sahib, Mian Muhammad Shafi, Tayeb Sherif, Tariq Solaija.

Dr Z.H. Zaidi of the School of Oriental & African Studies, University of London, provided valuable advice and encouragement. Professor K.K. Aziz also offered detailed comments on the manuscript. I am indebted to both these historians while alone accepting responsibility for the conclusions in this book.

I am grateful to the library staff of many institutions and archives for their expertise. In particular I should like to thank the following and, where appropriate, acknowledge permission to quote from collections: India Office Library & Records, London; Royal Commonwealth Society, London; Lincoln's Inn, London; Greater London Records Office and Library, London; Public Record Office, Somerset House and Kew; University of London Library; St John's College, Cambridge; Kent Archives Office, Maidstone; Quaid-e-Azam Academy, Karachi; Quaid-e-Azam Library, Lahore; Punjab Public Library, Lahore; Anjuman-Himayat-ul-Islam, Lahore.

Mr and Mrs Brockbank kindly provided access to documents on Yusuf Ali's house in Wimbledon, London. Mrs Khalida Rahman applied her professional expertise in restoring unique photographic material from old newspaper cuttings.

Copies of Crown copyright documents in the Oriental and India Office Collection of the British Library appear by permission of the Controller of Her Majesty's Stationery Office. Formal acknowledgements are also due to the Master, Fellows and Scholars of St John's College, Cambridge, for permission to quote from Yusuf Ali's admission details; the Royal Institute of International Affairs, for permission to quote from *Modern India and the West* (published by Oxford University Press, 1941, for the Royal Institute of International Affairs, London); Michael Joseph Ltd and the British Library for permission to reproduce the photograph of Yusuf Ali from *A Venture of Faith* by Sir Francis Younghusband, published by Michael Joseph Ltd. (1937); Mr Muazzam Ali and the International Centre for Islamic Studies (ICIS), London, for permission to quote from the M.A.Bogra papers (due to be published by ICIS).

Abbreviations

The following abbreviations have been used in the notes that accompany each chapter:

AHI Register *Ru'idad Ijlas* Register of the Proceedings of the General Council of the *Anjuman-Himayat-ul-Islam* (Society for the Protection of Islam), Lahore.

IOL India Office Library and Records, London.

PP Punjab Press Abstract, Vol. XXXIX, 1926.

PRO Public Record Office, Kew, London.

YA Yusuf Ali's personal collection of newspaper cuttings, pamphlets, typescripts and letters in the author's possession. Yusuf Ali's numbering scheme has been retained.

The winter of 1953 was a harsh one in Britain. On Wednesday 9 December, a confused old man was found out of doors, sitting on the steps of a house in Westminster. The police took him to Westminster Hospital. He was discharged the following day and a London County Council home for the elderly in Dovehouse Street, Chelsea, took him in. He suffered a heart attack on 10 December and was rushed to St Stephen's Hospital in Fulham. Three hours after admission he died. Unusually, there were no relatives to claim the body and arrange for the funeral. However, the deceased was known to the Pakistan High Commission and as soon as the Coroner for the County of London had completed the inquest, an Islamic burial was arranged in the Muslim section of Brookwood cemetery, Surrey. So, in these enigmatic circumstances, ended the remarkable life of Abdullah Yusuf Ali, at the age of 81.

Yusuf Ali is best known for his monumental English translation of and commentary on the Qur'an, first published in 1934 and subsequently printed for sale and free distribution on an unprecedented scale. The voluminous 'Yusuf Ali' is a standard reference in mosques and homes in the English-speaking Muslim world, perhaps the most widely circulated work of twentieth-century Islamic scholarship. The reputation of the work appears to have been enhanced by the passage of time, a tribute to the author's accurate rendering of the Qur'anic Arabic, command of English expression and erudition.

The need for a biography of Yusuf Ali has been keenly felt, particularly by readers of his work on the Qur'an curious to know what sort of man was behind such a *tour de force*. Entries on him are to be found in a few biographical directories, but these are not commonly available and their contents possess a hagiographic quality. When Yusuf Ali died the obituary notices in the Muslim press contained far less factual detail than those in *The Times* or *The Daily Telegraph* of London. The Muslim world seems to have settled for an image of a quiet scholar with mystical leanings and left it at that, a gross injustice to a life of political involvement, prolific literary output and public service.

Yusuf Ali belonged to a brilliant generation of Muslims of the Indian subcontinent, all born in the 1870s, who acquired an Oxbridge education or underwent training for the Bar in London or, as in the case of Yusuf Ali, both. This was a generation which included Muhammad Ali Jinnah, Muhammad Ali Jauhar and Muhammad Iqbal, and lesser known but influential personalities like Fazli Husain and Shaikh Abdul Qader. Yusuf Ali did not possess the genius of a Jinnah or Iqbal, the dash of a Jauhar, or the political acuity of a Fazli Husain. These contemporaries were to take the star roles in the making of modern Muslim history, but it is a tribute to Yusuf Ali's versatility that he was never far from the centre stage and while the casts changed and the prima donnas burnt themselves out, he continued as a minor but persistent player. Yusuf Ali participated in a startling number of key events, from the 1919 Paris Peace Conference to the Unionist-Muslim League cold war prior to Partition. He presided over numerous educational conferences and was an acknowledged expert on Indian education. He served on the 1932 Punjab University enquiry committee, was a member of its senate and played a role in the Unionist government's far-reaching educational programme for Punjab. Yusuf Ali was not only acquainted with the leadership of his generation, but had met and was influenced by the great Muslim personalities who made their mark in the nineteenth century – men like Sir Sayyid Ahmed Khan of Aligarh fame; Justice Badruddin Tayebji, one of the early leaders of the Indian National Congress; and Sayyid Ameer Ali, jurist and author of *The Spirit of Islam*.

Yusuf Ali was a man of extraordinary industry and deep emotion. His personal turmoil and triumphs are of interest in their own right, but his life possessed a richness of experience which can be used to obtain a better understanding of a momentous period of modern Muslim history. By delving into his life, it is possible to relive some of these moments and appreciate the pressures of the time.

The second half of the twentieth century has witnessed a struggle for the reassertion of 'spiritual' and 'political' Islam as an integrated whole in Pakistan and elsewhere. Yusuf Ali's intellectual attitudes demonstrate how the truncated version of Islam was a consequence of colonisation. It was an approach to become well entrenched in the consciousness of Muslims. In recounting the circumstances in which such an attitude took root in the Muslim psyche in the first place there is perhaps an opportunity to better understand the condition and exorcise it.

This book is in two parts: the first is a chronological account of his personal and public life; the second draws out the themes which stand out most prominently in his activities, writings and speeches. There are also two appendices. *Appendix One* is a bibliography of Yusuf Ali's published work and includes reviews he received and obituary notes. *Appendix Two* is a selection from his writings between 1906 and 1942. Yusuf Ali's conception of Islam accompanied particular political preferences and the extracts have been primarily selected because they shed light on the type of synthesis of ideas that came about. Some extracts have also been included because the subject matter is of continuing historical relevance and Yusuf Ali's scholarship in these fields warrants their wider circulation.

The great Muslim personalities of this century have been inadequately researched by Muslim biographers. There is a genre of orientalist scholarship which has been quick to identify patterns of social change in Muslim society, but has paid a price for such broad-brush analysis in its ready typecasting of individuals. It will be a tragedy if the Muslims themselves cannot preserve the miniature portrait, so that when the time is right the collection can be re-examined without the preconceived notions of Western scholarship. Here is a challenge for Muslim historians to delve for themselves and do something about preserving our history.

Part I

Biographical Accounts

I

FOUNDATIONS

Muslim India effectively became British India after the Battle of Baksar in 1763. This military defeat in Bihar was to force the Mughal Shah Alam II to confer on the London-based East India Company the right to collect land taxes and administer civil justice, concessions which allowed Britain to introduce a class of English administrators in place of Muslim officers. The plunder of India then commenced in earnest, wealth both for the shareholders of the Company and to finance wars and annexations in and around India. The power of Tipu Sultan of Mysore was broken in 1799 and by 1818 most of India was under British control. The Hindus became the new confidants of the British administration and the Muslims were left outsiders in their own homeland.

Muslim influence was further circumscribed after the failed revolt of 1857. There was to be a terrible military and economic vengeance for this 'disloyalty' and the punitive measures included restrictions on the use of Urdu as an official language and even fewer employment opportunities in public services and government. The revolt, however, forced Britain to adopt a new regime for India, in which the authority of the Board of the East India Company was replaced by that of the British Parliament, exercised through a Secretary of State for India, to whom a Viceroy of India and the Indian Civil Service were made responsible. The Indian exchequer bore the cost of the India Office in London, the Indian Army and the Indian Civil Service.

The Muslims began to rebuild their institutions in the 1870s. A group in Bombay formed an *Anjuman-e-Islam* in 1876, which included a school project for their children. In 1877 Sayyid Ahmed Khan, better known as Sir Sayyid, founded a college at Aligarh in the conviction that Muslim survival rested on its standard of education.[1] The Central National

3

Muhammadan Association was also established in the same period by Sayyid Ameer Ali in Calcutta. Some years later in 1884 the *Anjuman-Himayat-ul-Islam* was formed in Lahore to work in the fields of education and social welfare, and it founded Islamia College. These decades of institution-building coincided with the emergence of Muslim scholars with a command of the English language which they deployed in the defence of Islam.[2]

Abdullah Yusuf Ali was born on 4 April 1872, in Surat, a textile town in Gujrat, Western India, which formed part of the 'Presidency of Bombay' in the days of the Raj. He belonged to a mercantile community known as the *Bohras*, who trace their Muslim ancestry to the efforts of preachers dispatched by the Fatimid caliphs in Cairo. Religious doctrine required the community to be led by a supreme leader, the *da'i*, though succession to this office was a frequent source of dissension. One such dispute led to the *Dawudi* and *Sulaimani* split, around the reign of the Mughal Emperor Akbar in the sixteenth century. The *Bohras* in general were deeply involved in trading activities in Surat and Bombay, though in 1920 Yusuf Ali was sufficiently well known to be cited as an example of a *Dawudi Bohra* who was an exception to this rule.[3]

In not following the traditional *Bohra* professions, Yusuf Ali was emulating his father. He was the second and younger son of Yusufali Allahbuksh, an official in Surat's police force. On retirement in 1885, Allahbuksh was given the title of *Khan Bahadur*, an award the Raj bestowed on Muslims for some act of public service or philanthropy.[4]

Yusuf Ali's name was to be subject to many variations. When applying to enter Cambridge in 1891 he used 'Abdullah Khan Bahadur Yusuf-Ali', unusual because it incorporated his father's title, not a hereditary rank. This could not have been an oversight because he repeated it when registering at Lincoln's Inn later in the year. When applying to join the Indian Civil Service (ICS) in 1894, Yusuf Ali entered 'Abdullah ibn Khan Bahadur Yusuf Ali' on the application form filled in in his own hand, but the signature used was 'Abdullah KB ibn Yusuf Ali', the variation reflecting an uncertainty in his own mind. The inclusion of *ibn* (son of) was again an unusual feature in the name of an Indian Muslim. The India Office administrator responsible for processing ICS applications deemed a

4

double-barrelled surname in order and 'Abdullah ibn Khan Bahadur Yusuf-Ali' came about.[5] Yusuf Ali settled for this cumbersome form for many years, sometimes even using 'A.I.K.B. Yusuf-Ali' in correspondence. It was from the 1920s that the far less formal 'Abdullah Yusuf Ali', in its unhyphenated form, came into common usage.

The young Yusuf Ali's concern with rank and status manifested itself in other ways. Yusufali Allahbuksh died in July 1891 and in October of the same year Yusuf Ali described his father's profession as 'formerly Government Inspector of Police'. However, by November 1891 this occupation had changed to 'deputy commissioner' and in 1894 Yusuf Ali would prefer 'municipal commissioner'.[6] Curiously, an Indian biographical directory published in 1911, in its entry on Yusuf Ali, described his father as Shaikh Yusuf Ali Shujauddin, Khan Bahadur, 'a prominent member of Surat Municipality'.[7] When Yusuf Ali died in 1953, an obituary notice even described his father as a former chairman of Surat municipality.[8]

Though the main *Dawudi Bohra* religious seminary, the *Jamia Saifiya*, was located in Surat, Yusufali Allahbuksh chose a separate route for his son's education. Yusuf Ali was sent away from Surat to Bombay, to attend the new school of the *Anjuman-e-Islam* and then a missionary school named after its Scots founder, John Wilson. He joined Wilson's School around 1882, so he was barely eight or nine years old when first despatched from home.[9]

There was a marked contrast between the two educational institutions attended by Yusuf Ali. The aim of the Anjuman was the 'amelioration of the Muhammadan community and to effect some improvement in their educational, moral and social state'.[10] The men behind it were Muhammad Ali Roghay, a rich shipbuilder, and the talented Tayebji brothers, Kamruddin and Badruddin, who were the first Muslim solicitor and barrister of Bombay respectively. In the only expression of political independence really open to the Muslims at the time, the Anjuman was enthusiastically pro-Ottoman. During the Russo-Turkish war of 1876-77, meetings to raise funds for the Ottomans were organised and on one occasion 20,000 rupees were collected on the spot.

The Anjuman's school opened in September 1880, after much lobbying, persuasion and petition to convince the Bombay Government that

5

Muslims genuinely needed their own denominational school. Fifty children were enrolled in the first week, but these grew to several hundred very quickly. Badruddin was dedicated to the Anjuman school and watched over its activities personally. Other pupils at the Anjuman included two of the Tayebji sons and for a while Muhammad Ali Jinnah, then known as Jinnahbhoi. Teaching was in Urdu and English, though the choice of the former was significant because the dominant language of Western India was and remains to this day Gujrati. However the teaching of Urdu was an important part of the Anjuman's case for a separate school, on the grounds that this was the Muslim language of India. The British-style education was also a basic *raison d'etre* of the school, because too few Muslim children were qualifying for further education. Both Yusuf Ali and Jinnah retained their respect and friendship for the Tayebjis. When Badruddin died in London in 1906, Yusuf Ali was present at the funeral, and in a moving speech recalled his days at the Anjuman school, 'under the wings of Badruddin'.[11] Jinnah too remembered the school and in a will drawn up in 1939 arranged for a sum to be left to it from his estate.[12] The ethos at the Anjuman was uplifting and forward-looking, exemplified by its leadership's attempt to unite the different Muslim communities of Bombay. The great aim of his life, Badruddin Tayebji once said, was to 'cement these discordant elements into one compact mass whose catchword will be "Islam" without any of the later differences.'[13] The Anjuman became a hub of activity which brought together *Sunni, Dawudi Bohra, Sulaimani Bohra* and reformist *Khoja* Muslims. It was a tradition which both Jinnah and Yusuf Ali, and other products of the Anjuman powerhouse such as Akbar Hydari – the first Indian accountant-general and active in the formation of Osmania University, Hyderabad – were to uphold.

Badruddin Tayebji became a judge of the High Court and a president of the Indian National Congress, the political party through which Indian aspirations for political independence were first expressed. The prosperous and confident Bombay Muslims' natural inclination was to seek out Hindu-Muslim cooperation in the struggle for independence. Sir Sayyid Ahmed Khan in Northern India and Ameer Ali in Bengal did not share this perspective. They were wary of such an alliance and felt that Muslims' political interests coincided more closely with those of the British and that

6

special safeguards were required to protect the community's interests.[14] This was a complex and keenly contested debate that was to spill over to Yusuf Ali's generation as well.

Allahbuksh did not leave his son long at the Anjuman, either sensing that political controversy would affect educational standards or at the prompting of his friend and superior in the police service, Frederic Lely. Yusuf Ali was enrolled in the school of the Free Church of Scotland, a matter easily arranged by Lely because his wife was a daughter of a missionary of this Church based in Poona.[15] Yusuf Ali was uprooted a second time, from the family-like atmosphere of the Anjuman school to the formal setting of a Scots-run institution. His new surroundings were stamped with the personality of its founder, the eponymous Rev. John Wilson, a noteworthy linguist, specialist in the antiquities of Western India and translator of the Bible into Marathi.[16] Yusuf Ali attended Wilson's School till the age of 15, matriculating in 1887, before moving on to its senior section, Wilson College, which was affiliated to the University of Bombay.

Yusuf Ali was one of those children who are born as adults. Educational institutions were to be his real home from a very early age, in which the memorable occasion was more likely to have been a dormitory function or a college ceremony, rather than a family festivity. It was an upbringing that bestowed on the young Yusuf Ali an early seriousness and maturity. A testimonial from his college principal, Rev. Mackichan – who completed the Marathi translation of the Bible commenced by Wilson – portrays a punctilious eighteen-year-old, 'I have known Mr Abdullah Yusuf-Ali for a number of years – all through his school and University course in Bombay – and have much pleasure in testifying to the excellent character which he has always borne in his private and student life.'[17] It is a testimonial to the determination of a young boy of humble origins to apply himself and grasp whatever opportunities came his way.

A staff member's account of the College a decade after Yusuf Ali's time provides some indication of the ethos of the institution: 'Wilson College students were the plain-living group of Bombay students then – St Xavier and Elphinstone attracted the richer people. Many of our students came from the Konkan villages - many were Chipawan Brahmins - and we had a good many Gujratis, Sindhis, and Parsees, a few Mussalman and

Beni-Israel as well as Christian and Anglo-Indian students. They were all hard workers. Examinations dominated their study.'[18]

Yusuf Ali's short-lived family years were immensely precious to him and there is a glimmer of a sense of loss in a passage written when middle-aged: 'It was between the ages of four and five that I first learned to read its [the Qur'an's] Arabic words, to revel in its rhythm and music, and wonder at its meaning. I have a dim recollection of the *Khatm* ceremony which closed that stage...My revered father taught me Arabic, but I must have imbibed from him into my innermost being something more, - something which told me that all the world's most beautiful languages and literatures are but vehicles for that ineffable message which comes to the heart in rare moments of ecstasy.'[19] Biographical references such as these are rare in his published work and the singular silence on his mother or elder brother is poignant evidence of an emotional void.[20] The self-discipline from an early age and a truncated childhood left other scars. Yusuf Ali could be inordinately effusive to those offering him friendship and there is a clue to a complex and sensitive temperament in this tribute to Sir Roland Wilson, a tutor at Cambridge: 'To have known him for 28 years, to have conversed with him in intimate talk in public and private questions in the changing kaleidoscope of the world, to have won his confidence and to have been associated with him in links of mutual respect and affection; these experiences are among the most cherished treasures of my life. May his soul rest in peace.'[21] Independence at an early age often fosters a resilience but in Yusuf Ali's case it left a vulnerable and brittle disposition. Though his public persona was charming, colleagues found him touchy and sensitive. He was quick to feel misunderstood and victimised, but immensely gratified when accepted as a confidant or initiated into a select circle.

The proselytizing Free Presbyterian missionaries of Wilson College were remarkable men, no less so than the founders of the Anjuman. Mackichan, for example, had distinguished himself in physics at the University of Glasgow. His teacher, Lord Kelvin, had personally presented him with one of the first Kelvin electrometers, which ended up in the physics laboratory at Wilson College. 'To the pupils who sat at his feet – among whom I had the privilege of being one,' Yusuf Ali was to write on

Mackichan's death, 'his beloved personality left at once a cherished memory and a fountain of inspiration.'[22] However, Wilson College, like other missionary schools, was about more than merely creating enthusiastic scholars, equipped to pass examinations successfully. In Mackichan's own words, 'The College stands for that which appeals to the religious mind of India and we believe that it is this contact of professors and students in the deepest and highest things of life that lies at the root of its influence on the lives of young men and women who fill its class-rooms and has made it in any degree effective in elevating the moral and spiritual tone of the present generation.'[23] There is little need to second-guess what was considered to be the source of the 'deepest and highest things of life'. In the words of University of Bombay's vice-chancellor in Yusuf Ali's time, 'The Indian people, by the Counsels of Providence, have been brought into contact with the most restless, progressive and enterprising nation of Europe - a people who have their very being in liberty and free discussion, and whose example is so contagious that it affects all who come within its sphere. Deliberately and without craven fear, we have invited the youths of India to study our history and our literature. We have permeated them with our ideas, and held ourselves as a worthy example for their imitation.'[24] In the face of this superior intellectual attitude, young Muslim minds had difficult choices to make. Those lacking confidence in their own culture and religion would mould themselves in their master's image. Yusuf Ali had been given a foundation at the Anjuman school, so he was slightly better equipped than most to tackle the onslaught.

Yusuf Ali had a brilliant academic record at Wilson School, matriculating top of his year for Bombay at the age of fourteen. He proceeded to obtain a first-class BA from Bombay University in January 1891, possibly in Classics because he won a Latin prize and was appointed to the Dakshna Fellowship in Greek history at his old college.[25] Yusuf Ali was awarded a Bombay Government scholarship for further studies in England, under a scheme instituted in 1868, in which nine students were sent annually from India for further studies in Britain. The scholars were free to select their course of study, and 'each scholarship would entitle the holder to an allowance of £200 per annum, payable from his date of arrival in England, and would be tenable for three years.'[26]

9

Khan Bahadur Allahbuksh died in July 1891, leaving his younger son few family ties in India. In September, Yusuf Ali arrived in England, still a teenager. It must have been an ordeal, alone in an unfamiliar world barely a few months since the loss of a father whom he revered. A civil service record notes, 'Herewith report arrival of Abdullah KB Yusuf Ali, Bombay Govt. Scholar. I have not seen him as he is living at Brighton but have written asking to be informed as to the day he is to be in London that I may make the necessary arrangements.'[27] Yusuf Ali chose to go up to St John's College, Cambridge and supported his application form with letters of testimony from his former principal Mackichan, as well as one from an M H Abdul-Ali, who wrote his letter of reference on notepaper of the National Liberal Club, 'I have much pleasure in bearing testimony – from personal knowledge – to the high personal character of Mr Abdullah K B Yusuf Ali, a distinguished graduate of the Bombay University.'[28] By 1913 Yusuf Ali himself would be clubbing at the National Liberal. Yusuf Ali studied law at St John's from the Michaelmas term of 1891. In 1895, he was awarded a Tripos with a good Second, coming seventh in second class in the Part I exams of 1894 and 4th in second class in Part II in 1895.

The prized career of the period was in the Indian Civil Service, the legendary ICS, the cadre which truly ruled India. In the words of Lord Macaulay, Victorian England's oracle on Indian matters, the ICS entrance examinations were aimed to receive only those who had 'the best, the most liberal and the most finished education' that Britain could provide. Standards were high, but there was a morbid preoccupation to exclude Indians, clearly seen in Viceroy Curzon's remark of 1900: 'Some day I must address you about the extreme danger of the system under which every year an increasing number of the 900 and odd higher posts that were meant, and ought to have been exclusively and specifically reserved, for Europeans, are being filched away by the superior wits of the Native in the English examination. I believe it to be the greatest peril with which our administration is confronted.'[29] The stratagems to make entry into the Service difficult for Indians included the limited scholarship period of three years, the upper age limit of twenty-two and the need to come to London for the examinations. In spite of these odds, or perhaps because of them, the ICS seemed to be a natural aspiration for bright young Indians of the time like Yusuf Ali and Muhammad Ali Jauhar.

While still based at Cambridge, not at the College but at 35 Thompson's Lane, Yusuf Ali applied to be a candidate in the ICS open competition examination held in August 1894. His College tutor, Rev. JT Ward, provided a reference. Yusuf Ali demonstrated his 'superior wit' by obtaining top marks in English composition and also excelling in Roman and English Law. However entry was a two-tier procedure and the short-listed 'probationers' were required to take a final examination in the September of the following year. The interim period could be passed at an approved university or college. Though Yusuf Ali's Bombay Government scholarship was for three years only, he was able to circumvent this financial hurdle and spent his probationary year with characteristic industry on the Part II law tripos at Cambridge, studies at University College, London, preparations for the ICS final exams and working for his admission to the Bar.[30]

The second round of examinations were more relevant to a career in India and included three compulsory subjects: Indian Penal Code and Criminal Procedure Code, Urdu and the History of British India. There was also a range of optional subjects. Yusuf Ali sat for the Code of Civil Procedure and Indian Contract Act, Arabic and horsemanship. He came top of the list, performing particularly well in languages, and gaining, out of 400, 385 in Urdu and 340 in Arabic.[31] He was informed of his success in October 1895 and assigned by the India Office to the North-Western Provinces of Agra and Oudh, later better known as the United Provinces (UP), even though his preference was for the Bombay Presidency.

The journey to India was in two legs, first by ship to the Adriatic port of Brindisi in Italy and second by ocean liner to Bombay. Yusuf Ali wished to delay his return to the end of the year. The changed plan required him to travel overland to Brindisi, which led to a slight wrangle with the authorities over expenses. One of Yusuf Ali's earliest letters to the India Office, written on 5 November 1895 from 20 Keppel Street, Russell Square, relates to this matter:

Dear Sir,
I am obliged to you for your letter of the 1st inst. As the Govt will not

be able to take my overland passage to Brindisi, I beg to ask whether it would make *any* allowance to me towards the expenses of the railway ticket.

I ought to mention that I cannot start from London much before the 27th Dec. for the reason I mentioned to the India Office when I obtained the extension of time within which I have to report myself in India; and starting on the 29th from London, if I went all the way by sea, I should hardly be in India in time. That is the reason why I find it necessary to go overland.

But of course I must and will most loyally abide by the decision of the India Office as to whether any allowance should be made towards the expenses of the railway journey.

I remain
faithfully yours

Abdullah ibn Yusuf-Ali[32]

The letter reveals a deference that was to be the theme of his relationship with Britain. Yusuf Ali had formalities to complete at Lincoln's Inn which may have prompted the postponement.[33]

By all accounts Yusuf Ali had an exciting, fulfilling and rewarding four years in England. He was to retain affection for his student days at Cambridge: 'The few years that I spent there were to make me a student in the real sense, awakening in me an insatiable urge to acquire knowledge and a love of study.'[34] There were also dramatic events to witness, like Dadabhai Naoroji's maiden speech in the House of Commons as the newly elected Liberal MP for Central Finsbury, and preparations for that grand event of pomp and display, Queen Victoria's Diamond Jubilee. It was a time when Indians were still a curiosity in Britain, politeness and gentility prevailed and racial prejudices were less on display. Yusuf Ali had been under age on arrival and was found a guardian, perhaps with help from his father's friend Lely. This guardian was 'a Christian Englishman in the highest sense of the term.'[35] The young Yusuf Ali was also befriended by two Englishmen who were to guide and encourage him in literary ventures in the years to come: George Birdwood, expert on Indian arts, and Roland Knyvet

Wilson, reader in Indian Law at Cambridge and an ICS coach in the same subject.[36]

Yusuf Ali, Jauhar and Jinnah were near contemporaries and though they would soon represent very different shades of Muslim opinion, there was a period when the three seemed interchangeable. All were Anglophiles, aesthetes, with a style and panache which came through in their sartorial elegance. Jauhar had been an ICS aspirant, but failed the examinations and ironically, on returning to India, commenced political activity in the UP and rapidly became a thorn in the flesh of the very same administration to which Yusuf Ali was attached.[37] Muhammad Ali Jinnah, who had joined Lincoln's Inn as a student in 1893, qualified within a few months of Yusuf Ali. Unlike the others he had not been tempted to the ICS, but then his early passion was to be a Shakespearean actor, before his father disabused him of these fanciful notions and he was saved for greater things.

Notes to Chapter 1

1   "I assure you that the only thing which can raise you to a high rank is education. Until our nation can give birth to highly-educated people it will remain degraded; it will be below others, and will not attain such honour as I desire for it. These precepts I have given you from the bottom of my heart"; from Sir Sayyid's speech delivered at Lucknow, 28 December 1887. See A.M. Zaidi, *Evolution of Muslim Political Thought*.

2   For example Ameer Ali's *The critical examination of the life and teachings of Muhammad*, published in 1873, was a response to Clark's *Ten Great Religions*; while visiting England in 1869, Sir Sayyid responded to Muir's *The life of Muhammad*.

3   A.A. Engineer, *The Bohras*, p.147, quoting from *Gulzare-e-Dawudi*.

4   In his application to St John's, Cambridge, in October 1891, Yusuf Ali stated his father's full name to be 'Yusuf-Ali Alabux', preceded with the following note in brackets, 'Khan Bahadur, title bestowed on him by Government about 1885?'. The entry on 'Father's rank or calling' is 'formerly Government Inspector of Police (retired about 1885?)'.

   The entry for Yusuf Ali in *Alumni Cantabrigienses*, compiled by J.A. Venn, University of Cambridge, 1954, notes that his father was formerly 'Government Inspector of Police, died July 22 1891'.

5   IOL: L/P&J/381, file 1673. Yusuf Ali's application form to join the ICS in 1894 bears red ink amendments made by India Office staff.

6   Yusuf Ali applied to the Bar at Lincoln's Inn in November 1891, providing his particulars as 'Abdullah Khan Bahadur Yusuf-Ali, second son of Khan Bahadur Yusuf-Ali, late of Surat, Bombay, India. Deputy Commissioner Surat Dish (Dist.?)'; see Lincoln's Inn Admission Register 1420-1893, p.437; see also IOL: L/P&J/381, ibid. where his father's occupation is recorded as 'municipal commissioner'. When Yusuf Ali married for the first time in 1900, the marriage register recorded his father's name and profession as 'Khan Bahadur Yusuf-Ali', 'Municipal Indian Commissioner'.

7   Entry for Yusuf Ali in *Who's Who in India*, Lucknow: Newul Kishore Press, 1911. A later directory, *Muslims in India - a biographical dictionary* Vol.1, Manoher, 1979, drawing on pre-1916 sources, also referred to 'Shaikh Yusuf Ali Shujauddin, well known in Surat'.

8   See Yusuf Ali's obituary notice in *Iqdam*, Lahore Urdu daily, 27 December 1953, p.12, which was based on a transmission by Radio Pakistan (undated). It also described Yusuf Ali's father as a leading poet of Surat.

9   IOL: L/P&J/381, ibid. Yusuf Ali's entry for 'Schools since the age of 12' is 'Wilson's School Bombay from 1882 to November 1887'. He underscored the '2' in 1882 with a question mark, which suggests it could have been 1881 when his age would have been nine. Attendance at 'Wilson College' is recorded to 1891. In his Cambridge application, the entry for 'School or schools, and masters' is completed as follows: Wilson School & Wilson College, otherwise called Free General Assembly's Institution, Principal Rev. D. Mackichan, M.A. D.D. about 3 years at the School & 4 years at the College, took B.A. degree in Bombay University January 1891; since then has been a Fellow of the College, & taught Greek History'. This would place Yusuf Ali's year of joining Wilson's School as 1884, not 1881-2.

10   This account of the *Anjuman-e-Islam* in Bombay is largely based on two sources: C. Dobbin, *Urban Leadership in Western India*; Husain B. Tayebji, *Badruddin Tayebji: a biography*.

11   Tayebji, ibid. p.353 quotes Yusuf Ali's speech reported in *The Times of India*, 8 September, 1906. Yusuf Ali's attendance of the Anjuman school is also noted in *Qamoos al-mashahir*, pp.73-74.

12   S. Wolpert, *Jinnah of Pakistan*, p.6 and p. 171. Jinnah's early law career was also to have a Tayebji connection: Badruddin's son, Faiz, partnered Jinnah in a famous Bombay *waqf* case.

13   Tayebji, ibid. p.232.

14   The objectives of the Central National Mohammedan Association founded by Ameer Ali in Calcutta in 1877 were "primarily to promote good feeling and fellowship between the Indian races and creeds, at the same time to protect and safeguard Mohammedan interests and help their political training...unless the followers of Islam prepared themselves they would soon be outstripped in the political race by their Hindu

fellow-countrymen." From S. A. A. Rizvi's *A Socio-Intellectual History of the Isna 'Ashari Shi'is in India,* Vol. II, p.432. Ameer Ali's Association anticipated the formation of the Muslim League in Dacca in December 1906.

15 Lely was magistrate and collector of Surat, who befriended Yusuf Ali's father. See Obituary note, *The Times,* 26 November 1934. Lely was fluent in Gujrati and Marathi.

16 See K. de B. Codrington, *Birdwood and the Study of the Arts of India,* Journal of the Royal Society of Arts, February 1970 pp. 135-150, for a portrait of John Wilson, 'who spoke six oriental languages and had travelled wide in India, [and] had no doubts that there was nothing better fitted than [our] Western knowledge to undermine the superstition of the country and open its mind to the Gospel'. The accounts of Wilson School and later Wilson College in this section are drawn from *Thoughts on Indian Education,* p.8,17.

17 Mackichan's letter of reference to St. John's College, Cambridge, dated 5 October, 1891, sent from Glasgow.

18 *Thoughts on Indian Education,* ibid., p.19.

19 *The Holy Qur'an - text, translation and commentary,* third edition (1938). See preface to the first edition.

20 Yusuf Ali crossed out the section in his Cambridge application form that asked for 'Mother's name in full' and 'Mother's maiden surname'. Surat was ravaged by cholera epidemics in the 1870s and he may have lost his mother while still an infant. He also does not mention her in any of his writings.

21 From the preface of *Wilson's Anglo-Muhammadan Law,* 1920.

22 Obituary note, *The Times,* 12 April 1934.

23 *Thoughts on Indian Education,* p.21.

24 William Wordsworth, vice-chancellor of Bombay University for a short period in 1890. From S.R.Dongerkerry, *A History of the University of Bombay 1857-1957,* p. 266. In the same vein, Lord Macaulay remarked: 'I am quite ready to take the oriental learning at the valuation of orientalists themselves. I have never found one among them who could deny that a single shelf of a good European library was worth the whole of native literature of India and Arabia'; quoted in Codrington, ibid.

25 *Who's Who in India,* ibid.; *Muslims in India - A biographical dictionary,* ibid; for reference to the lectureship in Greek history also see Appendix VII, *The Holy Qur'an,* ibid.

26 *Select Documents on the History of India & Pakistan,* Vol. IV, Ed. C.H.Philips, The Evolution of India & Pakistan; see Section D, 'Indianisation of the Civil Service 1858-1947', Government of India Resolution of 19 August 1867.

27 IOL: L/P&J/6/306 (1587), note of 23 September 1891.

28 The Abdul-Ali letter is dated 3 October, 1891.

29 *Select Documents on the History of India & Pakistan*, ibid. Lord Curzon to Lord Hamilton, 23 April 1900.

The first Hindus joined the Service in 1884, while Muslims were not to be appointed till 1890. For further details of Indian recruitment into the ICS see IOL: P/9368, The Royal Commission on the Public Services in India.

30 IOL: L/P&J/6/407, File 1856, contains Yusuf Ali's educational record, including the reference to studies in London. His other subjects in the 1894 ICS exams included French, Latin, English History, General Modern History, Political Economy and Economic History and Political Science.

31 ibid. and also IOL:L/P&J/6/406,409. Yusuf Ali obtained 40 marks more in the Urdu and Arabic papers than his nearest rival.

The 1895 ICS entry was a batch of 65, in which there were three Hindus and two Muslims, Yusuf Ali and Ali Ahmed Hassanally, also a Bombay University graduate who went to Oxford on a Sind Government Scholarship.

32 IOL: L/P&J/6/406/1714 and 408/1740.

33 The Inn's Council met on 25 November 1895, in order to receive motions in favour of candidates, who were then invited to sign their 'record of the call' at a separate meeting two months later. The requirement was for candidates to be proposed by a 'bencher' and Yusuf Ali had to make these arrangements prior to his departure. He was unable to attend the second meeting and, though admitted in his absence in January, did not formally sign his record till 1905. Yusuf Ali's call to the Bar was moved by Bencher John George Witt, on the strength of a written testimonial from a J. Westlake of Cambridge: "I should like to say a word in favour of Yusuf Ali, who was a student at Cambridge, and is a man of great ability." Detail from the archives of the Honourable Society of Lincoln's Inn, London.

Westlake was also responsible for nominating Muhammad Iqbal in 1908. Yusuf Ali's formal admission to Lincoln's Inn is recorded in the 'Lincoln's Inn Black Books', 27 January 1896. Jinnah was admitted in the next meeting of the Council held on 29 April 1896.

34 *Iqdam*, Lahore Urdu daily, ibid.

35 *The Civil & Military Gazette*, Lahore, 19/7/1936 (YA115). The guardian may have been Reverend Ernest Foster, to whom Yusuf Ali gave a power of attorney in 1922.

36 George Birdwood was a member of the Birdwood clan, which had extensive Indian connections. Birdwood's *The Industrial Arts of India*, published in 1881, established him as the expert on Indian artisanship and he was also known for the friendship he offered to Indian students in Britain. Yusuf Ali would have had contact with many members of the Birdwood clan: a Justice Birdwood, who was vice-chancellor of Bombay University in 1891; George Birdwood himself, who had been a registrar of Bombay

University; William Birdwood, who was a distinguished general and commander-in-chief of the Indian Army in the 1920s and organiser of Indian League of Nations activities in which Yusuf Ali participated. The Birdwood family's tradition of encouraging promising Muslim students from the Indian sub-continent continued to the 1960s. Yusuf Ali's moving dedication to Wilson has been cited earlier.

37 Though Jauhar was to blame 'an English spring and a young man's more or less foolish fancy' for his performance, the ICS examinations in subjects like Indian History posed leading questions which could test candidates' suitabilities as loyal functionaries of the Raj. For example, a question like 'State what you know of Tipu Sultan', from the 'History of British India' paper in 1895, could easily establish whether a candidate approved of this Muslim ruler's actions against the British.

2

ENTANGLEMENTS

Yusuf Ali's first appointment commenced on 23 January 1896, as Assistant Magistrate and Collector in Saharanpur in the United Provinces.[1] A newly arrived ICS man was both judge and jury in the area under his control: 'He had power to inflict up to six months' imprisonment; within two years he could jail an offender for 24 months, decree whipping, and jail even a European for three months. From the start, with an Indian assistant at his elbow, he began adjudicating the amount of tax due on this or that crop from village headmen, with power to remit it if a crop failed.'[2] All quite daunting for a twenty-three-year-old, and this was only the bottom tier of an elaborate pecking order through which the British regime operated. There was much touring and land surveying involved, at a time when the main mode of transport was on horseback. It was not without reason that riding was an examinable subject in the ICS entry examination. It was said of the ICS class that they regarded India with a mixture of paternalism, exasperation and pride.

After two years in Saharanpur, Yusuf Ali received a transfer to Bareilly. It was not far from Aligarh, where the Muhammadan Anglo-Oriental College, better known as MAO, was located. This provided him an opportunity to come in contact with Sir Sayyid Ahmed Khan: 'I had the honour of knowing Sir Sayyid in the latter years of his life. I remember some conversations I had with him – alas too few – on the subject of Muslim regeneration. I was then on the threshold of my career as a public servant, and I placed my educational ideals with the zeal and assurance of youth before this educational veteran whose life measured the span between the Indian Mutiny and the close of the Victorian epoch.'[3] Sir Sayyid died in March 1898, much concerned that the community had few men of calibre.[4]

Yusuf Ali was rapidly climbing up the rungs of the ICS ladder and in March 1899 was given charge of the Karwi sub-division of the UP. For the next decade his superior in the service would be James Meston, Financial Secretary of the UP and later its Governor. An Aberdeenshire Scotsman, he affected an empathy for Muslims but the velvet glove concealed an iron fist.

The first expression of Yusuf Ali's literary abilities came with the publication in 1900 of *A Monograph on Silk Fabrics Produced in the North Western Provinces and Oudh*. The work contained cultural, technical and industrial information. It included a justification of the Islamic position: 'A man in a warrior race has no business with effeminate luxuries such as silk or gold.' A section on *ahadith* (sayings and doings of the Prophet) on the subject provided separate sub-headings for those derived from *Sunni* and *Shi'i* sources, an early example of his determination to transcend a sectarian outlook in the spirit of the Bombay Anjuman. Yusuf Ali's interest in the topic may have been prompted by his *Dawudi Bohra* roots – Surat was a traditional centre of the silk industry – perhaps with encouragement from George Birdwood, who was active in promoting an Indian exhibition in London at the turn of the century.

ICS officers normally only returned to Britain on 'furlough', a type of extended leave that was one-fourth of the period of active service, to a maximum of six years. Yusuf Ali's first formal furlough, according to the ICS service records, commenced in May 1905. However he also visited Britain in 1900 and wed Teresa Mary Shalders. The marriage took place on 18 September in Bournemouth, following Church of England rites. Teresa was twenty-seven, a year younger than the groom.[5] The marriage was solemnised by Canon Henry Slater in St Peter's Church, which had a claim to fame because the poet Shelley's heart was buried in its cemetery. Yusuf Ali signed himself in style as 'Abdullah ibn Yusuf Ali' on the marriage document, perhaps to show he was no commonplace native.

The exclusion of Indians from the social circle of English ICS officers led to very few knowing of the marriage, though the shrewd Meston might well have been aware. It was a bold and uninhibited act by the young couple, who may have looked at the dawn of the new century and thought everything possible – including the harmony of races, religions and continents. Teresa joined Yusuf Ali in the UP and their first child, Edris, was born in November 1901. She gave birth to a second son, Asghar Bloy, in October of the following year. By this time Yusuf Ali was the Assistant Sessions Judge for Saharanpur. Teresa and the boys soon left India, settling down in a house on Lemsford Road, St Albans.[6] Their home was named 'Kirwee', after the sub-division in the UP of which Yusuf Ali had once been in charge.

By the time his first official furlough commenced Yusuf Ali had just turned thirty-three, already a Deputy Commissioner and in the elite circle of Indians reaching high office in the ICS. Yusuf Ali arrived in Britain determined to utilise his two-year leave as effectively as possible. Amongst the tasks he completed soon after arrival was to belatedly record his call to the Bar at Lincoln's Inn, which he did in May 1905. There were also family matters to attend to in St Albans as another son, Alban Hyder, had been born in September 1904 and Teresa undoubtedly required support in coping with three boys, all under four years old.

It was in 1905 as well that Muhammad Iqbal arrived for the first time in Britain on a Government scholarship. Iqbal sought admission in Lincoln's Inn, following the path of Cambridge studies and Bar entrance favoured by Indian students. Also studying for the Bar was Abdul Qader, editor of the famous Urdu literary magazine *Makhzan* and later a close associate of Yusuf Ali. Iqbal already knew Abdul Qader very well and would stay with him in London when visiting from Cambridge. If Yusuf Ali, Iqbal and Abdul Qader represented the new generation, there were already two senior Indian Muslim figures also in London. Justice Ameer Ali had recently retired with his English wife to a country house in Berkshire – they married in 1880 – but forayed regularly to the Reform Club in London to pen robust letters to newspapers in defence of Indian and Muslim causes. The other distinguished Indian personality was the venerable Badruddin Tayebji, visiting London for medical treatment. It was a charmed circle with numerous social and family interconnections. Even Iqbal became doubly drawn to it through his editorial work indexing Ameer Ali's books and a friendship with Attiya Fyzee of the Tayebji clan.[7] Badruddin's death in September 1905 brought the small Muslim community together for the *janaza* (funeral) prayer. Mourners included the

Turkish Consul General in London, Hamid Baig. Called on to speak, Yusuf Ali reflected on Tayebji's happy family life: 'To see him in his family life was to see a perfect picture of devotion, domesticity and perfect union. It is such a picture which makes us realise what a power it is in our home life. To us of the younger generation his example is a most inspiring one to follow.'[8] He had cause to dwell on family matters because Teresa was now expecting their fourth child. There was also a poignancy in these remarks because of the marital problems soon to rock his world.

He tried hard to devote himself to domestic pursuit but the pull to the public stage was great. India was very much in the news, partly due to the visit there by the Prince and Princess of Wales – the future George V and his consort – and also because there was an air of expectation that the newly elected Liberal government would bring political reform: Australia after all had been a self-governing dominion since 1900. Yusuf Ali was brimming with ideas on what needed to be done in India. The twentieth century beckoned great social changes and it fell on the young generation of Western-educated Indians like himself to ensure their homeland kept pace. The ideas on religion and politics and Hindu-Muslim cooperation which Yusuf Ali first expressed in speeches and writings in the 1906-7 period were to form the cornerstone of much of his thinking in later life.

Yusuf Ali presented a lecture at the influential Royal Society of Arts on *The Indian Muhammedans: their past, present and future*, possibly at the suggestion of his mentor Sir George Birdwood, treasurer and trustee of the Society. The event was duly announced in the Society's weekly journal and took place in December 1906. It was a brilliant success for Yusuf Ali, who had lantern slides at hand depicting prominent Muslim personalities and examples of Mughal architecture.[9]

Lord Ampthill, a former Governor of Madras and an acting Viceroy of India in 1904, chaired the meeting. In the best of imperial style Ampthill hoped the audience realised 'what an amount of character, energy and enterprise it meant for a young man of India to come over to this country, pursue his studies here and enter into competition with Englishmen in order to get into the Indian Civil Service.'[10] He welcomed an Indian who 'should come to England and of his own free will endeavour to give information about his fellow subjects.' This suggests Yusuf Ali volunteered to speak at the Society.

Yusuf Ali responded to Ampthill's remarks with a display of loyalty. 'There is nothing,' he asserted, 'either in the religion or the history of the Indian Musulmans to prevent them from taking an honourable place as citizens in a free and progressive Empire.' He attacked the Indian *Wahhabi* movement, at the time a much criticised bogey in British circles, in much the same way attempted by Sir Sayyid Ahmed Khan thirty years earlier: their call for *jihad* (struggle in the defence of Muslims) against the British was not to be taken seriously.[11] He felt the movement was bringing Indian Muslims into 'disrepute' by acts such as 'the miserable assassination in 1871 of the English chief justice of Bengal'. He condemned it for preaching in a spirit of 'hostility and an uncompromising attack on the existing order of things'. He believed 'the majority of Indian Muhammedans have always rejected it.' Yusuf Ali wished to allay British suspicions of Muslim militancy.

Yusuf Ali's flush of admiration for the European way of life prompted some hasty proposals for Indian Muslims. 'The different Anjumans which they already possess are excellent institutions,' he observed, 'but the Muslims require a healthy organisation of their Church on a purely religious, though broad and non-sectarian, basis. Their social system requires organisation on progressive lines, with more valuable benefits of women's cooperation. I have an idea that the women in Turkey, Syria, Egypt and Algeria (especially the last) are far more advanced than the Muslim women of India.' The campaign of the British suffragettes was in its heyday and may have prompted this apologia.[12]

In the discussion that followed Ampthill congratulated Yusuf Ali on his excellent command of English. Whether Ampthill understood the witticisms the speaker had made in German in the course of the lecture is not known. The meeting also saw an interesting little altercation between Yusuf Ali and Justice Ameer Ali. In the course of his speech Yusuf Ali selected the example of *waqf* (endowment) as a Muslim institution needing reorganisation. 'Could not Mr. Ameer Ali,' he asked, 'give us a detailed and reasoned exposition of the subject, dealing not only with abstract generalities, but with concrete and specific instances?' The problem of Muslim endowments had been exercising the Justice's mind since 1892, so he made short shrift of what must have seemed to him a rather precocious young man. Ameer Ali replied during question time that he himself had no problem with the law on *waqf* – four hundred pages of his work on Muhammadan law were devoted to its elucidation. Ameer Ali added that he had been under the impression that it was only the English judges that had not quite appreciated this branch of Muslim law, so he was sorry to find 'the learned reader of the paper felt a similar difficulty. If Mr Yusuf-Ali would be good enough to explain to him the exact nature of his difficulty he should be very happy to offer such explanations as he could.'[13] Another disgruntled Muslim member in the audience was a Dr Sayyid Abdul Majid, who complained that the speaker had made the Muslims of India sound so antiquated.

When the Royal Society's Council held its next annual general meeting in June 1907, the Society's Silver Medal was awarded to Yusuf Ali for his talk. This was a significant public recognition because the Society fulfilled 'a most useful role in providing an opportunity for the discussion of Indian problems – often of the highest Imperial interest - before interested and influential audiences.'[14]

Yusuf Ali was invited to deliver a series of six lectures at the Passmore Edwards Institute, London. These were transferred to larger rooms because of the growing size of the audience. A book emerged from the series, published by John Murray of London in 1907, *Life and Labour of the People of India*, which contained an effusive dedication to George Birdwood.[15] Yusuf Ali's analysis in *Life and Labour* was consistent with the views expressed at the Royal Society of Arts. He painted a picture of an ancient 'immemorial' society now afflicted with decay and corrupt social and religious practices: 'One of the most marked tendencies of Indian social life is that all forms of institutions making for order and joint action are getting disintegrated or undermined.' Indian Islam had become an abstract term 'with no visible organisation and no persons or bodies in whom authority is vested and recognised.' Muslim practice was often no more than 'paroxysms of *tazia* [effigy of the tomb of Imam Husain] worship in the month of *Muharram*, and the aggressive slaughter of kine at one of their festivals, especially if it clashes with a Hindu festival.'[16] Yusuf Ali called for a process of social reform, but one which could only work if certain other forces were kept at bay. The ground must be prepared for social reform 'by eliminating the factors which blind our vision and warp our judgement.' Foremost of these was political activity which exploited religious differences. 'It is in the hands of such as these that religious animosities are aroused among His Majesty's loyal and law-abiding subjects,' he said. Yusuf Ali's Empire-Loyalism was leading him towards an apolitical notion of religion.

The other unavoidable issue for Indian Muslims was their encounter with the Hindu majority community. The Bombay Muslim intelligentsia, for reasons to do with their prosperity and level of education, did not feel threatened and actively supported political cooperation. In *Life and Labour* Yusuf Ali questioned the need for any special concessions for Muslims because of their minority status and asked: 'Why should Muslim appeals to Government be couched in terms, not of fair field, but of special favour?'

In a speech given to the British Constitutional Association in the Whitehall Rooms and reported in *The Times* in late January 1907, Yusuf Ali hoped that majorities would eschew arrogance towards minorities and declared support for 'secular education'.[17] It was not a particularly tactful remark to make at a time when the Muslims were campaigning for university status for Aligarh. Theodore Morison, MAO's recently retired principal, had remonstrated against him a month earlier for failing to raise the issue at the Royal Society of Arts.[18] Yusuf Ali's attitude towards the Aligarh campaign reflected the reserve of a Bombay man for denominational institutions, best expressed by his contemporary Akbar Hydari: 'the idea of a Muhammadan University filled me with fear that the already too great emphasis on caste and creed that has been the bane of our land might thereby be further accentuated.'[19] Jinnah too regarded proposals for a separate Muslim electoral roll with 'special creed' privileges as anathema. It is perhaps not surprising that when the Muslim League was founded in December 1906 to represent Muslim interests as a separate community, this was not to be in Bombay with its highly educated Muslim elite, but in Dacca.

Edwardian England was sure of itself and its destiny. The spirit of the times inspired Yusuf Ali to chart out his own future. His life work would now be to express in more detail proposals for India's role in the Empire and the type of politics appropriate for Indian Muslims. He was confident in his mission: 'Mrs Humphrey Ward, presiding at one of the (Passmore) lectures, was kind enough to mention three qualifications in the present writer for dealing with Indian life. In the first place, being born and bred in India, he is of the people. In the second place, his association with the Government of the country enables him to view life also from the administrative point of view – viz: as a whole, and with special reference to social organisation and cohesion. In the third place, a Cambridge education and a lengthened study of European life and methods should enable him to present facts in a form which appeal to European readers and be not unacceptable to Eastern traditions.'[20]

He might have added a further qualification for serving as a bridge between India and the West, which was marriage to an English woman. The self-commendation hinted at a showman's streak lurking somewhere in this industrious and brilliant young man's personality.

Yusuf Ali's life so far had been one of smooth progress and unqualified success, from one public distinction to another. In British circles Yusuf Ali was 'a very talented member of the Indian Civil Service and a representative of the great Muhammedan community', the description used in *The Times* in its January 1907 report of the meeting in the Whitehall Rooms. This was no mean compliment, made at a time when Britain was conscious that it had more 'Muhammedans' in the boundaries of its Empire than could be claimed by the Ottoman Caliph. The report itself took up six column inches on the leading page, an indication of Yusuf Ali's meteoric rise though it had not yet been a decade since he had left Cambridge. He was elected to the Royal Society of Arts and the Royal Society of Literature and had friends in the highest of places. He met Lord Morley, the Secretary of State for India, on several occasions to discuss issues of political reform. Yusuf Ali put to him the case for the introduction of parliamentary government but, for all his Liberal politics, Morley could not concede this. 'My arguments for some qualification of that position did not appeal to him,' Yusuf Ali noted ruefully.[21] Yusuf Ali even resided for

26

a while at Cromer House in Norfolk, indicating some connection with the aristocratic Baring family, best known of whom at the time was the Earl of Cromer.[22] The famous pro-Consul of Egypt and his kinsman Baron Revelstoke were confidants of Royalty, one becoming Lord Chamberlain and the other personal financial adviser to George V.

The furlough came to an end, and after the glitter and zest of London life Yusuf Ali must have dreaded returning to the humdrum chores awaiting him in the UP. Yusuf Ali had slipped into the Indian Civil Service's cherished image of itself, the enlightened public servant, administrator-cum-scholar, under whose paternalistic and patronising gaze India would gradually emerge from its slumbers. Unfortunately the realities of the ICS included its colour prejudice and while an Indian of his calibre could be feted in London, the doors of the white man's clubs and gymkhanas in India were closed to natives, however much Europeanised. Yusuf Ali made the journey back to India alone, leaving Teresa Mary with the boys and a baby daughter, Leila Teresa, born in December 1906. The gymkhana clique would only close ranks against such brazen violation of a sexual taboo.

By March 1907 Yusuf Ali had resumed duties as Deputy Commissioner of Sultanpur. When Meston moved from the UP provincial government to the finance department of the Government of India as Finance Secretary, his Muslim protégé also made a similar transfer. Yusuf Ali was for a time acting under-secretary and the deputy secretary in the Department of Finance, in effect one of the most senior civil servants to India's 'Chancellor of the Exchequer'. Meston, hard-working and shrewd, cultivated bright young Muslim administrators; his protégés included Ameer Ali's public school-educated son, Waris.[23]

The first signs of Yusuf Ali's domestic crisis appeared in 1908, when he took nine months of medical leave, from February to October 1908.[24] The event which so devastated him was news of Teresa's infidelity. The marriage had been bizarre from the outset. There was no record of Yusuf Ali taking official furlough in 1900 for the wedding in Bournemouth, while the church ceremony too seemed out of character. Perhaps the union was an impulsive affair, in which basic incompatibilities were overlooked in the headiness of the hour. A rapid succession of children did not strengthen a

27

faltering marriage and it is possible that Yusuf Ali, engrossed in his life of public activity, was oblivious to Teresa's dissatisfaction. In 1907 he returned to India with noteworthy achievements in public life and cause for happiness in the birth of a daughter after three sons, but then his world crashed around him on the news of Teresa's affair.

While Teresa may have been acting within the mores of Edwardian society – everyone knew of the *amour* between the reigning monarch and Lillie Langtry – her actions were inexplicable and deeply humiliating for an Indian Muslim. Yusuf Ali came from a respectable if humble Gujrati Muslim background in which the values of family life were unquestioned. There is no reason to imagine that he would have been anything but a decent and conscientious husband and father, though the circumstances of his childhood had made him a trifle egoistical. The hurt caused by Teresa was deep and still in evidence when he wrote the preface to the Qur'anic commentary in 1934: 'A man's life is subject to inner storms far more devastating than those in the physical world around him... such a storm, in the bitter anguish of personal sorrow which nearly unseated my reason and made life seem meaningless.'[25] When the marriage disintegrated he did not just experience outrage and hurt pride. The trauma was all the more intense because the partnership perhaps also represented many of his hopes of shared trust and confidence between East and West. She turned her back on him for another man and in a way this meant that the Empire too had signalled a rejection. If Teresa lacked integrity, could it be that the society and culture he idealised were also flawed? No wonder Yusuf Ali felt tormented to the extreme and experienced a nervous breakdown. He applied for medical leave and did not work for most of the year in 1908.

Divorce on the grounds of adultery required all the unsavoury details to be presented before a court, creating even greater anguish. However when the news came that Teresa was actually expecting her lover's child, Yusuf Ali was left with little choice. Nevertheless he regained his composure in these wretched months, presiding for example at the UP Industrial Conference in 1909, and the following year performing a similar role at the All-India Muslim Educational Conference held at Nagpur.

Teresa's illegitimate child was born in September 1910, and Yusuf Ali came to London to file for divorce. This was done in April 1911, citing one

Obed Thorne as co-respondent.[26] He did not stay at the family home in St Albans, even though Teresa was no longer living there, and instead lodged at the Ivy Hotel in Kew Green. The divorce petition was heard at the High Court's Family Division in June and made a decree absolute in January 1912.

The ages of the four children ranged from barely five years old to ten and Yusuf Ali asked for custody. He won this battle but then promptly left them in the care of an English governess and departed for India. As the years passed the children grew estranged and resentful of their father. Yusuf Ali was to disclaim all of them in the will he drew up in 1940: 'In spite of all I have done for them, [they] have to my sorrow persistently maintained an attitude of ill-will and hostility towards me, and have in-sulted and annoyed me and spoken to others against me,' he wrote in evident anguish and bitterness. Teresa was to marry again, though not becoming Mrs Thorne but a Mrs Astell. Yusuf Ali was fortunate the case was not reported in the press. It was to be a closely guarded secret, not known even to Meston or India Office staff in London till several years later.

By 1912 the worst was over for Yusuf Ali and he took up duties as the Magistrate and Collector for the UP district of Fatehpur in the month of March in that year. James Meston was now Lieutenant-Governor of the Province and his handling of Muslims in general and Yusuf Ali in particular revealed the darker, more manipulative side of his character. The unfortunate Yusuf Ali had to work in a UP in serious political turmoil, not helped by Meston's schemings. In 1913 the situation came to a head in Kanpur, a town only fifty miles from Fatehpur.

The Kanpur Mosque incident arose because Meston backed a munici-pal decision to demolish the *wudu* (ablution) area and toilets of a *Shi'i* mosque in the Machli Bazaar quarter of the town to make way for a road. The demolition took place on 1 July 1913, during the month of *Ramadhan*. It immediately became a *cause célèbre* for Muslims throughout India, of all religious schools. Muhammad Ali Jauhar rallied the Muslim community through the columns of his *Comrade* newspaper and the efforts of the *Khuddam-e-Ka'ba* (Servants of Ka'ba) Society. On the evening of 3 August about twelve thousand Muslims assembled at the *'id gah* (prayer ground) for a demonstration and proceeded to the mosque. The police opened fire, killing sixteen, several inside the mosque.[27] Meston invoked a criminal law to make Jauhar and another Indian Muslim leader, the fiercely intellectual Abul Kalam Azad, liable to arrest if found in Kanpur again. When court proceedings started against arrested activists like Shibli Numani, Muhammad Iqbal came from Lahore to act in their defence.[28] The Muslims sent Jauhar to Britain to protest to the Secretary of State directly.

The UP Government refused to accept any blame and instead interpreted the Muslim grievance as a plot against the Empire. Jauhar's support for Ottoman Turkey in the *Comrade* during the Tripolitan and Balkan conflicts of 1911-12 was used by Meston to raise the bogey of pan-Islamism: 'The true nature of the agitation is not, in my opinion, far to seek. The troubles of Turkey have, among other unfortunate consequences, brought to the front a type of young Muhammadan in India who will always be a problem to us...side by side with this type, we have the unforgiving religious bigot, who draws from the Turkish defeats a revival of his smouldering dislike of Christian and British ascendancy in India.'[29] Such attention only ensured Jauhar's popularity. Yusuf Ali's position must have been most awkward: a high-ranking Muslim in a provincial administration reviled for its high-handedness and brutality and, perhaps most damning, a confidant of the hated Meston. The Kanpur mosque incident was an important landmark which drew the battle lines between Muslims prepared to stand their corner and those preferring to remain quiet. The First World War would sharpen the divide and place Jauhar, the disappointed ICS applicant and Yusuf Ali, the Service's high-flier, on opposing sides. The dispute itself was eventually resolved by the Viceroy Lord Hardinge, responding to a compromise suggested by the diplomatic Raja of Mahmudabad.[30] Meston was unrepentant and continued to control Muslim activity in the UP through a network of informants for the rest of his tenure as Governor till 1918.[31] A few years later, in an article in *The Nineteenth Century & After*, Yusuf Ali made a passing reference to 'the Kanpur Mosque difficulty with the Muhammadans', a choice of words that marks his estrangement from populist Muslim opinion in this period of his life.[32]

In February 1914 Yusuf Ali decided to leave the ICS, but because the rules required twenty years' service before a proportionate pension could be permitted, he sought Meston's help. It is an indication of how centralised British rule was in India that the matter had to be referred to the Viceroy in Delhi and the Secretary of State for India in London.[33] Meston, for his own duplicitous reasons, was happy to oblige, and wrote a revealing letter to the Viceroy's Council member responsible for Home affairs:

I am sorry indeed for Yusuf Ali. He is a man of the most brilliant ability and the best intentions; and his literary work is of very high quality. He is however extremely touchy and sensitive; he has a bad manner with Indians, who regard him as tyrannical and unsympathetic; and he often runs up against Europeans as well without in the least intending to do so.

Although I used to regard him as terribly academic in his views, I must confess that he has made a very good district officer in a small district; but I am afraid to try him in a big district, especially where there is a military society; and not to put too fine a point on it, his future career is a decided anxiety to us all.

The reasons why he wishes to retire are very strong; he has told me them privately with much distress. He married an Englishwoman by whom he had, I think, four children. Things went wrong and he had to divorce her, I believe; the children were left in his custody. Realising as he does the difficulties attending children of this character in India, he very wisely is having them educated in England; and the lady in whose custody they were has recently died. He has not a relation or friend in Britain to whom he can entrust them, and he is genuinely anxious to be able to settle down in England and supervise their education himself. He would also try to get a practice at the Bar and I have no doubt that he will succeed, while he can make an income by writing.

In these circumstances, converging from public (early retirement to relieve the block in promotions) and private interests alike, you will see how strong a case there is for letting him have his way. It is a case

which I cannot very well put on official record, but I should be glad
if you could allow what I have now told you to influence the
decision.[34]

Though Meston's note was not a matter of official record, news of Yusuf
Ali's troubled marriage got round the India Office circles in London. Sir
Malcolm Seton, an assistant under-secretary, for example, wrote to his
superior, 'I have heard Mr Yusuf Ali lecture, and Sir Charles Lyall has told
me a good deal about him. He is a man of exceptional literary gifts, and, I
should say, very attractive personality. Perhaps you know him? I had not
heard of his domestic troubles.'[35]

Apart from the information it contains about Yusuf Ali's reasons for
resignation, Meston's letter sheds light on the discomfiture with which
Indian officers in the Indian Civil Service were regarded by their English
colleagues. Meston was only too happy to remove Yusuf Ali from the
hierarchy, 'to relieve the block on promotions' and to avoid loss of face if
a native could pull rank over an Englishman. Meston's line of reasoning
was typical of official thinking. The Viceroy Curzon himself had minuted
to the India Office in London in 1900, 'Wedderburn [Member of Parliament and Indian National Congress president, 1889] wrote to me the other
day, very civilly, and asked me why we do not employ more Natives in the
very highest ranks of the Service. I told him plainly in my reply, because
they are not competent, and because it is our constant experience that,
when placed in authority, if an emergency occurs, they lose their heads or
abdicate altogether.'[36] The Indians of Yusuf Ali's generation had extolled
the superiority of Western education, but once this was attained, found the
jobs commensurate to their training only grudgingly given.

After submitting his application for resignation but without awaiting a
decision on the matter of the proportionate pension, Yusuf Ali left India
for Britain to look after his children. On 4 August 1914 Britain declared war
on Germany. He was in Sevenoaks, Kent, and on 8 August wrote to the
India Office: 'I am prepared and shall be pleased to volunteer for temporary
service, in any capacity in which I can be useful on account of the War.'[37]
He also signed up in the local territorial force, the West Kent Fencibles.[38]
Like many Indians of his era, Yusuf Ali cherished Empire and Sovereign.

It was an unrequited relationship, as the Empire was foremost concerned with protecting its own interests. There was something about the British style in India and the self-confidence of men like Lely, the Collector of Surat who had befriended his family, or Meston, Governor of the UP for whom he worked, that commanded unquestioning belief. Even though treated with condescension, Yusuf Ali could not abandon the loyalties that bound him to the 'Mother Country'. At this juncture 'Mahatma' Mohandas Gandhi was also in London and, seeking to be both saint and politician, was no less loyal in urging all Indians residing in Britain to fall into line and show support.[39]

By September Yusuf Ali was running short of funds. His early retirement had not yet come into effect and no pension payments had been received. He wrote to the India Office for help with these financial difficulties, requesting some interim payment while the exact amount was still being finalised.[40] However, the India Office soon made a decision on his entitlement and accepted Meston's recommendation to grant a proportionate pension, which amounted to about £800 per year.[41] This was a comfortable income to live on and assured Yusuf Ali's financial future. He was now forty-one with an opportunity to take stock and chart out a new course for himself.

Ottoman Turkey, under the inept leadership of the Young Turks, found itself dragged into the conflict on the side of the Central Powers led by Germany.[42] During the Tripolitan and Balkan wars of 1911-12, Indian Muslims sent delegations with medical aid and women contributed their jewellery. Iqbal first recited his famous *Jawab-e-shikwa* at a meeting to raise funds for the Bulgarian campaign. He also brought a meeting to tears in Badshahi Mosque by his verses on the *shuhada* (martyrs) of Tripoli. Jauhar's own feelings at the Ottoman debacles of the time were so deep-felt that the thought of suicide crossed his mind. Indian Muslims were emotionally committed to their Ottoman 'Caliph of Islam', and this was a deep-rooted loyalty also to be found amongst those considered Europeanised like Justice Ameer Ali. When Britain declared war on Turkey in November 1914 Yusuf Ali, a 'representative of the great Muhammedan community', was a most valuable asset in the propaganda battle for Indian Muslim public opinion.

Notes to Chapter 2

1   IOL: V/12, Histories of Services - United Provinces.

2   Malcolm Darling, *Apprentice to Power 1904-8*.

3   From Yusuf Ali's presidential address to the University Section of the All-India Muslim Educational Conference, Golden Jubilee Session, Aligarh, March 27, 1937 (YA201).

4   Shibli Numani is quoted in Maftoon Ahmed, *Maulana Shibli Numani - aik mutala*, p. 103, "Sir Sayyid frequently told me that of all the British-educated (Indian) Muslims there is not one who could speak at a gathering or write. He only made three exceptions."

5   The marriage witnesses were Alice Mary Shalders, probably Teresa's mother and one W. Scott Evans. Prior to the marriage Teresa and her mother had lived in 'Pine Holme', Westbourne Park Road, Bournemouth West, one of the many hotels in this fashionable and genteel seaside resort. The marriage was not announced in the local newspaper, *The Bournemouth Observer*. The marriage register specifies the bride's father to be Isaac Noah Shalders, profession 'Gentleman'. The 'Shalders' surname suggests Dutch connections.

6   Edris's birth is not recorded at the General Register Office, London; Asghar Bloy and their third son, Alban Hyder, were registered in 1904 (October-December 1904 Volume of the Register). This suggests that for at least some of the time Teresa resided in India.

7   In the preface of an edition of *The Spirit of Islam* Ameer Ali writes, " I take the opportunity of expressing my gratitude to ....Mr. Muhammad Iqbal, Government of India Research Scholar at Cambridge, for his careful revision of the proofs and the compilation of the index." For references to Iqbal's friendship with Attiya Fyzee and her brother see Durani, *Iqbal Europe mai*, p.119, 198 and also Gandhi, *Eight Lives*, p.51. Miss Fyzee was also known to Yusuf Ali - see Note 9 below.

8   The funeral is described in Husain B. Tayebji, *Badruddin Tayebji: a biography*, p.353; Yusuf Ali's speech was reported in *The Times of India*, 8 September, 1906.

9   'The Indian Muhammedans: their past, present and future', *Journal of the Society of Arts*, No. 2824, Vol. LV, 4 January, 1907. Yusuf Ali's lantern slides of Muslim personalities included the Nizam of Hyderabad, the Aga Khan, the late Begum of Bhopal, Miss Fyzee, the late Badruddin Tayebji and Sir Sayyid Ahmed Khan.

10 ibid.; also for subsequent quotations.

11 *Wahhabism* owes its name to the eighteenth-century revivalist preacher of Nejd, Muhammad ibn Abdul Wahhab, who campaigned for a return to the authentic practices of the Prophet. Indian revivalists and reformists associated with the eight-

eenth-century Delhi reformer Shah Walliullah came to be known as *Wahhabis* because they too condemned customs that had entered the Muslim way of life, such as the excessive veneration shown to *pirs* (masters of *sufi* orders) and their tombs. The two best known of Shah Walliullah's intellectual heirs, Sayyid Ahmed of Rae Bareilly (1786-1831) and Shah Ismail (1781-1831), founded a movement known as the *mujahideen* to proclaim *jihad* against the Sikhs in north-western India in the 1820s. After Sayyid Ahmed's death the movement became anti-British.

Sir Sayyid Ahmed Khan argued that these early Indian *Wahhabis* were loyal to Empire, "the leader of the *jihadis* was Sayyid Ahmed, but he was no preacher. Maulvi Ismail was the man whose preaching worked marvels on the feelings of Muhammadans. Throughout the whole of his career, not a word was uttered by this preacher calculated to incite the feelings of his co-religionists against the English...he said that under the English rule Muhammadans were not persecuted and as they were subjects of the Government, they were bound by their religion not to join in a *jihad* against it...since 1857 however a band of desperate men and others...fled to the North West frontier...for the purpose of making a religious war against Government...the frontier colony...was scarcely one which could be designated a *jihadi* community." See G.F.I.Graham, *The life and work of Sir Sayyid Ahmed Khan.*

12 In the speech Yusuf Ali devoted a lot of attention to the prominent role of women in Muslim history, though adding an apologetic note, "in saying all this about Muhammedan women I am in no sense defending the abuses which have sapped the foundations of our social system and ended in the undoing not of women but of men. The rising generation of Muhammedans are becoming more and more conscious of the abuses." *The Indian Muhammedans*, ibid.

13 ibid.

14 *Journal of the Society of Arts*, 28 June, 1907. Yusuf Ali arranged for his paper and the discussion to be reprinted as a pamphlet published by Messrs. P.S. King & Sons, 2 Great Street, Westminster.

15 Dedication to George Birdwood:

> Who to his special insight of
> the inner consciousness of the East
> adds an ever-helpful sympathy
> with the artistic and literary life
> of the immemorial people of India
> This little book is dedicated
> As an affectionate appreciation
> of the many kindnesses and courtesies
> received from him
> by the Author.

It is an example of Yusuf Ali's overwhelming sense of gratitude to those who befriended him.

16 *Life and Labour*, p. 335; subsequent quotations are from pp. 335-339.

17 *The Times*, 24 January, 1907: "In the case of education, if it was impossible to agree about religion, why not follow the example of those States, which like India, left religion alone and had purely secular education?" Such a public statement from a leading Indian Muslim was a stab in the back for those campaigning for university status for Aligarh.

18 Yusuf Ali's responded to Morison: "As a controversial topic I could not discuss it." *The Indian Muhammedans*, ibid.

The British were reluctant to recognise a 'Muslim University' and there was a confrontation between the Government and an independently-minded group comprising of men like Shibli Numani and Jauhar. The Government not only wanted powers of veto in its administration, but objected to the name, preferring 'Aligarh University'. British interests in this debate were championed by personalities like the Raja of Mahmudabad, influential in the Muslim League. For an account of the tussle, see Maftoon Ahmed, *Maulana Shibli Numani - aik mutala*, pp. 70-71.

19 See *Eminent Mussulmans*, Madras: Natesen, 1922, for details on Hydari's life and views on Aligarh. University status was finally accorded in 1920. Both Hydari and Yusuf Ali later served on the court of Aligarh University.

20 *Life and Labour*, preface. The extract continues in enigmatic fashion "If a fourth qualification may be added, it is the possession of an open mind and the consciousness that in private and public life the influences that go furthest are not those that are most talked about, but that in any case, there can be no finality in the discussion of social problems."

21 Indian reforms, letter, *The Times*, 16 November 1928. Morley's attitude is a reflection of the deliberate steps taken to retard the evolution of political institutions of India even by liberal reformers. A very different standard applied to Australia or Canada.

22 The Earl of Cromer was a keen Greek scholar and Yusuf Ali's early distinction in this field could have been the basis for their association. Yusuf Ali's association with Cromer Hall is referred to in the divorce papers he filed in 1911.

23 Meston was a relentless judge of character. His remarks on Waris Ali were penetrating: " He is neurotic and very easily takes alarm if he thought we had designs upon him...he is still dreadfully introspective and interested in minute details of his own symptoms... at one time I feared that it would be quite useless trying to keep him in India, and had written to his father a hint to that effect. After talking the matter over with his parents, whom I met in London last autumn, I decided to make another effort to keep the boy, whom we all like and who is full of brains and good qualities..." See MSS Eur F136/3, letter dated 17 June 1914. At another point Meston described Waris as a 'weak reed'.

Waris was educated at Wellington College, a public school with military traditions located in Berkshire. He served in the ICS from 1911-1929 and on retirement lived in Britain.

24 IOL: V/12/232 (1913) Histories of Services - United Provinces.

25 *The Holy Qur'an - text, translation and commentary*, Third edition, 1938. The quotation is in the preface to the first edition.

26 Divorce details obtained from the Public Record Office, London by permission of the Senior Registrar. The divorce petition was submitted by Yusuf Ali using his full name 'Abdullah ibn Yusuf-Ali'. The document includes information on the addresses where the married couple had resided in the past, which were in St. Albans and Cromer House, Norfolk and at 'divers other places' and the names and dates of birth of their four children. At the time the petition was raised, Teresa Mary was not residing at 'Kirwee' in St. Albans but at Halesowen, Grove Park Road, Chiswick. The divorce petition documents the sordid details: "the said Teresa Mary Yusuf Ali had frequently committed adultery with Obed Thorne. That on or about the 23 December 1909 at Grange Cottage at Markyate in the County of Bedford, the said Teresa Mary Yusuf Ali committed adultery with the said Obed Thorne. That on the 23rd September 1910 the said Teresa Mary Yusuf Ali was delivered of a child of which your petitioner (Yusuf Ali) is not the father, but of which the said Obed Thorne is the father...."

27 IOL: Meston Papers, Mss. Eur F 136/3, and particularly Meston's official minute in 136/15 which provides full details of the incident.

28 Mian Amiruddin, *Yad-e-Ayyam*, p.38.

29 IOL: MSS Eur F136/15. This antagonism cannot be disassociated from Meston's membership of the Freemasons. In 1926 he was installed grand superintendent of the provincial grand chapter of Royal Arch Masons of Berkshire. *Dictionary of National Biography 1941-50*, Oxford University Press, 1959. The Masons had long conspired to weaken Ottoman Turkey and hence opposed pan-Islamism. A Masonic journal recorded in 1907 " ...the so-called Young Turks or Reform Party in Ottoman Empire, which includes many princes of the Imperial house, are masons to a man...[but] Sultan Abdul Hamid remains apprehensive as ever of Freemasonry, convinced that as far as his Empire is concerned, its activity is directed towards political emancipation and reform, which of course means the overthrow of his rule." *The Freemason*, 29 June, 1907, held at the British Library, Colindale. Meston's later career included supervision of the League of Nations' financial committee. He was also one of the founders of the Royal Institute of International Affairs, Chatham House.

30 In the Raja of Mahmudabad's proposal to the Viceroy, Muslims would 'admit they had been wrong and ask forgiveness...(while) the Viceroy would allow them to erect an arcade on the site of the demolished *wudhu khana* and to utilise the top of the arcade as a part of the mosque and that the rioters and all other persons under trial would be released.' IOL: Meston Papers, ibid.

31 A notable informant was Fateh Ali Khan, Nawab of Qizilbash, who provided Meston with inside information on the Muslim League and sought to influence the Nawab of Rampur, in whose court relatives of the Ali Brothers were employed. Fateh Ali Khan left an amusing glimpse of life in Rampur: "I only wish I could find more time to stay with his Highness (the Nawab of Rampur) to make him turn out in my presence some undesirable men and get rid of his uncommon habit of keeping awake till very late at night and asleep till very late in the day and having no exercise and consequently food only once in 24 hours." From Fateh Ali Khan's letter to Meston, 31 January 1914, in IOL: MSS Eur F136/5.

32 *The Nineteenth Century & After*, March 1916; the Kanpur Mosque reference is in Yusuf Ali's article on the outgoing Viceroy of India, Lord Hardinge, who returned to London as Permanent Secretary at the Foreign Office.

33 IOL: L/P&J/6/1261 (1914).

34 IOL ibid. Meston to Craddock, February 1914.

35 IOL: L/P&J/6/1261 (1914) Seton to Holderness, 27 April 1914.

36 See *Select Documents on the History of India & Pakistan*, Vol. IV, Ed. C.H.Philips, Lord Curzon to Lord Hamilton, 23rd April 1900.

There was great reluctance to allow Indians into the decision-making circles of the Raj. The first Indian member in the Viceroy's Council, Sir S. P. Sinha, was not appointed till 1909, thirteen years after Yusuf Ali joined the ICS. Sinha's presence resulted in fewer papers being circulated at Council meetings, for fears that state secrets would be jeopardised.

37 IOL L/P&J/6/1261 (1914). Yusuf Ali to Seton; the letter was sent from 'Bradbourne', an estate in the parish of Riverhead near Sevenoaks. Records at the Kent Archives Office indicate there was a Bradbourne Hall, owned and occupied by one William Gore Lambarde and also a Bradbourne House, occupied by Jacob William Hills. Yusuf Ali may have lived in either.

38 From *The Times*'s obituary on Yusuf Ali, 15 December, 1953: "Settling in this country Yusuf Ali did much useful work for the 1914-18 War effort in platform appeals for recruitment, in written propaganda both in English and Urdu, as a private in the West Kent Fencibles, and as a president of the Indian Students' Prisoners of War Fund."

39 Gandhi writes in his autobiography, "I felt that Indians residing in England ought to do their bit in the war. English students had volunteered to serve in the army, and Indians might do no less...I thought that England's real need should not be turned into our opportunity, and that it was more becoming and far-sighted not to press our demands while the war lasted. I therefore adhered to my advise and invited those who would list as volunteers....I wrote a letter to Lord Crewe, acquainting him with these facts and expressing our readiness to train for ambulance work." M.K.Gandhi, *Gandhi- An autobiography*.

40 IOL:L/P&J/6/1261 (1914) Yusuf Ali to Holderness, 7 September 1914: "Sir, I have the honour to thank you for your letter J&P 3252, d.3 Sept. 1914. I take it that my retirement will take effect from the 20th Sept. 1914. On that date the amount standing to credit in the General Provident Fund will become payable. I request that the amount may be paid to me with interest on that date. In case it will take time to calculate & verify the exact amount, I request that some approximate amount may be paid to me, leaving the balance to be adjusted when the verification is complete."

41 IOL ibid. Memorandum from Finance Department, Pensions and Gratuities, Government of India, to the Secretary of State for India, 23 July 1914: "We agree therefore with the Lieutenant Governor in thinking that the case is deserving of special consideration and support his recommendation that Mr Yusuf Ali should be allowed to retire on a proportionate pension [which] will amount approximately to £748 a year."

42 The astute Sultan Abdul Hamid II was forced to abdicate by the Young Turks in April 1909. A minute prepared by Sir F.A.Hirtzel, Secretary, Political Department, India Office, provides background to Turkey's entry into the War, "The coup d'état of January 23 1913 [which consolidated the Young Turks' hold] was financed by a Hungarian notable M. de Szemere, and a band of German Jews. Its success was followed by a steady increase of German influence, culminating in the appointment of Liman V. Sanders Pasha as Military Advisor to the Porte with greater powers than had been conferred upon any foreigner in Ottoman Service. German officers now advised the expulsion of the Greek population from many parts of Turkey, which was carried out with unnecessary vigour, and marked by a number of outrages. In May 1914 the German Cruiser *Goeben* visited Constantinople for the second time. Admiral Souchon, Commander of the German Mediterranean Squadron, flew his flag on this power cruiser. A number of mysterious conferences took place between him and Enver Pasha [the thirty-four-year-old Minister of War] at some of which Liman Van Sanders was present...on August 9 the *Goeben* and *Breslau* entered the Dardenelles and remained in Turkish waters under cover of a nominal sale". See IOL: MSS F 136/15. In response to this naval provocation Britain immediately impounded two Turkish ships that were being built in British shipyards. There was no compensation and this brusque action increased Turkish hostility at the public level, especially as the ships cost seven and a half million pounds, much of which had been raised by mass subscription. By October 1914 Admiral Souchon was leading the Turkish fleet in naval forays and it did not require a formal declaration of war for Britain to respond by bombarding the forts at the entrance of the Dardanelles.

3

IN THE SERVICE OF THE CROWN

The early years of the Great War saw massive military campaigns which did not yield the quick success expected by Lloyd George and other leading British politicians of the day. Instead there was stalemate and near defeat, best marked by the Allied retreat from Gallipoli in the face of determined fighting by the Turks. The turn of events raised the importance of propaganda on both sides. If Britain could propagate the story that the Kaiser ate babies, the Germans responded by spreading the rumour that the King-Emperor had taken flight and been sighted in Lucknow or Delhi. The propaganda war was crucial to Britain to woo the neutral countries to the Allied side. It was responsible for winning over the United States and ensuring the continued neutrality of Sweden, crucial as a munitions supplier. Every stratagem was needed to make certain the Balkan states would not side with the Central Powers.

With Turkey's entry the great conflagration commenced in earnest and there was a groundswell of sympathy and loyalty amongst Indian Muslims for the Caliph. The government in India adopted various tactics to bring the situation under control. There were deportations and arrests, and assurances to Indian troops in the British army that holy areas of Arabia would be immune from attack.[1] Prominent Muslim princes like the Nizam of Hyderabad were persuaded to make public declarations justifying the British action against Turkey: 'It is the duty of the Muhammadans of India to swerve not a hair's breadth from their devotion to the British Government...and that in no case allow themselves to be beguiled by the wiles of anyone into a course of open or secret sedition against the British Government.'[2] Indian soldiers were deployed in immense numbers on many fronts and a disaffection in their ranks, or a drop in Indian recruitment, would have been a death-blow at a time when prospects of victory seemed to be slipping away.

It is against this backdrop that Yusuf Ali wrote to the editor of *The Times* on 17 November 1914, almost proposing a role for himself:

> The vagaries of popular rumours cannot at a time like this be a matter of indifference to lovers of India and the Empire....in the dissemination of news as in tactics, the first comer holds the field. Cannot our Press Bureau in London, with the assistance of someone who understands the mind of rural India, cable out daily bulletins for the Viceroy for free circulation in the vernaculars through the notice boards of all *thanas* [police stations] and *tahsils* [councils], in addition to the Press. We are quite secure of enlightened opinion in India. Is it not worthwhile also to appeal to the sentiment and news hunger of the masses, the home folk of the Indian soldiers who are shedding their blood in the battle line on the Aisne and in Flanders?

Yusuf Ali made a further unabashed declaration of loyalty in an extraordinary speech at Caxton Hall a week later, on 23 November, 1914. It would have been a daunting occasion for anyone else, particularly as the former Commander-in-Chief of the Indian Army was chairman. Yet Yusuf Ali was in no sense subdued and the power and language of his expression would have taught his audience a lesson or two on the arts of propaganda:

> *Chairman* (General Sir O'Moore Creagh VC): Ladies and gentlemen, I beg to introduce to you this evening Mr Yusuf Ali. He had a very distinguished career at Cambridge and also a very distinguished career in the Indian Civil Service, which he has lately resigned. He will give you a paper tonight on 'India's Rally round the Flag'.
>
> *Yusuf Ali*: Mr Chairman, ladies and gentlemen. When I was asked to read a paper before the East India Association, my first idea was to write a simple, business-like paper; but when I took up the pen, and the subject warmed on me, I found the occasion was so great that I had to write a paper more or less to the occasion. The result is that I have

to apologise to you for the style in which the paper is written. It is somewhat emotional, and looks upon the emotional and the sentimental side of the question more than upon the business side.

The rally of India round the flag has been so splendid, so spontaneous and so unanimous, that it is well both for India and England to realise the full meaning of this epoch-making achievement...What does the rally mean for India?...let a simple Indian soldier speak for himself: 'The Empire in self-defence has appealed to all its subjects. If it has been threatened in India, British soldiers would have gone there; but as it is threatened in Europe, we have come here.' And then he added, converting into a glorious sentiment new to India an obvious formula embodied in his instruction in a wholly matter of fact sense: 'We are indeed Indians, but also Britishers.' But most heart-stirring of all is the appeal of one who knows intimately every part of his Empire as no Sovereign before him knew it - one whose *chahra-e-mubarak* [auspicious face] was seen with pride and glory by millions of men in Bombay, Delhi and Calcutta less than three years ago...the King-Emperor calls. India salutes and falls in, ready to die for country, Padishah, flag and Empire.

... and what made it [the link between India and the Empire] such a living dominant force? The personality of India's gracious Sovereign, who resolved, with his noble Consort, to enthrone himself in the heart of India in waking a new life and force from the echoes of historic Delhi.

The Sovereign speaking to his people, the Sovereign in the midst of his people, the Sovereign smiling and trusting when Prudence spoke of danger and wiseheads appealed to precedents, the Sovereign who gave dignity and splendour by the magnificent simplicity of his own daily life, and rescued Court functions from their terrors by kindly words, gracious smiles and quiet acts of practical charity - this was the influence which captivated India.

Fight, ye glorious soldiers, Gurkha or Sikh, Muslim, Rajput or Brahman! Fight for the name of India and make it glorious with your blood! Great are your privileges. You have comrades in the British

Army whose fellowship and lead are a priceless possession to you
They have fought and conquered in these very fields for centuries.
They are as staunch and steady against the crushing weight of
numbers as they are bold and enterprising in the hour of dash and
gallantry. They have something of your own mystic sentiment and
spirituality, however different may be their manner of showing it.
Their chivalry in the most trying turns of fortune will open your eyes
to those knightly qualities which your ancestors enshrined in their
legends...

Your King-Emperor has told you that he has drawn the sword for
a righteous purpose, and that he will not sheathe it until that purpose
has been achieved. Be yours a share in the achievement!

As I stated at the outset, my object in reading the paper was to
sound what our energetic secretary [of the East India Association]
calls the trumpet call. I have myself had the privilege of appearing at
certain recruitment meetings in this Country, and have invariably
been received with great courtesy and attention. I found that enthusiasm in one sphere begat enthusiasm in another, and I thought
perhaps from an Indian view one might be allowed to speak one's
mind freely on the side of sentiment and poetry. Remember that
business is always with us, but poetry rarely is.[3]

The war-time atmosphere in Britain may have evoked strong emotions, yet
the strange rhetoric belies the impression of a self-composed and intel-
lectually disciplined civil servant. Yusuf Ali's inspired piece of jingoism
and showmanship would have left the distinguished audience in no doubt
of his value as an Indian publicist for the British and Allied cause. It was
the perfect response to Lord Kitchener's poster appeal that confronted
Londoners everywhere: 'Your country needs YOU'.

Yusuf Ali's adoration of George V brings to mind the notion of *fanaa*:
the annihilation of one's own personality so as to become united with
something far superior, the King-Emperor's *chahra-e-mubarak*, or auspicious face, to use Yusuf Ali's quaint Urdu phrase. Curiously, the King,
according to a biographer, 'for all his commonsense and realism, was not
impervious to the mystery of monarchy, to the divine responsibilities of

Kings...that there existed some almost mystical association between the Sovereign and the common people.'[4] The expectations of the monarch certainly evoked the desired response from one subject. Yusuf Ali's devotion was not entirely unrequited. When George V instituted the Order of the British Empire in 1917, its inaugural list included Yusuf Ali as a Commander of the British Empire – CBE.

Yusuf Ali's faith in Empire in the winter of 1914 was not widely shared by other Indian Muslims in London. The loyalist *Islamic Review and Muslim India* published in Woking only offered qualified support, 'as long as the war remains a secular war and nothing is done to interfere with the status quo of the caliphate or the Hejaz...the Musalmans...will remain faithful to their obligation and will be ready to fight under the flag beneath which they have lived and been sheltered.'[5] Some prominent Indian Muslims steered a middle ground, most notably Iqbal and Jinnah, the latter already a thorn in the flesh of the British for his demand that Indian Army recruitment should only proceed if the bar on Indians serving as commissioned officers was removed. Yusuf Ali was different because his loyalty was unconditional. Muhammad Ali Jauhar – on opposite sides to Yusuf Ali in the Kanpur Mosque incident – was locked away with his brother in May 1915 for 'expressing support and sympathy with the King's enemies'.[6]

Yusuf Ali's enthusiasm for the Crown made him the right man for the moment. His offer to assist the War effort 'in any capacity in which I can be useful' did not go unheeded for long. Some of his literary activities in 1915 contain clues to the nature of his work. In June he wrote a letter to the editor of *The Times*, which touched on India's potential in supplying Britain with essential supplies: 'Not only shells, but uniforms, bags and leather goods are in demand. Home industries are working overtime, and orders are flowing to neutral countries. Should not India get the word? With textiles, leather goods and canvas, she is in a position to help immediately. Her industries are waiting for the call of the Empire, as her Armies did at the beginning of the War....' The letter was addressed from 6, New Square, Lincoln's Inn. By 1916 he was involved in supply work for the Imperial Institute, acting as 'chairman of special committees on gums, resins and essential oils'.[7] Additionally, his article in the prestigious journal *The Contemporary Review* on 'India's Services in the War', contains references to other war-related activity, in particular involvement in welfare activities for Indian soldiers on the European fronts: 'A word of cordial acknowledgement is necessary for all that has been done for wounded and convalescent Indian soldiers in this country, and the admirable manner in which local conditions have been adapted for their needs and habits is an eloquent tribute to the resource and skill with which their experienced administrators have met the novel situation....the camaraderie of the Indian soldiers with their British confrères has been mentioned in the letters of soldiers from the front, both British and Indian. Battalions of British troops from India are brigaded with Indian troops in the Indian Corps, as well as English Territorials. I have met British soldiers, on short leave from the front, returning with quite a collection of watches, electric torches and trinkets for their "Indian comrades" in the battle line.' Yusuf Ali also writes about one particular soldier who won the Victoria Cross: 'Amid a tornado of fire – with asphyxiating gas – he led his platoon with the greatest gallantry in attack, and subsequently brought in eight wounded British and Indian officers. His calm heroic figure, in a Brighton hospital for wounded, on his way to recovery from wounds and asphyxiating gas, made an impression that makes one proud to be an Indian.'[8] The British authorities kept a careful watch on Indian soldiers in British hospitals, for fear that their accounts would adversely affect recruitment. Apart from a careful censoring of mail, steps were taken to dissuade visits by 'unreliable' Indians. There was a War Office instruction that ex-ICS officers were the most suitable type of visitor.[9] It is apt that when Yusuf Ali was buried in Britain in 1953, his grave was to be close to a neat, serried rank of tombstones, the graves of First World War Indian soldiers who died in Britain, on parade in death as they were in life.

Like the Caxton Hall speech, *The Contemporary Review* article was in blatant jingoistic style, sharing with it a spiritual undertone: 'This war has taught us more geography than we ever learnt at school or college. But it has opened the door of knowledge in a far more important direction. It has brought self-revelation and the inner appreciation of others, which can only come in great crises.' The tension in the trenches did inspire a famous genre of Great War poetry, but Yusuf Ali was nowhere near the excitement

46

and danger of the actual shooting war in the frontline. The spider web world of propaganda was able to trap its very creators.

By this time Yusuf Ali had still not remarried. The youngest of his sons, Alban, was now thirteen years old, while Leila Teresa, the only daughter, was ten. His emotional devotion to the cause of the Empire cannot be separated from these personal circumstances. He had been absent from his children's lives for three years and on his return in 1914 they may have demanded some proof of commitment. Perhaps his exaggerated patriotic gestures were an attempt to redeem himself in their eyes. There could also have been other subtler factors at work. The King was the distant, kindly father commanding obedience from his children, loyal subjects of the Empire. It may be that Yusuf Ali craved for the same filial adoration from Alban and his siblings which he himself offered to George V.

He had resigned from the ICS for his children's sake but it was unlikely that he would eschew public life for them. They were old enough to be placed in boarding schools and perhaps he expected them to persevere much like himself in his own childhood. Among his circle of friends in this period were Sir Frederic Lely, the former Collector of Surat; and E.W. Perera, a historian from Ceylon.[10] There was an active Muslim community which held regular meetings at a centre near Notting Hill Gate as well as at the Shah Jahan Mosque, Woking. In January 1917 Yusuf Ali was invited to chair a meeting at which Marmaduke Pickthall, who had not yet formally declared his Islam, spoke on the life of the Prophet. In his own remarks Yusuf Ali invited the audience to reflect 'in sober earnestness' on the gifts of the Prophet's personality and the Muslims' good fortune to be heirs to his teachings.[11] He joined the staff of the recently created School of Oriental Studies at Finsbury Circus, lecturing in 'Hindustani, Hindi, and Indian Religious Manners and Customs', though he also retained the office at New Square, Lincoln's Inn. On 8 March 1917, *The Times* carried a report of a lecture he gave at the School on 'The importance of Hindustani', the fifth of its general introductory lectures. It was of topical interest because moves were afoot for the creation of a university in Hyderabad with Urdu as the medium of instruction. Also teaching at the School at this juncture was Sir Thomas Arnold, author of *The Preaching of Islam* and an editor of the *Encyclopaedia of Islam*, to which Yusuf Ali would later make a number of contributions.

In May 1917 Britain set up a Department of Information which included a Propaganda Section and a Bureau of Intelligence.[12] The brightest scholars of the day who knew something of the Muslim world were involved in the Department's work, including Arnold Toynbee, who headed Section E of its Bureau of Intelligence, in charge of counter-propaganda in Turkey and the Middle East. Toynbee had already produced a piece of 'black propaganda', a pamphlet on 'atrocities' inflicted on Armenians. The Bureau's Section D under Allen Leeper was responsible for the three strategic countries in the Balkan Group – Bulgaria, Rumania and Serbia. Britain had an interest in stoking Serbian nationalism in 1916, because a strong Slav state would act as a barrier against German advances towards Arabia and even do something for the Allied cause in the disastrous Dardenelles campaign. An oft-repeated slogan in *The Times* was: 'Serbia is holding the Gate of the East. Let us help her with all our might.' Yusuf Ali seems to have developed a sympathetic interest in Serbian affairs in this period. In November 1916, he published *Mestrovic & Serbian Sculpture*, ostensibly about Ivan Mestrovic, the Serbian sculptor exhibiting then in London, but really a paean to Serbian nationalism. The booklet was dedicated to 'the speedy success of the Allies and their intimate mutual understanding'. The subject and style suggest that this work could have been commissioned by Section D. Its head, Leeper, himself wrote a pamphlet in a similar vein on Rumania, *The Justice of Rumania's Cause*, in 1917. The Serbian authorities were grateful to their sympathisers and amongst the fifty honours awarded by the Prince Consort of Serbia to British subjects in 1919, a recipient of the Order of St. Sava, Class IV, was Yusuf Ali.[13]

A section in *Mestrovic & Serbian Sculpture* indicates how willing an accomplice Yusuf Ali was in the British plan to glorify Serbian nationalism:

Withal [in the work of Ivan Mestrovic] there is a national consciousness that amounts to more than religion. This consciousness can build its dreams both on the past and the future...when the events of the nineteenth century gradually won autonomy for the Balkan States, these dreams were revived. Such dreams necessarily involve conflict of nationalities, but it is for the artists to interpret them, to invest them with new meaning, to purify them of the lust of bloodshed, and with their magic to feed the strength of Hercules with the radiance of Apollo and the Muses. Such is the meaning of Mestrovic and his Serbian sculpture. The art is not mainly religious; it is not mainly personal; it is national. Its whole ideals are bound up with the growth and glory of a united Serbian nation...we have seen that his heroes and his ideals have a direct bearing on the Balkan movement of today. The exhibition in London has brought home to the English people the intense patriotism and national feeling of the Southern Slavs. Following on the Rodin exhibition, it has cemented the highest thought of the Allied nations by means of their art...such is the power of art; while it lays emphasis on national characteristics, its truth illuminates dark places and serves to bring nations together.

Yusuf Ali dismissed the Muslim population of Serbia in the following terms: 'the half-million pure-blooded Serbian Muhammadans of Bosnia represent a religious revolt. Their temperament is naturally one which protests against the established order. When they were members of the Roman Church they broke away into Manichean and other heresies.' The Muslim founders of the *Anjuman-e-Islam* would have been incredulous to hear their distinguished protégé describe how 'Serbian independence was extinguished in the onrush of the Osmanli Empire from the East' after the battle of Kosovo in 1389. Yusuf Ali's unwillingness to sympathise with the Ottomans was a renunciation of the values held by the Bombay elders: the Anjuman had collected funds for Turkey during the 1870s and as recently as 1906, when Badruddin Tayebji, founder of the Anjuman school, died in London, the funeral was attended by the Turkish Consul. Even staunch Empire-Loyalists like the Aga Khan (Aga Sultan Muhammad Shah III), who for doctrinal reasons could have been expected to be indifferent, respected these traditional pan-Islamic allegiances. It was an act of intellectual treachery by one who knew better.[14] Mercifully Yusuf Ali was not to dwell on Serbian art and politics ever again.

From several articles which Yusuf Ali wrote in the 1916-1918 period it is clear he awaited some change of heart in Britain's imperial attitudes. In January 1916 he declared: 'I have addressed many public meetings in England, and it seems to me that the British Democracy and the British people are willing and anxious to understand Indian needs and Indian aspirations, and to do justice to India.'[15] His hope was that Britain would acknowledge India's war sacrifices and so elevate her to the self-governing status of Australia and Canada. Yusuf Ali would seek every opportunity to highlight India's readiness for responsibility. The presence of three Indian delegates (the Maharaja of Bikener, Sinha and Meston) to the Imperial War Conference of 1917 was one such occasion: 'Now that the Imperial War Conference has finished its labours, a short retrospect of its work will enable us to see how India stands in the Empire. In the first place it must be made clear that the position of India's Representatives at the Conference was not that of mere advisers, but they were full members like the representatives of the dominions...His Majesty the King-Emperor, with the tact that characterises his Royal House, and Her Majesty the Queen, did them the honour to entertain them at Windsor. The Indian Representatives are to be congratulated on a very comprehensive programme of work in which they have worthily represented the cause of India.'[16] In December 1917 Yusuf Ali was deservedly made a CBE – for services to the Empire. The next *Who's Who* contained a thirty-line entry about him, which few other Indians could surpass. It provided no references to his previous marriage or four children, but there were details of his club - the National Liberal – and recreations – 'walking, riding, travel, chess'.[17] In the month he was awarded his honours, the Zionists organised a grand event at the London Opera House to mark the conquest of Jerusalem by Allenby. The Liberal politician Herbert Samuel – to be appointed the first British High Commissioner of Palestine after the war – called on the gathering to rejoice wholeheartedly because 'the achievements of the British arms in Palestine have lent new significance to the traditional Jewish prayer "Next year in Jerusalem" '. There were shrewd forces at work who sacrificed relatively little in comparison with Indian army losses in the Gallipoli, Somme and Kut-el-Amara campaigns, but gained everything.

Yusuf Ali's enthusiasm for the Empire was now in full torrent. In February 1918 the *Overseas* journal, published by a club of the same name in collaboration with the 'Patriotic Club of Britons Overseas', contained this testimonial:

> The Empire provides India with many gifts of incalculable value. After the constant internal wars of the Eighteenth Century the *pax Britannica* has enabled India to develop her moral and material resources. Membership of a great and liberal Empire has expanded her vision and brought her into intimate touch with the greatest thought and the most practical movements of the world. Her social organisation is moving gradually, from an archaic or medieval base to a democratic basis. There is no department of her life which has not been vivified by the Anglo-Saxon love of freedom and practical love of order and organisation....When we think of the Empire now, we think of a great and composite political association, in which each part has its rights and privileges as well as duties, and which is held not by force, but by consent of intelligent public opinion and by a desire to give honest expression to the great ideas of liberty, responsibility and ordered growth, which are the contribution of British History to the progress of mankind.

The war years had given Yusuf Ali time to place his emotional and passionate devotion to the King Emperor within an intellectual credo. The pamphlet he had written on Serbian sculpture called for 'intimate mutual understanding' of nations. No culture could afford to be insular and it was his belief that India's progress relied on its contact with the Empire in general and Britain in particular.

The greatest of Yusuf Ali's wartime adventures was a hazardous trip to Scandinavia at the behest of the Foreign Office and the newly formed Ministry of Information. Sweden had been made a centre for anti-British propaganda by an assortment of Irish, Egyptian and Indian groups and in January 1918 the British ambassador, fearing some change in the country's neutral position, despatched a telegram to the Foreign Office 'for a friendly native Indian to come here to deliver lectures on British rule in India'.[18] Sweden was also of strategic importance as a swing towards a pro-German stance would affect munitions supplies to Britain. The Foreign Office consulted the India Office, which characteristically preferred to send a European: 'The Secretary of State for India agrees that it is very understandable to arrange a counter campaign of lectures (as well as of publications) against the enemy activities now having their centre at Stockholm. It is understood that Mr W Archer, who is a distinguished Scandinavian scholar and has lately published a book on India, has been employed recently in dealing with some of the Indian publications at the Centre; he would perhaps be more effective than an Indian lecturer with a Stockholm audience. But if stress is laid on the engagement of an Indian, the Secretary of State for India would suggest that Mr Yusuf Ali (lecturer in the London School of Oriental Studies) ICS retired, or Mr N C Sen of 21 Cromwell Road might be approached in this matter.' The Ministry of Information, also a party in these discussions, preferred Yusuf Ali as it was 'imperative that a native should be sent', failing which it would settle for Mr Archer.[19]

In due course – a wit in the Foreign Office scrawled on the file that he hoped a decision could be made before the war was over – Yusuf Ali was to have discussions with John Hose, an official at the India Office, and on 4 March responded to the most elegant of invitations from Stephen Gaselee of the Foreign Office, addressed to him at the School of Oriental Studies: 'We should be pleased if you could see your way to undertake this work and if there is any possibility of your so doing, might I trouble you to call on me any week day between 11.30 and 1 or 4.30 and 6.30.' The bureaucrats had decided that Yusuf Ali was their man, particularly because William Archer, who worked on Scandinavian matters in the Ministry of Information, could not be spared. At the meeting Yusuf Ali raised the question of payment. He mentioned the recent purchase of a house, most likely referring to plans to move out of Chiswick to Bedford Park, also in West London. Once Yusuf Ali's services had been secured, the Foreign Office started telegraphic correspondence with its legations in Denmark and Norway, to see whether they too might be interested in lectures on India. This process took several weeks, during which time Yusuf Ali was kept in the dark. Finally, on 23 March he wrote to the Ministry of Information enquiring whether the trip was still on. Everything was now in order, and he was told to be prepared to go out on an Admiralty boat to Copenhagen in early April. Prior to departure Yusuf Ali requested a special briefing, to which Gaselee replied in his inimitable style:

Dear Mr. Yusuf Ali,
Mr. Hose of the India Office tells me that before you start for Scandinavia you would like to have a short talk with somebody at the Foreign Office on general questions of propaganda in that country. If you could come here and see me some morning about eleven o'clock I will do my best to tell you everything you want to know, or more probably, to find the person who is really an expert on the subject.[20]

Yusuf Ali's professional approach was not matched by the Ministry of Information. The civil servant responsible for Scandinavia, Herbert O'Neill, sent a solicitous note to the British Legation in Copenhagen with the following instructions and advice: 'I think it will be advisable to let him draw on the Legation for any monies that he may require up to a certain amount, but we shall be very glad if you will kindly arrange for a room for him in a hotel. You realise of course that he is a Hindu [*sic*] and I do not know whether there is any colour question in Denmark, but I trust that adequate arrangements can be made for his hospitality. He is a very charming man and should do us a lot of good. He is most anxious to help in any way.'[21] The next day the Foreign Office sent a separate telegram to its own man in the Legation, which rectified the obvious mistakes. The Copenhagen trip did not augur well. Yusuf Ali's lantern slides were not prepared in time and he had to leave without them; the boat by which they were later despatched was sunk. The journey was across a war zone and not far from the waters followed by Kitchener on his ill-fated Russian mission. In the course of this trip, Yusuf Ali addressed audiences in various Scandinavian cities including Copenhagen, Stockholm, Uppsala, Lund and Christiania. One of the lectures, 'Features of Indian Culture', was translated into Danish and published as a booklet.[22] Not unexpectedly, the propaganda lectures led to a crossing of swords with anti-British Indian nationalist groups. Yusuf Ali issued a brief but combative statement to the Swedish press describing one such group, the Indian National Committee, as comprising only 'two anarchists, both of whom can in no way be regarded as neither representing India nor are they in touch with that country'.[23] The issue dated 29 May 1918 of the Swedish paper *Aftontidning* contained a long and cleverly phrased response berating Yusuf Ali:

> In your issue of the 8th instant you were kind enough to publish an article under the sensational title 'The Indian National Committee shown up' written by an Indian, Mr Yusuf Ali....for every impartial reader of the article it must have been clear that instead of having shown us up it was Mr Yusuf Ali himself who was shown up. We can only regret that he left Stockholm the evening before his article was published. It is therefore not our fault that this our answer cannot reach him personally... the Swedish public...learns from your paper that Mr Yusuf Ali is a 'politician' and a 'patriot'. In his own lectures and speeches he makes it appear that he is commissioned by some such body as the Indian National Congress or the All-India Muslim League to speak on behalf of India. We challenge him to show how he is justified in calling himself a politician, and whether any political organisation in India commissioned him to come to Sweden and make the false statement to the Swedish people that India is happy, flourishing and satisfied under England's sceptre, and to mention a single organisation or a single leading politician in India who maintains anything of the sort. And we protest most emphatically against the word 'patriot' being used for a man who during his whole life has only furthered the interests of India's Foreign Government.
>
> ....Mr Yusuf Ali says: 'I have taken trouble to place myself in communication with the persons concerned.' This is not true. If he had wished to see us, he could have got our address from the English Legation. It was we who took the first step towards making his acquaintance, in the hope, which unfortunately proved vain, of arousing in him a sentiment of patriotic self-respect. But after a very short conversation, we discovered that his aim was only to induce us to give him information as to our organisation etc. naturally in the interests

of his Government...Mr Yusuf Ali is kind enough to invite us to live in our own country and come under the humanising influence of its literature and philosophy...but why does not Mr Yusuf Ali himself put his doctrine into practice? If our philosophy teaches us not to use force to win back our freedom (which seems to be what Mr Yusuf Ali means) why does he help England by recruiting soldiers and giving money for the slaughter in France?[24]

The feeling of contempt was mutual and on his return to London Yusuf Ali wrote to the British press referring to the 'enemy' he contended with in Scandinavia.[25] The Indian National Committee men were well informed, evidence that Yusuf Ali's propaganda work had not gone unnoticed. His link with the Muslim League, referred to in the *Aftontidning* letter, was tenuous and limited to lectures delivered at the London branch, though in the circumstances he may have elevated it to something more significant.[26] It would also be in character for him to solicit further information on the National Committee's membership in order to pass this on to the authorities. The 'enemy' for Yusuf Ali was not just Germany and Turkey but revolutionary societies trying to break the link between India and Empire.

Gaselee sought to obtain official recognition for Yusuf Ali's Scandinavian mission in the form of a letter of appreciation to be sent from Lord Hardinge, the former Viceroy and now Permanent Secretary at the Foreign Office. Perhaps because three government departments were involved, nothing happened, till Gaselee revived the issue with O'Neill at the Ministry of Information after reading the review of Yusuf Ali's Danish lecture in *The Times Literary Supplement*. By this time the file on the matter had been 'lost'.[27] The inter-departmental correspondence was overtaken by the declaration of Armistice Day on 11 November 1918. With the Great War over, niceties like a formal letter of thanks rapidly became less urgent. The 'representative of the great Muhammadan community' had risked life and reputation but was quickly forgotten. Yusuf Ali is unlikely to have minded. His devotion to the Allied cause was idealistic rather than prompted by pecuniary considerations. It was part of an elaborate intellectual credo and trust in the Allies. Allied victory would yield a new world order: 'The Great War is supposed to have killed Imperialism, Militarism and Racial Domination.'[28]

The Allied plans for imposing settlements on the vanquished Central Powers soon stirred the Muslim world. Schemes were mooted to divorce Constantinople from the rest of Ottoman Turkey. Muslims knew they had to speak out, for if it was the 'City of Islam' today, what were to be the prospects for the institution of the Caliphate? Yusuf Ali too may have felt a passing disillusionment at the persistence of the imperialist imperative in Allied plans. He wrote a carefully worded letter to *The Times* in November 1918, venturing to admonish Britain, yet affirming essential loyalty: 'Those in whose hands lies the direction of British policy would incur a grave responsibility if they ignored in the coming settlements, not only the interests but the sentiments of the Muslims of India, British and Protected, Egypt, Afghanistan, British Malaya and other territories owning his Britannic Majesty's sway.' The letter contained a suggestion: 'Would it not be well to have in the inner counsels of the Government one or two Muslims of sufficient standing, experience and independence to keep in touch with and advise on the great Muslim interests that have loyally and steadfastly supported the cause of the Empire and the Allies in the trying four years through which we have just passed?'[29] His polite expression masked the crisis in India as the famous Khilafat movement mobilised public opinion to protect the Ottoman Caliphate's authority and power in the Arabian peninsula – *jazirat ul-arab*.[30] Yusuf Ali had never agonised much about the conflict of loyalties between Caliph and King-Emperor. He resumed teaching at the School of Oriental Studies, but this was mundane activity after the cut-and-thrust of the war years. Yusuf Ali's offer to return to public life was soon to be taken up at the highest levels.

The authorities needed a 'moderate' faction of Muslims not only to fight the anti-British nationalists but also to prepare public opinion for the dismemberment of the Ottoman Arab provinces. Whether by design or accident, a group of Muslims living in Britain took it on themselves to assure the British Government that they would not make a fuss over the partitioning of the *jazirat ul-arab* – provided some other safeguards could be given. Writing from 41 Sloane Street, London, they despatched a letter to the Foreign Secretary on New Year's Day, 1919. It began: 'We the undersigned Muhammadan subjects of His Majesty the King-Emperor beg respectfully to represent to His Majesty's government that we have read with great concern the suggestion recently put forward in the Press from various irresponsible quarters regarding the future of Constantinople to the effect that it should be taken from its present possessors.' The style was typical of the Indian Empire-Loyalists and its signatories included Ameer Ali, the Aga Khan and Pickthall, but not Yusuf Ali.[31] About the Ottoman Arab provinces, the respectful petitioners desired to 'express no opinion'. As if on cue, four days later, Prime Minister Lloyd George addressed Parliament in order to 'reassure' Muslims that Ottoman Turkey would not be deprived of Constantinople or Asia Minor, but the Arabs were entitled to a recognition of their 'separate national conditions'.

The Peace Conferences, at which the victors decided the fate of Germany, Turkey and the other vanquished Central Powers, lasted from 1919 to 1923, and redrew the map for the Muslim world. The 'Big Four' of the Conferences were Lloyd George, President Woodrow Wilson of the United States, Georges Clemenceau of France and Orlando Vittorio of Italy. To strengthen her bargaining position vis-à-vis the remaining allies, Britain not only secured voting rights for the self-governing dominions like Australia, but also for colonies without home rule like India, giving the British Empire block seventeen representatives to everybody else's four or five. The Indian delegates were the same as those selected for the Imperial War Conference of 1917: Sir James Meston (soon to be elevated to a peerage), Sir S.P. Sinha (also later Lord Sinha) and the Maharaja of Bikener. In spite of the particular interest of Indian Muslims with the settlement terms with Turkey, or perhaps because of it, a Muslim was not included. The Indian delegation's contributions do not appear to have been particularly weighty; the Maharaja of Bikener made a big hit in February 1919 by inviting the seventy-year-old Clemenceau to India to shoot tigers. The unrepresentative nature of the Indian delegation and the serious discontent in India over the well-publicised designs against Ottoman Turkey and its Arab provinces troubled Edwin Montagu, the Secretary of State for India and official leader of the Indian delegation. He took steps to rectify this by calling on the India Office's most favoured 'moderate' Muslim contacts. His letter to the Governor of Madras, Lord Willingdon, conveys some of the drama in Paris in May 1919:

> I am writing to you again from Paris where I came on an urgent summons from the Prime Minister, with a view to representing the case of the Indian Muhammadan in regard to the settlement with Turkey. Bikener, Sinha and I had our audience with the Great Four last Saturday, and as it was clearly desirable that we should be accompanied by some Indian Muhammedans, I took the Aga Khan, Aftab Ahmed Khan of my Council and Yusuf Ali along with me. We stated our case and were listened to with attention...what the result will be is not yet known, but anyhow I can fairly claim that so far as the Indian delegation is concerned, we have left nothing undone to bring the point of view of the Indian Muhammadan home to the powers that be.[32]

Yusuf Ali's self-advertisement in *The Times*, for the government to appoint 'one or two' Muslim advisers, had not gone unnoticed. His selection for the Paris Peace Conference would be the highpoint of a glittering career in service of the crown. It was a brilliant success for one not born into the aristocracy of India to reach the cockpit of world affairs, in the splendour of the Palace of Versailles with its mirrored halls and ante-rooms and elaborate gardens in spring foliage. It was no mean feat for the son of a police inspector. He rubbed shoulders with the great and famous, possibly even forming an acquaintanceship with Prince Faisal, son of Sherif Hussein and leader of the Arab delegation.[33]

This stage of the Paris Peace Conference ended with the signing of the Treaty of Versailles in June 1919 which, though concerned primarily with Germany, had significance because it was the occasion for the creation of the League of Nations. The mood at Paris was to punish the vanquished severely – a most savage burden of financial reparations was placed on Germany. Much of the behind-the-scenes committee work was managed by a handful of British civil servants, notably Maurice Hankey, Secretary to the Committee of Imperial Defence, and staff of the Foreign Office's Bureau of Intelligence – men like Leeper, Toynbee and Zimmern. The

League of Nations grew out of these cabals which, behind a high-sounding covenant, gave the victors a legitimacy for imposing their hegemony over German and Ottoman territories.

If the Empire-Loyalists had 'no opinion' to express on the future of the Hejaz and the Ottoman Arab provinces, this was not the case with the Ali Brothers and others in the Indian Khilafat movement. They regarded Sherif Husein as a renegade who 'assumed with the concurrence of the British the title "King" in a land in which the Sultans of Turkey were content to be merely servants of the Holy Places'.[34] There was much at stake for the Muslim world because the Caliph's religious authority was inextricably bound with governance of the holy cities of Mecca and Medina. 'Khilafat' committees rapidly sprang up the length and breadth of India in a remarkable demonstration of unity, culminating in the formation of an 'all-India Khilafat Committee' at a conference in Delhi in November 1919. The conference declared it a religious duty to withdraw cooperation from the government if the Caliphate was compromised by an unjust settlement. Jauhar was an undisputed hero of the Khilafat movement. The scene was set for confrontations at the Paris Peace Conference, to involve both Yusuf Ali and Jauhar.

The terms of the German settlement did not hold any hope for Indian Ottoman sympathisers, but back in India the Viceroy Chelmsford used the Muslim presence at the Paris Peace Conference to assuage a distinguished Khilafatist Delegation which met him in Delhi in January 1920:

> I venture to think, gentlemen, that there is no relevant argument on behalf of Turkey which was not fully utilised by the Indian Delegation. The Delegation received a full hearing from the Peace Conference in the middle of May, and as a result of previous representations of my Government and the efforts of the Secretary of State, it was accompanied on this occasion by three prominent Indian Muslims His Highness the Aga Khan, Sahibzada Aftab Ahmad Khan and Mr Yusuf Ali.[35]

The Khilafatists were not satisfied and despatched Muhammad Ali Jauhar, Maulana Sayyid Sulaiman Nadwi and Sayyid Husain to Europe to present

59

their case for the preservation of the authority of the Ottoman Caliphate. The delegation was in London in February 1920, at the time when the terms for Turkey were being drafted in London.

Jauhar worked furiously, conducting his campaign in a manner which earned him Montagu's stricture: 'Mahomet Ali has done us a lot of harm here by the extreme nature of his demands.'[36] Every move of the delegation was monitored by the security services, including each luncheon appointment; there is no record of a meeting with Yusuf Ali even though he would later claim a connection with the Khilafatists: 'As you know I have myself taken part in the rejuvenation of the Khilafat movement.'[37] Jauhar had caused trouble for Meston in the Kanpur Mosque incident of 1913 and like a bad penny had turned up again, making Montagu fear that Khilafatist 'extremism' would disrupt the Government's own timetable for Indian political reform. Yusuf Ali was more likely to have been at pains to avoid contact with a 'revolutionary'.[38]

On 19 March 1920, the Khilafatist delegation had an appointment with Lloyd George at 10 Downing Street. Jauhar and Sayyid Husain argued as powerfully as they could against the partitioning of the Arabian peninsula:

> Quite apart from the main claim for the preservation of the Khilafat with adequate temporal power, the Muslims claim that the local centre of their faith, namely, the 'Island of Arabia', should remain inviolate and entirely in Muslim control. This is based on the dying injunction of the Prophet himself...the *jazirat ul-arab*...includes Syria, Palestine and Mesopotamia as well as the... Arabian Peninsula. Muslims can acquiesce in no form of non-Muslim control, whether in the shape of mandates or otherwise, over any portion of this region.[39]

It was a vain attempt. The Prime Minister had a deep antipathy towards Turkey and spent a lot of time at this historic meeting dwelling on the Armenian problem and the right of victors to do what they pleased with the vanquished. Just as the Viceroy and the Secretary of State in the past had claimed that Indian opinion was consulted, so too did Lloyd George: 'When we were in Paris we took great care to consider the Mussulman representatives who came from India. They were represented in the first instance with very great force by two able Indians who were not Muhammadans, but who were still very much imbued with a sense of what was fair to their Muhammedan fellow countrymen...then delegations were arranged from Muhammedans, some residing in Britain and some who came from India, and at my request the Supreme Council heard their case.'40 The two 'able Indians' were Lord Sinha and the swashbuckling Maharaja of Bikener, both Hindu, while 'their fellow Muhammedans' referred to the three Muslims appointed by Montagu, the Secretary of State for India, as advisers to the India delegation to the Peace Conference. These were the Aga Khan, Yusuf Ali and Aftab Ahmad Khan.

When the Peace Conference reconvened in Paris the mood was anti-Turk and anti-Muslim. Constantinople and the Bosphorus coastline had been occupied by the Allies in March. The dismemberment of the Ottoman provinces was sanctioned in the Treaty of Sèvres in May 1920. Turkey was required to give up Thrace and Smyrna to Greece, the Straits were to be internationalised, there would be close financial supervision of the Turkish Government and independent states of Armenia and Kurdistan were to be created. Britain acquired League of Nations-backed mandates over Palestine and Mesopotamia. Sir Herbert Samuel was immediately appointed as British High Commissioner of Palestine. As a prominent journalist of the day noted, 'There are no annexations made if you are acting on behalf of a League of Nations, give yourself a mandate...So Great Britain obtained her Mesopotamia, France her Syria and Italy her Adalia, all from the benevolent League of Nations.'41

Though some of the decisions of the Treaty of Sèvres were later to be reversed, with credit due to Mustafa Kemal for his military successes, Indian Muslims were deeply angered by Britain's cold indifference to their religious sentiments. The League of Nations became a byword for deceit. It was this resentment which gave a new militant turn to the struggle for independence. The Khilafatists turned their back on constitutional reform and injected the Indian freedom struggle with a fresh impetus. They combined forces with Gandhi and the Congress Party on the grounds that the greatest enemy of Islam was Britain. A powerful though short-lived Muslim-Hindu alliance was born which called for strikes and the non-payment of taxes. Gandhi was initially reluctant to force a showdown with the government but found his hand was forced by the Khilafatists.[42] Rather than seeking to defuse the tense Indian domestic situation by accelerating political reform, Britain extended the state of martial law imposed during the war to peacetime.[43] It was a characteristic gesture of imperial arrogance that equated with nothing India's war-time sacrifices.

The situation in Britain too had changed after the Great War, with significant industrial unrest as troops returning home demanded a fairer society to replace the old aristocratic order. The industrial mobilisation generated by the war had to be sustained and the Indian markets and commodities were of paramount importance. Just as national interests had prevailed in the *jazirat ul-arab*, so too did they affect the promises of Indian home rule or self-government that had been held out in the heat of the moment. In any case the Liberal Party, supported by many Indians like Yusuf Ali as the champion for Indian reform, was in rapid decline. India's war effort had never been sufficiently publicised or appreciated in Britain, but Yusuf Ali continued to hope that 'the British Democracy and the British people' would 'do justice to India'.[44] While India was convulsed by incidents such as the Jallianwala Bagh massacre, in which Indians protesting against martial law were killed indiscriminately by troops, Yusuf Ali engaged himself on the fate of the Peacock Throne rumoured to be in Constantinople: 'What a priceless possession it would be for Delhi and India under her new status after the War.'[45] The Hashemite revolt, Sèvres and continuing martial law had shaken many Muslims of his generation to their senses but his idealistic faith in Britain held through.

He was not party to a petition 'praying for a reconsideration of the Turkish Treaty' submitted by a group of Muslims and their sympathisers in Britain to the League of Nations on 22 November 1920.[46] One reason may have been travel because in December he was in Bombay putting the finishing touches to *Wilson's Anglo-Muhammadan Law*.[47] He was also soon to take up a new post in Hyderabad Deccan. Yusuf Ali maintained a silence on Sèvres till 1925, when a book on Indian history made a passing reference to the 'humiliating terms' the Treaty imposed on the Turks.[48]

His reasons for returning to India at the end of 1920 at the age of 47 may have been personal. Around the early 1920s he married Gertrude Anne

Mawbey, the daughter of Thomas Mawbey, a Derby magistrate and printer. Unfortunately the children from his earlier marriage were becoming increasingly resentful towards him. In particular Bloy, now almost twenty years old, took to tormenting his father. In his will, Yusuf Ali singled him out: 'Indeed my son Bloy has gone so far as to abuse, insult, vilify and persecute me from time to time.' By moving to India, Yusuf Ali could at least spare his young wife this unpleasantness. He gave her the Muslim name of *Masuma*, the innocent, a touching choice given his first wife's infidelity. The last five years for him had been one of public bravado and private anguishes. Now there was to be a new phase in his life that afforded greater personal contentment and fostered the generation of a vast literary output over two decades.

Notes to Chapter 3

1. Viceroy Hardinge had pledged that the sacred regions of Arabia, the shrines of Mesopotamia and the port of Jedda would be "immune from attack or molestation by the British Naval and Military Forces so long as there is no interference with pilgrims from India to the Holy Places and Shrines in question." The Viceroy's pledge reassured Indian Muslims and recruiting for the army improved. See Niemeijer, *The Khilafat Movement in India*, p.80.

2. Zubaida Yazdani, *The Seventh Nizam: the fallen empire*, p. 103. The Nizam had been leant on heavily by the all-powerful Political Resident, Sir Stuart Fraser, to issue the manifesto in 1914.

3. *Asiatic Review*, Vol. 6, 1915; pp. 26-33.

4. Harold Nicolson, *King George V*, p.86.

5. See article by Al-Kidwai, *Islamic Review & Muslim India*, Vol. III, No.1, January 1915. This issue also includes a report of a meeting held on 20 December 1914, at which Maulvi Sadruddin, editor of the magazine and *imam* of Woking Mosque, took the same line, "It was a matter of great regret that Muslim was pitted against Muslim; but Islam also teaches us loyalty and so we serve His Majesty the King, whose subjects we are."

6. PRO: FO371 4231 (1919-20). The Ali Brothers saw their only crime to be "freely expressing and promoting sympathy with our Muslim brethren, and maintaining our allegiance to the Caliph of our Prophet (on whom be God's benediction and peace) and Commander of the Faithful."

7. Entry on Yusuf Ali in *Muslims in India - a biographical dictionary*, Manoher, 1979.

8. *Contemporary Review*, Vol. CVIII, 1915; pp. 446-456. This article is of historical value because of the details on India's military and financial contribution to the Allied cause by 1916. This included over 200,000 soldiers (to rise to about one million in subsequent years - the end of many was to be in the killing fields of the Somme and the Kut-el-Amara campaigns) and a contribution which stood at about fifty million pounds sterling by April 1915 alone.

9. IOL: L/Mil/7/17347. This file, on the War Office's censorship of the mail of Indian soldiers in Europe and related issues, includes extracts from these letters. These official extracts, prepared by the Censor, were circulated to the India Office, the War Office and the Foreign Office, including a copy for the King. They provided a measure of the level of loyalty amongst the troops and were also used to weed out trouble-makers. Some of the letters make very moving reading and capture most vividly the bewilderment of Indian troops thrown into the French front.

10.In 1936 E.W. Perera made a mysterious reference to "the help I had received from Mr. Ali during the dark days of 1915" and said that by referring to it he had to "break the vow of silence he had taken." This comment was reported in the Ceylonese press in reports on Yusuf Ali's visit in that year to attend the All-Ceylon Muslim Educational Conference. *Times of Ceylon*, 15 September 1936 (YA128); also *Ceylon Daily News* of the same day (YA131).

11.*The Islamic Review*, Woking, 15 September 1936. Vol. 5, Nos. 2-3, February-March 1917. Yusuf Ali chaired a meeting held to celebrate the birthday of the Prophet at Hotel Cecil on 6 January, 1917.

12.On its creation in 1917, the Department of Information reported directly to the Prime Minister. In 1918 the Propaganda Section, located at Wellington House, London, was incorporated into the newly formed Ministry of Information. Yusuf Ali was to have further contact with this Ministry in the Second World War. The Bureau of Intelligence, better known as the Political Intelligence Department, came under the umbrella of the Foreign Office.

13.PRO: FO372/1322 (1919) contains details of the St Sava award. *Mestrovic & Serbian sculpture* was one of a series of artistic and literary booklets in the 'Vigo Cabinet' series.

14.It was only twelve years later, as his perceptions changed, that Yusuf Ali made it a point to draw attention to the inappropriateness of the term 'Muhammadan'. Evidence of his knowledge of Ottoman administration can be found in *Life and Labour of the People of India*, published in 1907: "the autonomy of *millats* in the Turkish Empire has done much for the consolidation of Turkish rule among diverse subject populations...there were two elements of failure in the otherwise admirable institutions granted by the Ottomans...one was the weakness of machinery and the laxness of methods. The other was the omission of a supply of safety valves to facilitate automatic expansion and development, and to bring an ancient civilisation gradually into line with modern ideas." p.348.

15. *The Hindustan Review,* January 1916; 'Our Immediate Future'.

16. *The Hindustan Review,* August 1917; 'The Imperial War Conference, 1917'.

17. *Who's Who 1918.* Yusuf Ali's addresses are given as 6 New Square, Lincoln's Inn, and 25 Sutton Court, Chiswick.

18. PRO:FO395/190 (1918) contains details of Yusuf Ali's Scandinavian trip of 1918.

19. ibid. File note signed by H.C.O'Neill of the Ministry of Information, 18 February 1918.

20. ibid. Gaselee's letter to Yusuf Ali is dated 5 April, 1918. Yusuf Ali's home address was now 'Chelwood', 3 Bedford Road, Bedford Park, London W4.

21. ibid. H.C.O'Neill to L.C.Marten, the British Legation, Copenhagen, letter dated 5 April, 1918.

22. Yusuf Ali's Danish booklet was *Traek af Indien Kultur* (Features of Indian Culture), translated by David Grunbaum with the assistance of L.C.Marten. It received a review in the *Times Literary Supplement* of 5 September, 1918.

23. Reuters report, 'Bogus Indian Committee' in *The Times,* 11 May 1918.

24. FO395/190: the *Aftontidning* letter was signed by Virendranath Chattopadhaya on behalf of the Indian National Committee. The extracts quoted here are based on the translation contained in the Foreign Office file. The translated letter was sent in full to Yusuf Ali by the Foreign Office on 12 July, 1918. He responded by enquiring whether the full letter or only an extract had been published in the Swedish newspaper.

25. *The Times Literary Supplement,* 19 September 1918.

26. Yusuf Ali had been invited to deliver some lectures to the London Branch of the Muslim League in the 1915-17 period. "I compared the Indian Muslims to a flock without a shepherd. There were those present who expected me to take them as their guide. They were even annoyed when I did not." From: All-India *Tanzim* conference, Urdu text of Yusuf Ali's presidential address, December 1925.

The London branch of the League was formed in April or May 1908 with offices at 42 Queen Anne's Chambers, Westminster. There are a number of reasons for suggesting Yusuf Ali could not have been as closely involved in its activities as he would have liked his audiences to believe. First, the Bombay Muslim intelligentsia - which included Yusuf Ali - inherited Badruddin Tayebji's advocacy of Hindu-Muslim co-operation and the notion of special privileges advocated by the Muslim League was an anathema. Second, Yusuf Ali's contacts were with Liberal Party politicians - for example Lord Morley - while Justice Ameer Ali, founder of the London Branch of the Muslim League, was more closely associated with the Conservative Party. Ameer Ali and Yusuf Ali were therefore allied to different sections of the British establishment, a feature reflected in their choice of clubs - the Reform for one and the National Liberal for the other. Perhaps the 'annoyance' referred to by Yusuf Ali in the above quotation was Ameer Ali's.

See also K.K. Aziz, *Britain and Muslim India*, p. 71, and *Memoirs and Other Writings of Sayyid Ameer Ali*, pp.74-75.

27. FO395/190, ibid. A hapless O'Neill offered this roundabout explanation to the Foreign Office on 10 November 1918, one day before Armistice Day:

> Mr. Gaselee,
>
> I very much regret to have to admit that what you say is true. The files are lost - or so I have been informed. I cannot think this my fault. Indeed if I were not constitutionally timid, I would submit that they last went to you for submission to the India Office. As it is I dare not make this suggestion and the episode becomes one of those singular occurrences which Providence sometimes permits to humiliate those who boast themselves efficient. I mean, of course, myself, but can we do nothing without the files?

If Yusuf Ali's file was truly lost, the final irony is perhaps that Gaselee went on to become the Foreign Office's official Keeper of Documents.

28. Preface of *India and Europe*, 1925. By 1925 his idealism had come to be tempered and the quotation continues, "Our descendants three generation hence will be better judge of that than we are."

29. On Constantinople, letter, *The Times*, 29 November 1918

30. Throughout this account, the word "Caliphate" is used to designate the institution and the word "Khilafat" to mean the Indian Muslim movement led by Muhammad Ali Jauhar and his elder brother Shaukat Ali. Though Sultan Abdul Hamid II had been deposed in 1909, the Caliphate itself was not abolished in Turkey till 1924.

31. The petition in *The Times* continued: "The Musalmans who have shed their blood or helped with their resources in the defence of the Empire are entitled to expect that the principle of national unity and freedom will be maintained in the case of Turkey as in the case of the European peoples. Any other course would give rise to a most painful impression that the high principles and lofty ideals which secured for the Allied cause the adhesion and loyal cooperation of the larger part of the Muslim world were abandoned in the case of Turkey because she is a Muslim state. We feel confident, however, that no racial or religious prejudices will be allowed to impair the trust of the Muslim nations in the good faith of the Allies and that the settlement of this momentous world problem will be based on the principles of justice and equity, and of national unity and national rule laid down by the Prime Minister of Great Britain and the President of the United States... We respectfully submit that the whole of this territory with Constantinople as its capital should be left in the hands of the Turkish nation....With regard to the other Provinces of Turkey we desire at present to express no opinion." Letter from some British Muslim subjects to the British Foreign Secretary, reproduced in K.K.Aziz, *The Indian Khilafat Movement 1915-1933*, pp.26-28.

32. IOL: Mss Eur D 523/16, Montagu Papers. The letter is dated 21 May 1919. Montagu is remembered as a reform-minded Secretary of State for India, a member of a distinguished circle of Liberal Members of Parliament of the Jewish faith who were close to Prime Minister Lloyd George in both political and business alliances. These included Herbert Samuel and Rufus Isaacs, war-time ambassador to the United States and Viceroy of India in 1921. Unlike Samuel and Isaacs, Montagu did not subscribe to the Zionist scheme for Palestine and fought many battles in Cabinet to obtain better peace terms for the Turks. He resigned in March 1922 and died a year later. His desperation is apparent in this letter to the Viceroy Chelmsford dated 25th June 1919, "...as regards the Turk I am fighting desperately...Balfour is my most redoubtable enemy. Milner is my only assistant. The Aga Khan has been most useful. I am not yet sure that we have failed. Much now depends upon America"; IOL: Mss Eur D 523/3.

    For details of a business scandal in 1912 involving Lloyd George, Samuel and Isaacs see *The Marconi Scandal* by Frances Donaldson.

33. Faisal became King of Syria in May 1919 but was banished by the French five months later. He sought refuge in London and was made King of Iraq under British sponsorship in 1921. Yusuf Ali wrote an obituary note to *The Times* on Faisal's death, published on 11 September, 1933:

    > As one who was hospitably received by King Faisal in Baghdad, and was greatly impressed by his simplicity, soldierly bearing and courtesy, will you permit me to pay a brief tribute to his memory?

    > The secret of his success lay in his realistic appreciation of facts and his adaptability to new situations. His palace was thronged by Beduin Arabs who came to visit him and expected from him Beduin standards of democratic equality. He did not deny them their reasonable demands, while at the same time he won the confidence of his city-dwelling subjects and of the *Shi'is* who form a large proportion of the population of lower Iraq. He had a reasoned belief in the value of the British connection. His interest in education was keen. Thanks to the facilities he offered me, I was enabled to study his nascent system of education. He was anxious to learn of the British educational system in India, and was moved almost to emotional interest when I spoke of the negative warnings which the system affords. He had an embryonic university scheme which I hope his Harrovian successor King Ghazi will be able to develop on lines suitable to Iraq.

    Yusuf Ali's reference is to his travels in Iraq in 1929. It is unlikely that Faisal so unburdened himself unless they met previously in Paris. If this inference is correct, Yusuf Ali would have also known T.E. Lawrence, advisor to the Arab Delegation at the Paris Peace Conference. While covering his visit in Canada in 1938-39, a newspaper did state that Yusuf Ali was a 'personal friend of the late Col. Lawrence of Arabia'; *Free Press*, London, Ontario, 6 January 1939 (YA265) .

34. PRO:FO371/4231 (1919-20). The quotation is from the Ali Brothers' memorandum of April 1919 from prison to the Viceroy. The document provides a vivid contrast to the obsequious petitioning of the Empire-Loyalists. It began *Bismillahir-Rahmanir-Rahim* and concluded with the Qur'anic verses: "O Ye that believe! Seek assistance in patience and prayer...and do not speak of those that are slain in Allah's way as dead". In their view Sherif Husein carried much of the blame for the loss of Muslim control of Islam's heartland. The memorandum documented the reasons why the British fanned the Hashemite rebellion in Hejaz: "On the 21st October 1915, less than a year after the pledge of 2 November 1914 [Viceroy Hardinge's undertaking, see Note 1 above] we find the Secretary of State for India telegraphing to the Viceroy as follows: At the present moment...our position and prospects are most uncertain...Arabs are wavering, and will probably join the Turks unless we can offer them great inducement. We are therefore in great need of striking success in the East...It is suggested that we should occupy Baghdad giving assurances to Arab leaders that we favour creation of an Arab State independent of the Turks." While this memorandum is an oft-quoted document, some orientalists have glossed over its Qur'anic references. For Minault, 'pro-Turkish sentiment made good political sense...the feeling of Islamic brotherhood ...gave them [Indian Muslims] a basis for solidarity among themselves to counteract their minority status in the political arena.' *The Khilafat Movement*, p.57. Such scholars impose their own censorship on historical documents, in this case to bolster the thesis that religion in the sub-continent merely provided a convenient rallying point for opportunistic Muslim politicians.

35. The Khilafat Deputation's memorial to the Viceroy and the Viceroy's reply, reproduced in S.S. Pirzada (ed.), *The Collected Works of Quaid Azam Mohammad Ali Jinnah*, pp.374-382.

36. IOL: Mss Eur D 523/4, Montagu Papers; Montagu's letter to Chelmsford of 1 April 1920.

37. An example of the close monitoring is this excerpt: "March 8, 1920 - (Jauhar) lunched with Captain Bennet, who is very friendly with Ameer Ali, and is responsible for pro-Turkish advertisements in the press." IOL:L/P&S/18/B361; Yusuf Ali claimed association with the Khilafatists in his speech to the All-India *Tanzim* conference, ibid.

38. In *The Making of India* published in 1925 he observed that Aligarh was 'saved' from the Ali Brothers' 'revolutionary' campaign aimed at cutting financial dependency on the Government; p.298.

39. IOL:L/P&S/18/B361; 'Minutes of Proceeding at a deputation from the Indian Khilafat Delegation to the Prime Minister'.

40. IOL:L/P&S/18/B361, ibid.

41. From Vernon Bartlett's *Behind the Scenes at the Peace Conference*. Bartlett was Reuters's correspondent at the Paris Peace Conference.

42. "Gandhi felt uneasy at the increasing impatience for action on the part of his Muslim allies....Now the Muslims were forging ahead of him in espousing his own technique of non-cooperation...He disagreed, furthermore, with the proposed boycott of European goods." See Minault, *The Khilafat Movement*, p.96 and also Niemeijer, pp. 107-108, for details of Congress's wavering over the non-cooperation campaign in mid-1920. The Khilafatists demanded resignations from the Police and non-payment of taxes, measures far too bold for the Congress at the time.

43. This was the outcome of a report by Judge Rowlatt, that lead to the Rowlatt Act of 1919. Yusuf Ali was characteristically uncritical: "the telegraphic summary of the Rowlatt Committee's report raised a few questions of criminal procedure in India which require considerations of their bearing on the larger questions of policy and judicial administration. The Committee's criticism and recommendations are no doubt confined in their application to special trials in connection with sedition...." *The Times*, 6 August 1918. When the Rowlatt report became the basis of a Bill there was an outcry of protest throughout India in the spring and summer of 1919. Jinnah was to say of the Rowlatt Act, "there was no precedent or parallel in the legal history of any civilised country to the enactment of such laws." S. Wolpert, *Jinnah of Pakistan*, p.61.

44. *The Hindustan Review*, January 1916; 'Our Immediate Future'.

45. Peacock Throne, letter, *The Times*, 10 September 1919 in which Yusuf Ali mooted the idea of raising funds in India for the purchase of the Peacock Throne, "would it not be well to acquire it for India and her new Imperial capital?" The Jallianwalla Bagh massacre occurred on 13 April 1919. At the command of General R.Dyer, ninety soldiers fired steadily for ten minutes at a crowd of 20,000 protesting against the Rowlatt Act. The summer of 1919 also saw the aerial bombardment of protesters in Gujaranwala. See P.G. Robb, *The Government of India and Reform*, p.177 for details of both incidents.

46. IOL: L/P&S/11/190, File 8342, 'Memorial sent by British subjects to the League of Nations'. Signatories included many of those who lent their names to the earlier, equally respectful memorial of January 1919. The memorial pleaded that the mandates would not be used as a cover for the exploitation of weak and small nations. Among the signatories were Lord Abingdon and Lord Lamington who in later years embraced Islam. The Labour leader Ramsay Macdonald also signed the memorial.

47. The preface of the fifth edition of *Wilson's Anglo-Muhammadan Law* ends with the note 'Bombay, 1st December 1920'. It was published the following year by Thacker & Spink, Calcutta.

48. *The Making of India*, 1925; p.295.

4

MAN OF MANY PARTS

The young prince Mir Osman Ali Khan ruled over his large kingdom in the Deccan with a gentle autocracy, ever mindful that effective power rested with the Political Resident appointed by Delhi. Yusuf Ali served briefly as a counsel in the Nizam's *Sarf-i-khas*, a body which administered the 'crown' lands, and later in 1921 became Revenue Member of the Executive Council of the State.[1] This made him responsible for land revenue, famine and revenue inspections, forests, customs and excise, and the police. It was a job that suited him ideally after the years as ICS collector and deputy commissioner in the UP. The Nizam exercised a careful watch over affairs, successfully curbing the excesses of a large and feuding aristocracy and forcing key ministers to consult advisers of his appointment. His particular achievement was patronage of Osmania University, founded in 1918, which attracted scholars from all over India. Hyderabad became an island of relative affluence and stability for Indian Muslims in comparison with the UP. Yusuf Ali would also have found the Nizam's politics to his liking because the Khilafatists were not tolerated.[2]

Osmania University included a bureau for the translation of textbooks and scientific literature from English to Urdu. Yusuf Ali was to be a participant in these cultural activities and would later describe his own literary contribution in the following terms: 'When I was in Hyderabad, I had the privilege of participating in the initial stages of the Urdu movement and Osmania University. The aim was to enrich our language with translations of original works and authoritative books, which could be used at the University for teaching. I also produced a small handbook [Urdu: *risala*] for them on Urdu orthography [Urdu: *kitabat*] which was meant to systematise the writing, spelling and printing of Urdu.'[3]

Yusuf Ali resigned abruptly from his post in 1922, in spite of everything appearing to be just right for him. Perhaps it was his insistence that things be done according to procedure rather than the fiat of the Nizam or the whim of some *nawab* (Indian aristocrat). Yusuf Ali was 'extremely touchy' – Lord Meston's assessment based on observing him in the ICS – which would have made life doubly difficult in the face of court intrigues. His departure from Hyderabad coincided with the appointment of a Bombay contemporary, Akbar Hydari, as Finance Minister. Thicker-skinned than Yusuf Ali, he proceeded to hold high office in the state for the next twenty years. It was a model career that Yusuf Ali could so easily have made his own. A story gained circulation that Yusuf Ali was still working for the ICS at the time and the resignation came about because of a dispute between the Nizam and the Viceroy, Lord Reading.[4] It may not have been easy for him to set the record straight on the real reasons for leaving the Service in 1913, for fear of exposing the dark secret of the scandalous divorce. Yusuf Ali was not to bear any ill will towards Hyderabad and later contributed several articles to *Islamic Culture*, a journal which had Hydari's patronage. He also attended the Nizam's Silver Jubilee celebration in 1937 and retained a friendship with Hyderabad notables like Nawab Imad-ul-Mulk Husain Bilgrami, Nawab Sir Amin Jung Bahadur and Nawab Sir Nizamat Jung.[5] Yusuf Ali's brief sojourn also saw the birth of a son, Rashid, in August 1922.[6]

Yusuf Ali left Hyderabad to practice at the United Province's Lucknow Bar and to write, possibly after a brief journey to England to settle his family.[7] Though a qualified barrister with the oratorical skills and show-manship essential for success in the profession, he was at heart a man of letters. He was particularly interested in Mughal history and collaborated with W.H. Moreland, formerly director of land revenues in the UP, on a study of Akbar's land revenue system. In March 1923 he read a paper on Babar based on the king's diary at a meeting of the United Provinces Historical Society. Yusuf Ali recognised many qualities in Babar: 'thus lived and died a brave and generous man. His hardy life filled in with his love of nature. His adventures, failures and successes never dried up the milk of human kindness in him. The sincerity of his soul, in strength and weakness, shines from every page of his self-revealing record.'[8] This movingly phrased admiration for a great Muslim monarch was indicative of Yusuf Ali's changing attitudes. Ten years ago George V and his *chahra-e-mubarak* had been the object of Yusuf Ali's veneration. Now at least his pantheon of heroes included a king from the Muslim past. Like Babar girding for a military offensive, Yusuf Ali was preparing for a subtle but combative campaign to shape Indian Muslims' way of thinking.

An invitation to address the Punjab Muslim Educational Conference in April 1923 in Lahore marked the start of this campaign. He presented an analysis of the intellectual and political choices confronting Muslims. The speech indicates that he had commenced thinking afresh about Islam and his mind was absorbed with the problem of accommodating this new factor with other ideas he held on Europe and progress:

> Now Islam finds itself confronted on all sides with the taunt that it is an unprogressive or a narrow religion. You and I, and all who understand Islam, know that the charge is false. But we have got to show by our institutions and our practice that we are prepared to modernise and liberalise our education...the aim is to bring the Islamic intellect into touch with modern learning of the West, and to give us a fresh stimulus to grapple with our peculiar problems, social and political, with the weapons of modern education, and the methods of modern communities.....the dangers connected with the thirst for modernity have sometimes claimed too much attention from our *ulema* and our satirists, but they should not be lost sight of...one is that the new wine may burst the old bottles, and so we may lose both the wine and the bottles.[9]

If Sir Sayyid had been satirised as *ibn ul-waqt* (son of the times) for his ready acceptance of European superiority in the 1890s, there was a respectful silence by the 1920s. Yusuf Ali also addressed the problem of Muslim religious identity and Hindu-Muslim cooperation in a single nation:

> For our part we are content to view religious questions from our own religious standpoint, and to cooperate in politics with all communities and parties which believe in well-ordered progress. We do not

consider Indian Nationalism of the right sort to be inconsistent with progressive Islam. On the contrary we consider that progressive Islam has a large service to contribute to the growth of a stable Indian nationality.

Yusuf Ali's intellectual scheme would allow Muslims to retain their religious identity while preserving the notion of Indian nationhood, all within the umbrella of western-inspired progress. It is not known whether Iqbal was in the audience, but the drift of the argument and its optimistic vision would have made him increasingly restive.[10]

Yusuf Ali's host in Lahore was most likely to have been Mian Fazli Husain, the province's Minister of Education who owed his post to the special patronage of the Governor, Sir Edward Maclagan.[11]

Yusuf Ali left Lahore for Bombay in June 1923, *en route* to Britain. He next devoted his time to two books on India, *The Making of India* and *India and Europe*. These works presented a sanguine picture of India, with the minimum of detail on the problems which had arisen in the last decade: the Kanpur Mosque incident of 1913 and the anguish caused by the war against Turkey; the Rowlatt Act and its bloody aftermath at Jallianwalla Bagh in 1919; the role of the Khilafatists and the worsening relationship between Hindus and Muslims. He was diligently non-controversial, portraying India as a land of contentment with only the minor hiccup. Even a British reviewer could not help observing of *The Making of India* that the author 'touches lightly on what he calls atrocities and unedifying facts'.[12] The book was dedicated to Viscount Willingdon, former Governor of Bombay, and his wife, in characteristic effusive style. It was a gesture that scored a few political points and reflected an insensitivity to Jinnah's feelings and his continued contempt of the Ali Brothers. Willingdon was despised by Jinnah, and as Governor had vowed to shoot or deport the Ali Brothers. As if to reaffirm his aloofness, *The Making of India* contained no reference to works by contemporary Indian scholars, with the exception of Ameer Ali's biography of the Prophet, first published in 1891.

The one facet of British administration which grieved Yusuf Ali was racial discrimination. His harshest words were reserved for those 'British non-officials' in India who regarded themselves as a ruling class: 'Their

74

claim gave the more offence, as, without being rulers, they claimed the status of a ruling race.' He took the opportunity to present Islam's enlightened code:

> Muslims are taught by their faith to rise above prejudices of race. All races are equal in the Muslim brotherhood. Other universal religions have similar ideas of brotherhood, but none carries it out to the same extent as it is carried out in Islam...it was so in the days of the Prophet and his immediate successors. It is so now, when the number of races and countries is infinitely larger within the pale of Islam.[13]

Just as India had much to learn from Britain, so too could Islam contribute to the West. Such cooperation was becoming a central feature of his emerging world view. A further passage in *India and Europe* reveals an interest Yusuf Ali was acquiring in the notion of a spiritual fellowship to cement harmony. Foreshadowing his involvement in the World Congress of Faiths ten years later, he wrote, 'In my view the religion of all thinking men is the same, however different may be the philosophy by which they explain their spiritual instincts, or the moulds in which they cast their spiritual hopes.[14]

It was now the era of Indian political reform in which certain 'subjects', like education, agriculture and health, were transferred to the control of provincial ministers responsible to elected legislatures. To the chagrin of those seeking more fundamental change, the important function of law and order was still with the Governor and his official executive council. The Viceroy and the Governors also retained the power of certifying bills even if these had been defeated by the provincial assemblies. In November 1923, elections were held on the basis of these arrangements and Yusuf Ali, back in India after passing the summer months in England, played a minor and inconclusive role in electoral activity in the UP.[15] It was a matter which Jinnah took far more seriously, winning a seat in the Bombay legislature as a Muslim Independent.

Yusuf Ali returned to Lahore in 1924 on the occasion of the fortieth anniversary of the educational and welfare body, *Anjuman-Himayat-ul-Islam.* Its main educational venture was Islamia College, an institution for

Muslim boys set up in 1892 to fulfil for Western India what Aligarh was achieving for the Muslims of North India - an institution for boys, which, in the aims of its founders, would 'provide both the *deen* and *dunya* types of education'.[16] The Anjuman's college committee, chaired by Shaikh Abdul Qader, was seeking a principal and the post was offered to Yusuf Ali to take up at the start of the next academic year. He accepted an offer which provided opportunity for public service in apparently congenial circumstances. The party in power in Punjab was Fazli's Unionist Party, an opportunistic ensemble of the landed gentry united against the town-based Hindu moneylenders. The British provincial administration of the Punjab needed such a rural-urban divide for its own ends and provided more electoral seats to the landlords and fewer to the urban areas. The underlying reason for conferring political patronage on the *zamindar* (feudal landlord) class was to ensure regular access to army recruits from the Punjab, 'the Prussia of India'. These types of mutual interdependencies were at the heart of the cosy relationship between the Unionist politicians and the British governor. Coincidentally, the new governor of the Punjab was now Malcolm Hailey, of the same batch of ICS entrants in 1895 as Yusuf Ali. As on so many other occasions, Yusuf Ali possessed all the important contacts. With his plans for the following year settled, Yusuf Ali returned to his family in London.

The summer of 1925 was also taken up moving to a new home in Chiswick. It had been a glorious summer enjoyably spent with Masuma and Rashid, and they had many friends to entertain.[17] Before leaving for his new post, Yusuf Ali organised a publication programme with Luzac in London for a series with the title 'Progressive Islam Pamphlets'. The first of these, *Greatest Need of the Age*, was published in August 1925, while the second was based on his lecture, *Islam as a World Force*, presented the preceding year in Lahore on the occasion of the Anjuman's anniversary. His debut as an Islamic scholar had commenced. He also contributed two articles to the formidable *Encyclopaedia of Islam* on the term *Khodja* and the nineteenth-century shaikh, Karamat Ali Jawnpuri.[18] The latter only thinly disguised the author's ideological preferences. The shaikh belonged to the *Ta'yuniyya*, an offshoot of the *Tariqa Muhammadiya*, and clashed with Haji Shariatullah's *Faraidi* movement. An important point of dispute

76

related to the legality of *Juma* and *'id* prayer in British India, which the Faraidis had declared illegal. Karamat Ali held that Bengal could not be regarded as _Dar-ul-Harb_ and so these prayers should be compulsorily observed. Yusuf Ali also took pains to refute the claim that the shaikh was a *Wahhabi*, by inference denigrating the 'militant' *Faraidis*. Karamat Ali had competed for a prize offered by Sir Charles Trevelyan for the best Urdu essay on the influence of the Greeks and Arabs on the Renaissance in Europe. On this Yusuf Ali noted with approval: 'He was thus interested, unlike the majority of contemporary Indian *Mawlawis*, in the relation of Islam to the wider questions of the world at large.' This was precisely what Yusuf Ali's own recent literary effort had been about as well.

Yusuf Ali's contacts and eminence immediately gave him a wider role in the Punjab. He was invited to the Syndicate of Punjab University and in a surprising development also accepted presidency of the *Jamiat-e-Tanzim*. This organisation had been set up by Dr Saifuddin Kitchlew a year earlier in 1924 with the specific aim of countering militant Hindu revivalist *sanghatan* activity in the Punjab. Yusuf Ali addressed the organisation at its conference in Aligarh in December 1925 in a speech with many nuances, such as a quest for a role in Indian affairs beyond educational service in the Punjab. Trusting neither the Congress nor the Muslim League for bringing about 'well-ordered progress', he saw an opportunity for *Tanzim*:

> This organisation is not based on the thoughts or emotions of a few individuals or a narrow class, neither does it present any sectarian views or plans. Its purpose is to overcome the centrifugal forces that are at work, and seek a unity of organisations that differ in their aims. Its purpose is to serve the community [Urdu: *qaum*] and nation [Urdu: *mulk*] in a spirited manner and with the end in view that we seek to work with other organisations rather than to oppose or boycott them... Our organisation was born in the lap of the Khilafat movement, therefore there is no rivalry between the two and there should be none. It is our duty to proceed wisely so that the Khilafat people do not think we are against their leaders and I believe we can sincerely support them personally and collectively.[19]

Yusuf Ali did not follow up this eloquence with further work for the organisation. The olive branch to the Khilafatists was made at a time when Kitchlew, a former Khilafatist, stood accused by Jauhar of showing 'partisan narrowness'.[20] The ground had been cut away from under the feet of the Khilafatists by the Turks' own decision in March 1924 to abolish the Caliphate, albeit forced through by Mustafa Kemal. Gandhi too had proved a fair-weather friend, leaving the Ali Brothers in the lurch on many a crucial occasion.[21] The Khilafatists were fighting for their political survival and regrouping to form the nucleus of the Punjab Muslim League, which was bitterly opposed to the pro-British Unionist Party. They could not react kindly to being written off. It was only a matter of time before the principal of Islamia College would be sucked into controversy.

Yusuf Ali provided the opportunity for confrontation through his involvement in League of Nations activities. The League of Nations was despised by the Khilafatists as the instrument that dissected the *jazirat ul-arab*. It was a tainted body, which Iqbal had described in acerbic verse as 'an organisation of thieves for the distribution of shrouds, sitting in a graveyard'.[22] The League was all the more obnoxious because of the large financial contribution which India had to make to its budget. Moreover, League of Nations activities in India were championed by Sir William Birdwood, the British Army general in the Gallipoli campaign against the Ottomans. In marked contrast, Yusuf Ali and his Lahore circle of Unionist friends were keen supporters of Birdwood's work. The *Zamindar* newspaper run by the Khilafatist Zafar Ali Khan had some caustic remarks to make on the participation of the Shaikh Abdul Qader - who had succeeded Fazli Hussain as education minister - and Yusuf Ali at a meeting of the League of Nations Union held in Delhi in February 1926:

> The League of Nations constitutes a conspiracy against the Muslim world and we want to proclaim it by beat of drum that the Indian Mussulmans do not like to hear one word in support of the League. If the League commences work in India we shall oppose it tooth and nail, in which crusade the entire Muslim press of India will be on our side. The office-bearers of the Lahore Union should have compassion on Islam and at least show some regard for their Muslim names.

78

Shaikh Abdul Qader and Mr. Yusuf Ali may cooperate with Government and get posts for themselves but they should not join a movement whose object is to crush the liberty of our Muslim brethren.[23]

When Abdul Qader was sent to Geneva as Indian delegate to the League of Nations conference in 1926, he was to receive further admonishments from sections of the Lahore press.[24]

Yusuf Ali's response would come at the Punjab Educational Conference held in December 1926. He made it a point to praise the League of Nations: 'it has given the lead to international action in various matters in which all States are interested, and it has materially helped in bringing out that spirit of international co-operation which must lead more and more to the harmony of nations.'[25] Yusuf Ali pursued controversy with dogged determination. His address included a fulsome expression of the Unionist Party's creed, which 'cherished the Imperial tie'.[26]

With characteristic industry Yusuf Ali participated in numerous public engagements between 1925 and 1927 while also serving as principal of Islamia. He jointly edited 'Glimpses of the Punjab: a souvenir of the 14th Meeting of the Indian Science Congress', held in Lahore in January 1927. In the same year he published a booklet for students, *Three Travellers to India*, which contained accounts of India as seen by Hiuen Tsiang, Ibn Batuta and the seventeenth-century Frenchman, François Bernier. Yusuf Ali also published another school text for use at the matriculation level, *Outlines of Indian History*. He was one of the brightest of men in a city already luminescent with a generation of formidable intellectuals. Sulaiman Nadwi left a roll-call after a visit to the city:

> For men of letters and men of learning, Lahore is today the best centre in India. It has the presence of talented men like Dr Sir Muhammad Iqbal, Shaikh Abdul Qadir, principal Abdullah Yusuf Ali, Professor Hafiz Mahmoud Sherani, Professor Iqbal, Professor Muhammad Shafi, Professor Sirajuddin Azar, Maulvi Muhammad Ali MA, Khwaja Kamaluddin, Professor Sayyid Abdul Qadir, Maulvi Zafar Ali Khan, which cannot be found in any other city. From the older generation there are Sayyid Mumtaz Ali Sahib, Munshi

Mahboub Alam Sahib and Maulvi Insha Allah Khan, who, though in the autumn of their lives, leave us the memories of spring. The associations of humourists, writers and poets are no less active. Salik and Mehr, Tajwar, Abul Asar Hafeez Jalandhri, Ghulam Rubbani, Dr Taseer...and many other men of letters are busy establishing themselves and the future awaits their success.[27]

Inevitably tensions were developing in the *Anjuman-Himayat-ul-Islam* between the Unionists, who were the important officeholders, and the nascent Muslim Leaguers on the continued employment of Yusuf Ali as principal of Islamia College. The Anjuman proceedings record several acrimonious discussions: on 19 June 1927 a question was asked why Yusuf Ali did not undertake any teaching; a few months later another member wished to know why the principal arrived at the College at 10 o'clock in the morning rather than at 7 a.m. during the summer season.[28] Relationships were deteriorating and the College Committee convened an extraordinary meeting in October. Yusuf Ali complained that aspersions were being made about him at meetings in his absence. He gave them the ultimatum that matters relating to Islamia College should not be discussed unless he was present. Yusuf Ali left Islamia College soon after to pursue various literary projects. By February 1928 he had completed work on the sixth edition of *Wilson's Anglo-Muhammadan Law*, a widely used legal digest whose previous edition had also been edited by him. A month later Yusuf Ali was in Allahabad, delivering a series of lectures in Urdu to the widely known Hindustani Academy on 'Social and Economic Conditions in Medieval India'. In the same period he was also appointed a member of the Court of Aligarh University.

Yusuf Ali left India in the spring, this time not following the usual sea route westward via the Suez Canal. He travelled instead to Baghdad and visited Karbala, using the old boat bridge at al-Musib to cross the Euphrates. He wrote an eloquent account:

I remember starting my trip from Baghdad, in that part of the country which is irrigated by the river Euphrates. I crossed the river at al-Musib on a bridge made of boats. It was a beautiful April morning and I was engrossed in thoughts of the events of past centuries. To the left of the Euphrates were the historic and ancient ruins of Babel. These were previously buried in the desert and have revealed the glory and splendour of an ancient age. The Euphrates is a unique river. Its origins are in a multitude of streams in the mountains of Eastern Armenia. It meanders through rocky plains and then runs alongside the desert, intersecting it with rivulets and canals to produce a flourish of vegetation abounding in fruit and agricultural produce. After this it joins the marshes. There are lakes a short distance from the noble Karbala connected to the river which serve as great water reservoirs. Further down it meets up with the river Tigris and the confluence is known as Shatt al-arab, which falls into the Persian Gulf.

In spite of the abundance of water, thirst proved a great affliction! There have been gardens in the lower regions of the Euphrates from ancient times. It was the cradle of old civilisations. The Hamiri Arabs would meet here. It was here too that the Arabs and Persians met and established contact. This is a fertile and green country. Dates and pomegranates are plentiful. The abundance of fruits sustained whole cities. The nomadic Arabs with their cattle would come to the plains. One is particularly sorrowed and grieved to see the abundance of water in the land where *Hadrat Imam* Husain, peace upon him, and his companions, in a condition of thirst, undertook *jihad* against oppression and inequality and drank from the cup of martyrdom. With all this water and sand surrounding you the remembrance of the martyrdom of *Hadrat* Husain is overwhelming.

I was overwrought with emotion when I reached Karbala *sharif*. The rays of the morning sunshine were imparting to the dome of Imam Husain's shrine a particular beauty. Karbala is located in the desert at a point visited by the caravans. Kufa, which was once the capital of the Caliphate, is only present today as a small habitation on the banks of a river. The resting place for *Hadrat* Ali, may God be pleased with him, is in the city of Najf. It does not have much significance as a trading centre. Karbala is located in the desert and remains a market as well as being held a place of special respect. It is a port of the desert, just as Basra is a port of the Persian Gulf. Both Karbala and Basra are commercial centres. Goods and materials arrive here throughout the year from all parts of the world. The street leading to the shrine is unparalleled in beauty and grandeur. The shrine has a coloured roof. The inner and upper walls are decorated with mirror work. Lights flicker and reflect off these mirrors. The doors of the shrine remain closed and one can feel spiritually elevated. The shrine's buildings are not very high. There is a cellar underground where there is *Imam* Husain's shrine. It was at this spot that he was martyred. Forty miles from here is the most noble city of Najf, where there is the shrine of *Hadrat* Ali, may God be pleased with him. It is located on a height. The golden dome is visible from miles around. Kufa is four miles away from Najf and is today desolate. There is a tram which goes there from Najf. Kufa's Friday mosque is magnificent but lying empty and unused. It has a blue dome and a colourful *mihrab*, which bespeak its bygone glory.'[29]

Yusuf Ali's knack of knowing the right people at the right place led to an invitation to the royal palace in Baghdad for an audience with the King of Iraq. 'He had a reasoned belief in the value of the British connection,' Yusuf Ali wrote with unconscious understatement of Faisal. 'His interest in education was keen. Thanks to the facilities which he offered me I was enabled to study his nascent system of education.'[30] This suggests that Yusuf Ali's travels might have been officially sponsored as part of some information-gathering exercise. He also visited Turkey where he caught a glimpse of Mustafa Kemal. His impression was one of cautious approval: 'He is not without faults, and some of his reforms savour too much of extreme nationalism. But he saved them [his people] from total extinction. He safeguarded their liberty. He purged the country of many evil customs and evil traditions that had grown up in the course of centuries. He cleared out the elements which would have hampered the growth and development of modern life. He has built up new institutions without...too great a hankering for the past.'[31] Yusuf Ali and the famous poetess and politician Sarojini Naidu were the only two Indians to be sponsored on educational tours of this type as the cultural ambassadors of British India.

From 1921 to 1928 Yusuf Ali tried his hand in a variety of employments and ventures in India, many ending on an unfinished note. The period commenced as Minister of land revenue in Hyderabad but concluded rather abruptly within barely a year. This was followed by practice at the Lucknow Bar and a half-hearted foray into electioneering politics. The years in Lahore were the most fulfilling, though there again he did not follow through the opportunities which presidency of the *Tanzim* offered for someone serious about social reform in India. He might also have made more of the principalship at Islamia, but it was not his style to hold back his political views. Whether as writer or speaker he had been consistently combative in projecting his vision of a 'progressive Islam' compatible with loyalty to Empire. At the age of fifty-five he still had his most memorable achievement to come.

Notes to Chapter 4

1. *The Times*, obituary on Yusuf Ali, 15 December 1953. See also *Islamic Culture*, Hyderabad, Vol.XXVIII, No. 1, 1954. When serving as Revenue Member his secretary was Nawab Fasih Jung.

2. In May 1920 the Nizam prohibited all Khilafatist meetings. He wrote to Viceroy Chelmsford, "...it is impossible for me to countenance proceedings that have avowed intentions of resistance, euphemistically called 'passive', to British authority - indeed against all authority." See Niemeijer, *The Khilafat Movement*, p.89.

3. From Yusuf Ali's *Tarikh-i-Hind kay azmana-i-wusta mai ma'ashri aur iqtisadi halaat*; p.17. Lectures delivered on 2-4 March 1928, Hindustani Academy, Allahabad. Urdu text obtained from Quaid-e Azam Library, Lahore; this edition was published in 1939.

4. In this version of events the resignation came about because the Viceroy Lord Reading (Rufus Isaacs) insisted the Nizam appear before him in Delhi. Yusuf Ali, described as Hyderabad's 'Regent General', advised Mir Osman Ali Khan against this on the grounds that the Viceroy was merely a governmental appointee, while the position of Nizam was monarchical: it was the Viceroy who should be required to pay respects to the Nizam, rather than the other way round. The Viceroy however prevailed and the Nizam was obliged to go to Delhi. The British exacted their revenge by forcing the resignation of Yusuf Ali 'from the ICS'. For a written account of this version of Yusuf Ali's resignation from the ICS see Baidar Malik, *Yaran-i-Maktab: Tehrik-i-Pakistan aur Islamia College*, p.189. A similar oral account was also given to the author in Karachi,

January 1988, by Maulana Ismail Ahmed Meenai, a former magistrate in Hyderabad State.

There are many strands in this story that can be traced to actual happenings in Hyderabad but they do not add up: Lord Reading did issue a petulant edict summoning the Nizam, yet this was not in 1921 but 1926; a resignation did take place in Hyderabad in September 1922, but it was of Sir Ali Imam, president of the Nizam's Executive Council. No doubt the colourful tale involving Yusuf Ali gained popular appeal because it provided an example of a Muslim taking a principled stand against the British administration at the cost of high office. When the general tenor of Muslim behaviour was fawning and servile, there was need for uplifting examples. Yusuf Ali became a vicarious symbol of Muslim self-respect.

5. *The Holy Qur'an: text, translation and commentary*, third edition (1938) contains, in its section 'Translations of the Qur'an' a reference to Nawab Husain Bilgrami; the June 1935 instalment of *The Holy Qur'an* (first edition) contains a warm commendation by Nawab Sir Amin Jung Bahadur. Nawab Nizamat Jung published a poem in honour of Yusuf Ali in *Islamic Culture*, Vol. XXVIII, No.1, January 1954.

6. Rashid's birth is not on record at the General Register Office, Somerset House, London, suggesting that he was born in India. Yusuf Ali's will indicates that Rashid was to reach the age of majority, which at the time was twenty-one years, on 4 August 1943. It is on this basis that Rashid's date of birth is presumed to be 4 August 1922. After World War II, Rashid worked for the Hyderabad Police Force, suggesting a connection with the Principality.

7. In September 1922 he granted power of attorney to a Reverend Ernest Foster, presumably to care for his young family in his absence: "I George Brian Foster of 'The Brentor Hotel', Brentor near Tavistock in the County of Devon, hotel proprietor, retaining possession of a power of attorney dated 15th day of *September 1922* and under the hand and seal of the Very Reverend Ernest Foster relating to freehold property known as Number 3 Mansel Road, Wimbledon, in the County of Surrey and other properties hereby acknowledge your right to production of the said document and to deliver copies thereof and I hereby undertake for the safe custody thereof. As witness my hand this twelfth day of August 1928." [Author's emphasis.] This document was discovered by the owners of 3 Mansel Road, Yusuf Ali's final London address.

8. *The Self Revelation of Babar*. Paper read on Saturday 31 March 1923. Yusuf Ali also offered an explanation for the decline of the dynasty, "if only the Mughals had been able to purify their home life by avoidance of indiscriminate and polygamous marriage, the history of Mughal India might have been entirely different."

9. This and the quotation that follows are from Yusuf Ali's *Muslim Educational Ideals – Presidential address to the Punjab Muslim Educational Conference*, 1923.

10. As early as 1909 Iqbal had written: "I have myself been of the view that religious differences should disappear from this country and even now act on this principle in my

private life. But now I think that the preservation of their separate national identities is desirable for both the Hindus and Muslims. The vision of a common nationhood for India is a beautiful ideal and has a poetic appeal...but appears incapable of fulfilment." Rajmohan Gandhi, *Eight Lives*, p.54.

11. Ashiq Husain Batalvi, *Iqbal kay akhri do saal*, p.118-119. Fazli unsuccessfully tried to enter the ICS after studies at Cambridge.

12. *The Times Literary Supplement*, 3 December 1925. Yusuf Ali's determination to be non-controversial led to tortuous understatements which hid the drama of the times. For example: "When Lord Chelmsford was succeeded by Lord Reading in April 1921, Mr Gandhi was in the plenitude of his influence. Lord Reading analysed the factors in that influence, and his patience and skill gradually unravelled the knots. In November 1921, the brothers Muhammad Ali and Shaukat Ali were convicted of tampering with the loyalty of Muslim soldiers and sentenced to two years' imprisonment. The Prince of Wales's visit in the cold weather of 1921-1922 was marred by some ugly incidents which did not help to promote British and Indian unity." *The Making of India*, p.298.

13. *India and Europe*, p.82.

14. ibid. p. 97.

15. He was once asked in 1933 to describe his electoral experience and whether he had ever contested seats for the Provincial Council or the Central Legislature in the last twelve years. Yusuf Ali replied "I did not actually contest a seat, but I have been in touch all the time, and I was a candidate for a while in the United Provinces." See the statements of the All-India Muslim Conference delegation to the Joint Committee, reproduced in K.K.Aziz, *The All-India Muslim Conference 1928-1933 - A documentary record*, p.156.

16. *Faran*, October 1981 (magazine of Islamia College, Lahore); see article in Urdu by M. Siddiqui on the College's history, pp.76-137

17. Letter in Urdu to Sughra Humayun Mirza Sahiba, dated 2 June 1925; reproduced in *Nuqush - Makateeb Number*, Vol.2, p.843. Yusuf Ali's address was *Marash*, 12 Grange Road, Chiswick, London W 5. Their summer guests included 'Nawab Sada Noor and his wife' and one Mr Yaseen working at the Indian High Commission.

18. For the entry on 'Khodja' see *The Encyclopaedia of Islam Vol.II*, Leyden, 1927, p.960-962. It includes a reference to the 'sacred person' of the Aga Khan. The entry on Karamat Ali is in the same volume, p. 752-754.

19. All-India Tanzim conference, Urdu text of presidential address, December 1925, obtained from Quaid-e-Azam Library, Lahore.

20. Minault, ibid., p.199. Kitchlew is erroneously described as a physician, p.83. He was a barrister and obtained his doctorate by submission of a thesis at a German university.

21. There were at least two occasions when Gandhi betrayed the trust placed in him by the Ali Brothers; first in 1922 when he arbitrarily called off the civil disobedience campaign,

85

leaving many of his followers exposed to the authorities; second in 1924 when he commenced a hunger strike while a guest in Mohamed Ali Jauhar's house, in sympathy for Hindus affected in a communal riot in Kohat. The statement he issued worsened the situation, "There is no doubt in my mind that in the majority of quarrels the Hindus come out second best. My own experiences but confirm the opinion that the Mussulman as a rule is a bully, and the Hindu a coward. Where there are cowards, there will always be bullies." For further details see: Sharif Al-Mujahid's article *The Khilafat Movement* in *Mohamed Ali: Life and Work*, Karachi: Pakistan Historical Society, 1978; Rajmohan Gandhi's biographical essay on Muhammad Ali in *Eight Lives*, p.111.

22. Iqbal had slightly differing Persian and Urdu versions of this poem on the League of Nations. The quotation is the last sentence of the Persian version. In *Payam-i-mashriq, Kulliyat-i-Iqbal*,(Farsi) Lahore: Shaikh Ghulam Ali & Sons, 1973, p.363. The Urdu version is equally scathing:

> Since a long time the sickly creature is in its death throes I am afraid I may not utter the sad news.

> Though the end seems to be almost near, its Christian devotees pray that it may survive!

> Perhaps this lean structure of European diplomacy through the blessings of Satan may last for a time still...."

From Iqbal's *Zarb-i-Kalim, Kulliyat-i-Iqbal* (Urdu), Lahore: Shaikh Ghulam Ali & Sons, 1973, p. 618.

23. PP: *Zamindar*, 5 February 1926.

24. For example:

> "It is the duty of Khan Bahadur Shaikh Abdul Qadir to draw the attention of the League of Nations to the attitude by France and Spain towards the Riffs, the destruction of Damascus by the French and the inhuman tyrannies committed by them in Syria. He should also raise his voice against the Pharaoh-like policy pursued by the English in Egypt. It is important to invite the attention of the League to the fact that the English have acquired possession of the Hejaz through Nejd. At present the League is undoubtedly the slave of the English and no help can be expected from it. Nevertheless, if the Shaikh speaks out and Persia supports him, the world will come to know the grievances and feelings of Muhammadans." PP:Lahore *Siyasat*, 8 July 1926.

25. From Yusuf Ali's presidential address to the History and Civics Section of the Punjab Educational Conference, December 1926; Punjab Public Library, Lahore. These were similar sentiments to those expressed in *India and Europe*, published a year earlier: "The League of Nations, with all its faults and imperfections, and they are many, is going about in the right way in building slowly and rallying round its standard all the nations it can persuade of its good faith and its power to further the progress of mankind."

26. ibid. Yusuf Ali's Empire-Loyalism was in full swing: "Above the Government of India we have an Imperial tie, which is symbolised by the British flag, the flag of the British empire. The flag is a symbol. It is even possible for us to have a distinctive national flag and yet to recognise and cherish the Imperial tie...If you strain at the leash, the fault may possibly be yours. The leash is elastic. I know of no character more adaptable than the British character, and no institutions more responsive to local needs than British institutions. It is for you to understand them and then to adapt them to your needs in the common bonds of empire."

27. M.A.Chughtai, *Iqbal kay Suhbat mai*, pp. 212-213. Maulana Sulaiman Nadwi's visit took place in April 1927.

28. AHI: Volume for period 3 October 1926 - 22 December 1928

29. *Masjid*, Urdu weekly, Lahore, 16 April 1937 (YA105). Translated by the author.

30. Obituary note on King Faisal, *The Times*, 11 September 1933; reproduced earlier in Note 33, Chapter 3.

31. *The Eastern Times*, Lahore, 3 June 1936; article by Yusuf Ali with the title 'Mustapha Kemal Ata-Turk', describing his visit to Ankara in 1928 (YA4).

5

FROM GENEVA TO LAHORE

On 18 August 1928 Yusuf Ali received a letter at his home, 34 Woodside, Wimbledon, in South London, from Lord Birkenhead, the Secretary of State for India. It informed him of his selection as a representative of India to the forthcoming assembly of the League of Nations in Geneva the following month.[1] The other five members representing India included the Earl of Lytton, a former Governor of Bengal, the Nawab of Palanpur and Sir Kurma Reddi, a former minister of the Madras government. The Nawab and his entourage stayed at the grandiose Carlton Hotel, Geneva. The rest of the delegation were booked into the Beau Rivage Hotel.

The Indian delegation was briefed by the Foreign Office to press strongly for the adoption of methods for controlling League expenditure. This financial priority may explain Yusuf Ali's inclusion in the Indian delegation, even though he held no official position in either the central government of India or any of the provincial governments. His former superior in the ICS, Lord Meston, served on the League's financial supervisory committee and may have felt the need for a capable and reliable delegate to press for his policies. Meston's presence in the League was itself a curiosity: he was a member of this key committee from 1923 to 1937 as an Indian delegate even though his association with India had ceased in 1919.[2]

Britain together with her colonies contributed a significant proportion of the budget and in return expected to exert an influence on policy and obtain a lion's share of positions in the Secretariat. For India this situation was particularly ironic, because it was the sixth highest contributor to the League's budget, but lacked a permanent seat and obtained few benefits from membership. The excessive influence of the main powers led to heated debate, particularly when Britain and the Empire delegates attempted to block projects put up by other countries, by withholding budget sanction. At one point proceedings became so stormy that the Secretary General threatened to resign. Yusuf Ali was a member of 'Committee II' dealing with technical organisations and also of 'Committee IV' relating to financial questions. The politically sensitive committee responsible for the Middle Eastern mandates was attended by a Hindu, Kurma Reddi. The Indian delegation did not ask any awkward questions about Britain's intentions in Iraq or Palestine. Instead, the Indian delegation held to its brief on League expenditures tenaciously, with Yusuf Ali in the forefront of their presentations.[3] The Indian delegation duly made speeches in support of the financial supervisory committee as 'the most authoritative and effective organ for controlling the budget in the League's possession'. Later Yusuf Ali was to receive a letter from Viscount Peel, Secretary of State for India, appreciating his participation and the manner in which India was represented. Yusuf Ali duly notified *Who's Who* to bring his entry up to date.

By the end of 1928 the Ali household moved a few hundred yards down the road to 3 Mansel Road. This was a three-storeyed red brick 'semi', on the same street as a school and within walking distance of both the Common and the station. It cost Yusuf Ali £1750. Rashid was still the only child of the marriage and there was enough room for the fine collection of books Yusuf Ali had been building up for twenty-five years. The house possessed a large rear garden with a tennis court – a favourite sport. The garden would later even have room for a hut to store yet more books. By 1930 Yusuf Ali's collection of books at Mansel Road was so large that he insured his library separately for £500.

His work at Islamia College and educational tours of the Near East, together with presidency of numerous Indian educational conferences and membership of the Court of Aligarh University made him a leading spokesman on Indian education. Soon after Yusuf Ali returned from Geneva his next public engagement was at the Royal Asiatic Society, at whose meeting in October he read a paper on 'Education in India: the New Outlook', later published in *The Nineteenth Century and After*. With the death of Ameer Ali in August 1928 there was barely another Indian Muslim of his intellectual calibre with an entrée in British social life. His own contributions to the world of learning matched Ameer Ali's. There were half a dozen books to his name, just as many pamphlets, over a dozen learned articles and two entries in the *Encyclopaedia of Islam*.

The Muslim community of London was well aware of the distinguished scholar in its midst. On the occasion of *'id-ul-adha* in May 1929 it invited him to speak on the life of the Prophet. A 'Progressive Islam Association' also came into being for discussions and study under his direction.[4] When the phrase 'progressive Islam' was used at the Punjab Muslim Educational Conference in 1923, it referred to the need for a reawakening of the 'Islamic intellect'.[5] Muslim institutions and patterns of thinking had become moribund and obsolete, unable to cope with the challenges of the day. For Yusuf Ali 'progressive Islam' was a catchphrase which did not harbour a burning iconoclasm but possessed a gentler focus, conveyed in the titles published in the 'Progressive Islam' series since 1925: *Greatest Need of the Age; Islam as a World Force; The Fundamentals of Islam; Personality of Muhammad*. This was his frame of mind when he commenced his most ambitious literary venture yet – the great task of expressing the message of the Qur'an.

Later in 1929 Yusuf Ali was sponsored on another tour 'through America, Hawaiian Islands, Japan, China, Philippines, Straits Settlements, Ceylon and India.'[6] He would work by day extolling the British Empire and pore over his labour of love at night. In the preface of *The Holy Qur'an – text, translation and commentary* there is a comment on the manuscript being 'carried about, thousands of miles, to all sorts of countries and among all sorts of people.'[7]

Between 1930 and 1932 three critical though inconclusive conferences were held in London to discuss constitutional reform in India. Yusuf Ali was never a member of the Muslim delegations, though his acquaintance with the redoubtable Maharaja of Bikener, and Akbar Hydari, representing the Nizam of Hyderabad, could have led to service for the Indian princes at the conferences. He followed events closely and would not travel abroad for the next eighteen months, except for a brief trip to Paris where he served as one of the two rapporteurs at the fifth International Moral Education Congress in September 1930.[8]

The first Round Table Conference concluded on 19 January 1931 on a sombre note. There was mounting political violence in India, with Congress workers intent on cowing any independent Muslim voices into acquiescence to their campaigns. It was against such a backdrop that the East India Association, mainly comprising retired ICS officers, organised a meeting at Caxton Hall in May in London to discuss 'The Round Table Conference and after', with Lord Zetland, a future Secretary of State for India, as main speaker. Yusuf Ali also contributed and his remarks were reported in *The Times* of the following day. Yusuf Ali cherished 'well-ordered progress' for India and was aghast at the turn of events: 'So long as the contempt of law persisted in India the Conference could not succeed except on paper; it could not work out a solution that would endure.'[9]

When the second Round Table Conference convened in September the leading lights were assembled – Gandhi, Jinnah, Iqbal, the Aga Khan, Mian Muhammad Shafi, Shah Nawaz Bhutto – though not Jauhar, who had died during the closing stages of the earlier round.[10] The Muslim delegates were influenced from afar by Fazli Husain, now a member of the Viceroy's Executive Council in Delhi and the real power behind the scenes.[11] There was major debate on whether elections should be by general adult franchise or through separate electorates. The Muslim demand for separate electorates was opposed by the Congress and vilified by British Labour Party intellectuals like Harold Laski. He charged Muslims with displaying 'religious fanaticism (that) was terrible'; they would 'cheerfully cut my throat in the name of Allah'.[12] The bogeys of Indian *Wahhabism* and pan-Islamism were now outdated; a new brush had been found with which to tar Muslims.

Yusuf Ali's contribution to the political discussions of the day was a further historical study on India, *Hindustan ki tamaddun ki tarikh* (A Cultural History of India), completed in September 1931. It was a riposte to demands of Indian delegates for greater independence for India, particularly Iqbal's famous Allahabad resolution of 1930 that had called for a Muslim state, 'within or without' the British Empire. Yusuf Ali deprecated such assertiveness: 'The evolution of British Indian culture is dominated by British ideas, which lurk even beneath the protests of those who are in revolt against what they term foreign ideas.'[13] He provided the intellectual voice for Unionist and Empire-Loyalist tradition in Indian political opinion.

Yusuf Ali's role in Indian affairs was peripheral but not inconspicuous. Iqbal addressed a number of literary meetings in London in the winter of 1931, one a glittering banquet at the Waldorf Hotel which Yusuf Ali attended.[14] On another occasion, the India Society organised a lecture for Iqbal to speak on his poetry and philosophy, presided over by Sir Francis Younghusband, formerly of the Indian Civil Service.[15] Yusuf Ali took the chair and himself recited Iqbal's poetry and discussed its message. He likened Iqbal to the French poet Paul Claudel because 'both used analogies and their work was infused with religious feeling'. A day after the India Society event there was a function organised in London by the Iqbal Literary Society. This was attended by Dr Nixon, one of Iqbal's professors from Cambridge days. At this meeting Yusuf Ali read extracts from Iqbal's *Bang-e-dara* and later compared the poet to Nietzsche, remarking that, like the German philosopher, Iqbal had 'revitalised his people'.[16] There was a vast political gulf between Iqbal and Yusuf Ali but both maintained a gentlemanly cordiality with each other. The same may also have applied to Yusuf Ali's relationship with Jinnah. Soon after the Second Round Table Conference adjourned there was a gathering of Indian students at London University at which Yusuf Ali spoke on 'The Indian University'. Jinnah hosted a reception for those who attended at the best Indian restaurant in town, the Veeraswamy.[17]

The Round Table Conference reconvened the following year and a compromise of sorts was eventually agreed on the issue of electoral procedure and the weight to be given to Muslims in the provincial assemblies. Yusuf Ali was not in London to witness the close because of an invitation from the National Council of Education to tour Canada. It was at this juncture that Jinnah temporarily bowed out of Indian politics, despondent at the Hindu-Muslim impasse and the appointment of his old adversary, Willingdon, as the new Viceroy. Jinnah concentrated on a successful legal practice at the Bar, not returning to India until 1934 to stamp his authority on the Muslim League. Yusuf Ali viewed Willingdon in quite a different light and by September 1932 was back in India to fulfil public responsibilities. He presided over the Sind Azad Conference and, returning to Lahore, was appointed a member of the Punjab University Enquiry Committee which sat from October 1932 to March 1933. The committee, better known as the 'Anderson Committee' after its chairman Sir James Anderson, was set up on the occasion of the golden jubilee of the University and charged with examining the existing situation and conditions and making plans for the future. An official history of the University makes special reference to Yusuf Ali's contribution which, not unexpectedly, was about the efficacy of English in the Indian educational system: 'All the vernaculars have been deeply influenced by the study of English literature. Above all, English is the medium of communication between provinces and with the outside world. Indeed, the use of English is perhaps the greatest bond which has linked together Indians of all provinces and communities. Without this bond the federation of India will be an ideal dream.'[18] These were deeply held sentiments, which sustained his private scholarship to make the message of the Qur'an accessible in English. Throughout these months he was undoubtedly carrying with him the manuscripts and notes of his Qur'an translation and commentary, welcoming most of all the sedate ocean liner trips as an opportunity for uninterrupted work.

The most important public duty assigned to Yusuf Ali was presidency of the All-India Muslim Conference, held in Calcutta in December 1932. This was a body set up in 1928 by Fazli Husain to undermine the Muslim League and its President, Jinnah, though later it became a forum for various Muslim political groups to maintain contact through a delicate period of mutual suspicions and rivalries.[19] The Muslim Conference's attempt to maintain Muslim unity through this divergence was reflected in its selection of the Aga Khan, Shaukat Ali, Jauhar and Iqbal as past presidents. Yusuf Ali joined a distinguished band of Indian Muslim leaders, though he was an odd choice given his lack of experience in electoral politics. Perhaps it was because the more prominent leaders were away in London attending the Third Round Table Conference. Fazli Husain, stage-managing events as usual from his vantage point on the Viceroy's Council, organised important aspects of the Calcutta meeting like funding and is likely to have hand-picked the president.[20] Yusuf Ali would witness the bickerings and horse-trading, but his life of political involvement and his life as a religious scholar ran along parallel lines which did not intersect. *The Religious Polity of Islam*, published in January 1933, was rich in theory but short on implementation.[21] It was around this time too that the Urdu press commenced referring to him by the title *Allama* (most learned).[22]

Yusuf Ali was back in London in June 1933, on what must have been his seventh crossing since the first journey from Bombay over forty years ago. Commercial air travel over that distance was still five or six years away. A few days after his return the East India Association invited him to speak on 'Indian reactions to the White Paper' at Caxton Hall, its usual meeting place. He directed his comments at fellow Indians who did not believe the White Paper went far enough on self-government. 'A sort of dismay was produced on its publication even among the circles which were accustomed to support the Government,' he observed with reference to the Unionists in Lahore. 'The time that had elapsed since had sobered public opinion a little. Reasonable people were beginning to see the safeguards and the reserve powers in better perspective now that the first mist of disappointed expectations had been dissipated.'[23] For each notch popular opinion in India shifted towards demands for independence, Yusuf Ali would revert with greater determination to support of the status quo. His advice to 'impatient reformers' was to 'march slow and make sure of every step.'[24]

The presidency of the Muslim Conference led to further responsibilities being thrust on him. In August 1933 Yusuf Ali was a member of the delegation of witnesses representing both the Muslim Conference and the Muslim League to the high-powered 'Joint Committee on Indian Constitutional Reform' convened in London under the chairmanship of the Marquess of Linlithgow. Yusuf Ali and his four colleagues were subjected to an intense cross-examination – over five hundred questions ranging from issues of women's rights in Islam through the Muslim demand for separate electorates to education and taxation policy.[25] Yusuf Ali in his role as general spokesman for the delegation fielded the majority of questions. The Hindu delegates at the Joint Committee hearings attempted to put the delegation on the spot, and Yusuf Ali himself did not emerge unscathed.[26]

In the course of the proceedings, Sir Reginald Craddock, a member of the Joint Committee, put a question to Yusuf Ali on 'whether there is a scheme for [a] Federation of Provinces under the name of Pakistan'. Yusuf

Ali replied, 'As far as I know, it is only a students' scheme; no responsible people have put it forward.'[27] The reference was to a small group of Indian Muslim students at Cambridge who in 1932 had proposed a federation of Muslim provinces.[28] Craddock persisted in this line of questioning, drawing out Zafrullah Khan, a fellow committee member, to declare the Pakistan scheme 'chimerical and impractical'. Yusuf Ali expressed confidence in the emergence of alliances across communal lines. He cited the Unionists of the Punjab as an example of such a party in which both Hindus and Muslims were drawn from the same landowning economic class: 'My friend Chaudhri Chotu Ram leads a party of which it is said that the great number are Muslims.'[29]

The Joint Committee's report led to a White Paper and eventually the 1935 Government of India Act, which proposed provincial and central legislatures and other measures to create a federation with limited self-government. Yusuf Ali, for whom the 'imperial connection' was an inviolable principle, expressed his reservations in a roundabout fashion in a note to *The Times*. He suggested that policy had become confused since the days when men like his father's friend Lely administered India:

Sir Frederic [Lely], throughout his career in India, maintained the highest standards of social relations between the British and the Indian communities. His example showed that civilians of the old school could carry out the purposes of the British Administration more effectually by personal kindliness and interest in the lives of the people then by regulations and showy public acts or speeches. His knowledge and understanding of the inner life of India were wonderful, and accounted for his great popularity among all classes of people. If I may be allowed one topical remark, may I say: 'In all your political arrangements, do not forget or undervalue the human and psychological element'.[30]

His sentiments were like those of the Conservative 'diehards' in British political circles who believed that Indians did not need freedom, but rather a paternalistic hand that would guide them towards development and economic progress. The Act was to provide a basis for elections in 1937, though neither the Congress Party or the Muslim League were satisfied that it met their demands for autonomy.

Yusuf Ali crossed the seas yet again and was in Lahore in early 1934. His work on the translation and commentary of the Qur'an was taking shape and he could contemplate publication in parts. There is a section in the preface of the first edition which describes how the publication came about:

> In the city of Lahore, I happened to mention the matter to some young people who held me in respect and affection. They showed an enthusiasm and an eagerness which surprised me. They almost took the matter out of my hands. They asked for immediate publication. I had various bits ready, but not even one complete *sipara* [one-thirtieth part of the Qur'an]. They made me promise to complete at least one *sipara* before I left Lahore. As if by magic, a publisher, a *katib* (calligraphist to write the Arabic text), an engraver of blocks for such text, and a printer were found, all equally anxious to push forward the scheme...my plan is to issue each *sipara* as it is ready, at intervals of not more than three months. As the work proceeds, I hope it will be possible to accelerate the pace.[31]

More by design than accident the date he assigned to the preface of this first edition was 4 April 1934, his sixty-second birthday.[32] The publisher found by his young friends was Shaikh Muhammad Ashraf of Kashmiri Bazaar, Lahore. The first instalment was on sale in June, priced at one rupee. It had a light blue vellum cover and was exquisitely produced and printed.[33] The back page was astutely used to promote the venture: 'not a dull Sunday sermon, but a piece of English Literature. No Sectarian views propagated through the commentary...Arabic text produced on beautiful photo blocks on glazed paper of superior Quality, Clear Print and get-up pleasing to the eye.' Readers were invited to place a mail order for the remaining instalments. Yusuf Ali despatched two more instalments in 1934.

Muhammad Iqbal was president of the *Anjuman-Himayat-ul-Islam* and endeavouring to find the best staff for Islamia College, now a seven hundred strong Muslim boys' institution commencing at the senior school 'intermediate' level and also awarding BA, BSc and MA degrees in various disciplines. He was prepared to scour far and wide for talent, offering a position to Muhammad Asad in the summer of 1934 to teach *fiqh*.[34] A principal also had to be found. Iqbal was unwell and so unable to attend a meeting of the Anjuman's council in July but he sent this written statement:

> If Mr Abdullah Yusuf Ali could return to this high office then a lot of our problems would be solved. But there is no hope of his returning and as far as I can see it would be very difficult to find a Muslim principal in India. We need a principal not only knowledgeable and learned but also influential and with contacts; one who is sympathetic to Muslim aspirations; someone who could train our children in all those spheres which, because of the future political conditions, have become essential for the life of the community. If the Muslims of India are fortunate to find such a person it will serve a dire need. Unfortunately among the Indian Muslims at present there is no such person available. Therefore my personal opinion, following the dictum 'seek knowledge even if you have to go to China', is that we should not hesitate in our search. This *hadith* may be considered weak, but nobody can doubt the relevance of its application. God belongs to the East as well as West. We should seek out a person whom we need from the East or the West. Again this is a personal opinion. You will have to make the final decision.[35]

Though Iqbal expressed doubts on Yusuf Ali's return to Islamia College, this did come to pass.

By the time the fourth instalment was published in March 1935 Yusuf Ali had performed Hajj and was back in Lahore. It was important for him to be close to the printer and publisher. Perhaps still undecided about Islamia College, he took on the job of editing the English daily newspaper *Eastern Times*.[36] The instalments, of about forty pages each, became a runaway success. Soon favourable reviews were reprinted in the inside front cover and later in the inside back cover as well. The press reviews included in the fourth instalment were from local Lahore papers such as the *Civil and Military Gazette* and the *Eastern Times*, as well as from further afield, like the *Bombay Chronicle* and Calcutta's *Star of India*. A prominent *alim*, Sayyid Sulaiman Nadwi, also endorsed the work.

On 14 April 1935 Iqbal received a stream of guests, including Sarojini Naidu. After Mrs Naidu he was visited by Yusuf Ali and a group from the *Anjuman-Himayat-ul-Islam* for a lengthy discussion.[37] There was some hard bargaining as Yusuf Ali sought to ensure that some of the problems which had arisen during the last tenure would not be not repeated. A council meeting of the Anjuman the following day noted Yusuf Ali's appointment at a salary of 1350 rupees per month.[38] The amount was princely in comparison to the amount offered to Asad – 250 rupees, rising to 300 rupees after the probationary six-month period.

From 1935 onwards there was the opportunity for the acquaintance-ship between Iqbal and Yusuf Ali to blossom into a close friendship. While there was a mutual respect between the two – Yusuf Ali acknowledged Iqbal's poetic genius and Iqbal in turn appreciated Yusuf Ali's erudition – the political gulf between them was too wide. They did not see eye to eye on the League of Nations, but far more important was the problem of the Unionists. Iqbal was no longer on amicable terms with this party's leadership. Speaking at an anniversary meeting of the *Anjuman-Himayat-ul-Islam* in 1935, Iqbal condemned Fazli Husain bitterly for engineering a rift between Muslims in the rural areas and those in the city of Lahore.[39] His criticism was directed at the very feature which Yusuf Ali had commended at the hearings of the Joint Committee for Indian Constitutional Reform.[40] As the relationship between Iqbal and Fazli Husain deteriorated, so Yusuf Ali acquired greater prominence in Unionist activities. For example, in October 1935 he gave the inaugural address to officers attending the Local Self-Government Institute of the Punjab. He also served as an office bearer of *Idara Ma'rif-i-Islamia*, an institution set up by Iqbal for Islamic research, but whose annual conference held in Lahore in 1936 was presided over by Fazli Husain.[41] The Unionists looked on Yusuf Ali as an intellectual capable of providing a counter-weight to Iqbal.

An incident in early 1936 served to exacerbate popular Muslim discontent with the Unionists. This was the demolition of Shahidganj

Mosque under the sanction of a court order, because of a land claim by Sikhs. Iqbal had felt sufficiently strongly over the Kanpur Mosque violation in 1913 to travel to the town to defend arrested Muslims. At Kanpur it was the *wudhu* (ablution) area of the Mosque that had been demolished by a high-handed municipality; in Lahore it was an entire mosque. The court action predictably roused the Muslims, evoking from Iqbal some of his most memorable verses in Urdu. The inability of the Unionist Party to stand up to protect Muslim interests became obvious, and the popularity of the Muslim League was enhanced even further by Jinnah's visit to Lahore in March 1936. Violent street demonstrations were erupting in the city but his cool leadership succeeded in calming an explosive situation without further loss of life. Three key Jinnah supporters were Iqbal, Malik Barkat Ali and Dr. Khalifa Shujauddin. All were closely involved in the *Anjuman-Himayat-ul-Islam*, with Iqbal as President and Malik Barkat the College Committee secretary.

In May 1936 Jinnah called on Iqbal to join the Muslim League's Central Parliamentary Board. Fazli Husain deprecated this move because a national united platform was against the interest of a provincial powerbase like his. While Fazli Husain and Jinnah were to conduct their rivalry according to Queensberry rules, at the grass-roots level of Lahore politics and the Anjuman there were no holds barred, particularly in 1936. The troubles which were to embroil Yusuf Ali began after the summer holidays at Islamia College.

With elections due early the next year, Iqbal signed a public appeal with fourteen other Muslims which placed on record his opinion of the Unionists:

> You will not be unaware that in this province the Unionist Party is participating in the elections. You should know that these people are responsible for the un-Islamic and unholy division of Punjabi Muslims into urban and rural categories. These are the very people who have sold away Islam's wonderful brotherhood for economic gain. Alas! Are these people unaware that Islam did not come to this world to unite on the basis of economic interests but instead it seeks to build a lofty palace for humanity based on unity of thought and action. We

accept that the mutual understanding between Muslim, Hindu and Sikh is the first brick for our palace of freedom and once in the Assembly there will be political agreements with unprejudiced and nation-loving Hindus, Sikhs and Christians. But we will not for a moment set aside Islam's magnificent ideals. Neither will we sell our principles to non-Muslims merely to realise our selfish and materialistic dreams.[42]

Among Iqbal's co-signatories were Malik Barkat Ali and Khalifa Shujauddin. Iqbal had served in the Punjab Legislative Council from 1927 to 1930 and spoke with inside knowledge of Unionist politicians and their indifference to the plight of deprived Muslims.

In the summer vacation Yusuf Ali returned to the family home in Wimbledon. The holidays included a spell in Derbyshire. Yusuf Ali wrote an article in the Islamia College magazine which indicates the extent to which public interests dominated his life. These would have left the barest of time for Masuma and Rashid even though he had returned to them after the absence of almost a year:

As soon as I reached London I joined my work at the World Congress of Faiths in University College. The first paper read at the plenary meetings of the Congress was mine on the Basis of Religion. There was a fine spirit of goodwill in that international gathering, and everyone was desirous of understanding and sympathizing with everybody else's point of view. I have already given my impressions of this Congress at a meeting organized by the Inter-Collegiate Muslim brotherhood on the 16th October and therefore will say nothing about it now.

I also attended the International Conference of the New Education Fellowship at Cheltenham, where some of our educational people from the Punjab were also present. In that connection I preached a sermon at the Unitarian Church in Cheltenham to a full congregation.

After that I went to Oxford to the Montessori Conference, where the great Italian Educationist Madame Montessori was present in person and delivered three important addresses.

My real holiday with my family was passed at Matlock in the Peak of Derbyshire. This is a beautiful part of England, with hills and dales and some interesting and famous historical mansions, like Haddon Hall and Chatsworth.

During all this time I continued my studies of the Holy Qur'an and went on writing my Translation and my Commentary; I am in hopes that the work will see its completion next year.[43]

Fazli Husain died in July 1936 while Yusuf Ali was in London. He called for a moment of silence at a meeting he was chairing at the conference of the World Congress of Faiths and in an obituary note paid tribute to 'one of the most brilliant sons of India who did wonderful work on the Executive Council of the Punjab, and again in representing India at the League (of Nations)'.[44] Later in the month, Yusuf Ali and his wife hosted a reception at the Waldorf Hotel for Feroz Khan Noon, the Unionist Minister appointed Indian High Commissioner to London. The distinguished guests, according to *The Times*, included 'the Saudi Arabian ambassador, Sir Atul Chatterjee, Sir Francis and Lady Younghusband, Sir Abdul and Lady Qader and Sir Hassan Suhrawardy'.[45] It was a world apart from the struggle of the Muslim Leaguers in Lahore.

Yusuf Ali returned to Lahore in September 1936, via Ceylon, where he presided at the All-Ceylon Muslim Educational Conference at Zahira College. The Qur'an instalments had become internationally known. The seventh instalment included favourable comments from *The Times Literary Supplement* and also from Pickthall, whose own translation had been published in 1930. Pickthall was gracious but there was a sting in the tail: 'It goes without saying that his translation of the Qur'an is in better English than any previous English translation by an Indian.' Reviews were also quoted from the *Shanghai Recorder*, the Arabic magazine *Al-Arab* of Jerusalem, Dr Khalid Sheldrake of 'The Western Islamic Association, London' and an Esperanto enthusiast. Interestingly there was never to be a commendation from Muhammad Iqbal, much closer to home. By September 1936 the work was more than half completed.

While working at Islamia College, Yusuf Ali lived alone at Nedo's Hotel on the Mall. An association of students known as the Inter-Collegiate Muslim Brotherhood invited him to lead the *juma* (Friday congregational) prayers at the Cooper Room in the Crescent Hostel, which he did regularly. Its secretary, Muhammad Shafi, remembered him as someone with a powerful physical presence 'like a boxer', who cut a glamorous figure in student circles. He had his own motor car and always wore a suit. He would speak English 'like an Englishman' and also Urdu clearly and distinctly. Shafi has no recollection of his using Arabic. Yusuf Ali's Friday address would be in either English or Urdu. He would come to the Friday congregation with his own mat and wore a cap for prayer. He had a reputation for not suffering fools gladly but was also 'an isolated figure, preoccupied in the translation'.[46]

Yusuf Ali's social circle in Lahore was quite selective. He was vice-president of a Lahore association, 'The Society for Promoting Scientific Knowledge'. On the cultural front he was chairman of the Lahore Art Circle and a member of various clubs such as the Rotarians and the International Fellowship Society.[47] He did not particularly care to have his privacy disturbed and was reserved to the point where few in Lahore were aware of his earlier accomplishments. Even a distinguished contemporary who was Principal of Oriental College, Lahore, and to whom Yusuf Ali would turn for advice on Arabic scholarship was to remain ignorant of his service as a Minister in Hyderabad.[48]

The storm broke in November 1936. Provincial assembly elections were due in January 1937, and the new Unionist leader succeeding Fazli Husain, Sikander Hayat Khan, asked Yusuf Ali to stand for a rural seat from Shaikhpura. Yusuf Ali accepted and submitted his candidature papers.[49] It appears that when he had taken the appointment of Principal the previous year, the thought of standing for election was there. He had reserved the right to stand for the legislature and had 'expressly repudiated' any condition that would bar him from politics.[50] The scene was all set for a confrontation between the pro-Unionist Principal and Jinnah's supporters on the Anjuman's College Committee.

Barkat Ali was a candidate in the elections on the Muslim League ticket. A feeling emerged that Yusuf Ali was encouraging Islamia College staff to seek elections on the Unionists' behalf.[51] Yusuf Ali admitted objecting to staff taking a prominent public part in 'party caucuses and party meetings' so as to 'exclude unseemly party wrangle from the atmosphere of my College as long as I have anything to do with it.' In a charged environment a ban on political activity within the College, coupled with the Principal's known support for the Unionists, would have been provocative. Yusuf Ali invited further trouble by removing some lecturers connected with the Barkat Ali faction on the grounds of incompetence.[52]

In the run-up to the elections Barkat Ali started his own weekly paper, *The New Times*. On 11 November the paper carried an article criticising Yusuf Ali. A further article of criticism appeared in the Urdu paper *Ihsan* on 19 November, written by Hafiz Firozuddin, a member of the general council of the Anjuman. The tenor of the attacks became vituperative. In a re-enactment of the criticisms he had had to undergo in 1927, he was asked to defend his teaching record at the College. Yusuf Ali used the columns of *Eastern Times* to fight his corner:

> It is true that I do no teaching work. In my agreement with the Anjuman I declined to accept any condition about teaching or anything else, but stated that as a matter of fact in order to get contact with boys a certain amount of teaching was desirable, and this statement was accepted as sufficient by the Anjuman at the interview which took place in the presence of Sir Muhammad Iqbal at his house. I am happy to think that the Honours work in English which I taught last year in the BA Class was able to show such excellent results in the University Examinations. Apart from class teaching, I have done a great deal to supervise the organisation and teaching by the staff, with excellent results, to which many boys bear testimony. Moreover I preside regularly every week once or twice during the Sermon Period and at general cultural or religious lectures in the College, and my lectures are a familiar feature in the College.[53]

A second charge against Yusuf Ali related to his work on the Qur'an during official school hours. Yusuf Ali's response was that there would be no great sin if this was the case, but the truth was that he had never corrected the proofs in the College. These were only delivered to the College because this was convenient for the printers.[54] He was also criticised for drawing a monthly salary of 1350 rupees, which was higher by far than that of the Principal of any College in the Punjab, excepting the Principal of the Government College of Lahore.[55] Yusuf Ali's lack of competence in Arabic was also raised: 'He is publishing an English translation of the Qur'an, though I am informed by those who know him personally, he does not know a word of Arabic, his translation being based wholly on other English and Urdu translations.'[56]

Faced with such personal attacks the inevitable came about, and on 6 January 1937 Yusuf Ali resigned, handing over responsibility to the vice-principal, Mr Ghani. The moment the students heard the news there was a spontaneous protest.[57] Windows were smashed and students assembled in the College's main hall, Habibiya Hall. *The Civil & Military Gazette*, favourably inclined to Yusuf Ali, reported cheering in his support and the condemning of Barkat Ali, Khalifa Shujauddin and Mian Amiruddin, Muslim League activists within the Anjuman. The same report said that Yusuf Ali called upon the students to restrain themselves and preserve the reputation of the College. It was an emotional moment, with students and their former Principal in tears. He was confronted with the persistent cry: 'Promise to stay.'[58]

After Yusuf Ali had left, the students marched to the offices of the Anjuman and then to various main points in the city shouting their slogans, before returning to the College grounds. A participant was to describe the next step: 'This was the first strike I had experienced. I do not know whether Allama Iqbal was President of the Anjuman or not, but he was the one to whom we turned. The students marched to "Javaid Manzil". The Allama was ill. Four student representatives went in and met him.'[59] The Anjuman responded to the crisis by calling a meeting of its College Committee at 6 p.m. the next day, Thursday 7 January 1937.

A delegation of striking students called on Yusuf Ali at his hotel that evening and he expressed a willingness to return if his demands were acceded to by the College Committee. The College Committee met at 6 p.m.: 'At this meeting, which lasted for nearly two hours, considerable discussion and exchange of views took place and ultimately it was decided unanimously to record a resolution of confidence in both the Secretary of the College Committee as well as the Principal.'[60] A large body of students who were waiting outside the office of the Anjuman responded to the decision with shouts of 'Principal Yusuf Ali *zindabad.*' Tempers cooled and normal college activities were resumed on the Saturday.

Polling day was 28 January 1937. The elections proved an anticlimax for Yusuf Ali. Apparently a local *zamindar* had also declared his intention to contest the seat. In order to bring in his own man, Maulvi Ghulam Mohiuddin Qasuri, Sikander had manoeuvred Yusuf Ali into accepting the nomination. He then shamed the *zamindar* into withdrawing in deference to Yusuf Ali. Similarly, he persuaded Yusuf Ali to withdraw by impressing on him the local popularity of the *zamindar*. Both candidates declared their unavailability and Qasuri was elected unopposed.[61] The Unionists did well in the elections, winning an overwhelming number of Muslim seats in the Punjab. If the account of Sikander's scheming is true Yusuf Ali remained unaware of it or turned a blind eye. Writing to *The Times* in London after the elections, he had a commendation to make: 'On the Indian side I may point with pride to the success with which the Unionist Party, under the leadership of Sir Sikander Hayat, has formed the first Government of the Punjab under the new Constitution.'[62]

Barkat Ali's tactics at Islamia College against Yusuf Ali were not wholly supported within the Anjuman. There were certainly other Muslim League activists in Lahore who at the height of the troubles came out in support of Yusuf Ali. Muhammad Shafi, then secretary of the Inter-Collegiate Muslim Brotherhood and in close contact with Iqbal, retained cordial relations with Yusuf Ali and admired him.[63] The veteran journalist Zafar Ali Khan, not known for holding back his opinions on people, also spoke highly of Yusuf Ali at a meeting in Islamia College which took place in the middle of the troubles. Zafar Ali Khan reminded the student body that their Principal was a man who did not tolerate 'time-serving or flattery'.[64]

Yusuf Ali continued as principal for the rest of the academic year and there were no further controversies. He was invited to Hyderabad to attend the Silver Jubilee celebrations of the Nizam, Mir Osman Ali Khan, in February 1937, and found the pomp and pageantry much to his liking:

New Hyderabad, the creation of His Exalted Highness Mir Sir Osman Ali Khan, links itself so well with its antiquities, historical associations and natural beauties that they form, all together, a fitting background for the commemoration of the twenty-five eventful years of a memorable reign.

At the express command of His Exalted Highness the celebrations were arranged as simply as possible, but the ardent enthusiasm of his subjects and well-wishers added a grace and dignity to the proceedings, which reflected in a remarkable manner the noble sentiments expressed by His Exalted Highness in his replies to the various addresses presented to him.

Who will forget the earnest words in which His Exalted Highness addressed his subjects in the newly constructed Jubilee Hall at the very first function of the Silver Jubilee? To serve his subjects and win their love - what nobler ideal can a Ruler set before himself? His worthy sons, the two Princes, have also been entrusted with important tasks in the administration of the State, and their noble consorts, the Turkish Princesses, lend charm and dignity to all movements for the amelioration of the education and environment of the gentler sex. The little grandson, Nawab Mukarram Jah Bahadur, inherits and unites in himself the traditions of the House of Sir Osman Ali Khan on the one hand, and on the other, of the Osmanli Dynasty of Europe and Asia.

In replying to the addresses of the various communities, associations, jagirdars etc., His Exalted Highness used felicitous words which evoked spontaneous cheers throughout the body of the Hall, and will find a hearty echo throughout the length and breadth of the land. Speaking of the untouchable cast he said: 'Under my rule there are no high and low, touchables and untouchables, and this has been the tradition of my House; rank and position depend upon virtue and merit alone.' Words like these will be prominently inscribed in a special pavilion to be erected in the Jubilee Gardens, open to all, so that the humblest of his subjects may come and read and profit by them.

The religious earnestness of this large-hearted Ruler was typified by the wonderful silver casket presented to him by the citizens of Sucunderabad and Bolarum. This was an accurate model, prepared to scale by a Hyderabad engineer of the *Haram Sharif* of Medina, which is now lighted by electricity installed by Hyderabad.

A word may be said about the illuminations. A number of houses, especially in the region of the Banjara Hill, have been built on hills, with wide spaces between, affording extensive views on all sides. The blaze of illumination is therefore visible for miles around. Illuminated Hyderabad presented a fairy scene. There is much romance in its modern as well as its early history. The hard work which was behind the splendid organisation that planned and effectively carried out the celebration reflects the highest credit on all concerned. His Exalted Highness' own simplicity and dignity of character, and his ceaseless solicitude and work for his people are matched by his religious earnestness of character, which fully entitles him to the appellation with which the National Anthem of Hyderabad closes:

Siraj-id-din-Islami, Amir-i-Muminan bashi
[Lamp of the Islamic faith, leader of Muslims]
May he be granted long life and every blessing.[65]

His mind seemed ready to set aside the political realities and settle for a fantasy, in which Hyderabad became transformed into the ideal kingdom with an enlightened prince, strict hierarchy and mutual respect.

Two months after his visit to Hyderabad, Yusuf Ali was in Aligarh presenting the presidential address to the All-India Muslim Educational Conference. Lahore's own social and literary life also kept him busy. As a member of Lahore's elite, Yusuf Ali was frequently invited by the Premier, Sikander Hayat Khan, to important state functions. His services were widely in demand by the Unionists, who had embarked on an ambitious educational programme. In April 1937 he was once again president of the annual educational conference for the Punjab. His regular activities included a *tafsir* class at Islamia College, at which a member of staff would read from the Qur'an, then Yusuf Ali would follow with a commentary in English, an arrangement that often led to a mix-up.[66] There were also articles for the local Urdu press, such as an account of the martyrdom of *Imam* Husain.[67]

Yusuf Ali had one more year to complete of his contract at Islamia College but decided against this. The purpose for staying in Lahore had been achieved. The manuscripts for the remaining eight instalments of the Qur'anic translation were complete and left with Shaikh Ashraf for publication at monthly intervals. His parting message to Sikander Hayat Khan was unequivocal. Like a medieval scholar saluting some royal patron he resorted to superlatives: 'The present Punjab government was a perfect example of true international fellowship because it was comprised of men of different communities.'[68] Yusuf Ali left a rebuke to his critics in Lahore, which only appeared in the final instalment published in December 1937. Responding as one who had been sinned against, he grieved, 'I had not imagined that so much human jealousy, misunderstanding and painful misrepresentation should pursue one who seeks no worldly gain and pretends to be no dogmatic authority.'[69] Yusuf Ali had lived in the eye of a storm but also completed his greatest creative act.

Notes to Chapter 5

1. IOL:L/E/7/1526, 1928, contains details of Yusuf Ali's participation in the 1928 League of Nations Conference.

2. I OL: L/E/7/1371,4112. The records note that "Lord Meston's provenance is described as India for convenience, but he serves in complete independence of either the Indian or the British authorities." So while Meston had ended his Indian connections in 1919, it was as India's delegate that he held the position on the financial supervisory committee from 1923 to 1937. Meston possibly also exercised influence through Zimmern, formerly of the Foreign Office and now at the League's Institute of Intellectual Cooperation. For evidence of their intimacy see IOL: Meston Papers, F136/12; letter from Zimmern to Meston dated 15 May, 1918.

3. IOL:L/E/7/1526 ibid. In Committee IV, Yusuf Ali was involved in a protracted argument with the Dutch delegation on their proposal to host a conference in the Hague in 1925 on the Codification of International Law. He proposed that this conference should be held in Geneva, as the additional costs of moving staff and the other arrangements in the Hague would result in an extra expenditure of 128,500 Swiss francs. According to the delegation's report, "this view did not however prevail and a very long and at times somewhat embarrassing discussion followed both in the full committee and in a sub-committee of which Mr Yusuf Ali was a member. Eventually it was agreed that the credit should be suppressed, and that the Codification Conference should not be held in 1929 unless the Disarmament Conference failed to take place in that year, in which case 208,500 francs of the credit voted for the Disarmament Conference might be used for the Codification Conference. The Dutch Government undertook responsibility for the additional 128,500 francs which the Conference would cost if held at the Hague...this was the only saving of any magnitude achieved in the course of the Budget debates."

   Yusuf Ali was involved in a similar acrimonious debate when he attempted to block a proposal to create new posts in the International Labour Organisation. "Yusuf Ali proposed the motion that new posts would serve no useful purpose...his proposal to reduce credit for 219,000 francs for new posts was defeated by 21 votes to 3."

4. Yusuf Ali refers to the association in the preface to his Progressive Islam Series pamphlet No. 5, *Moral Education*, dated December 1930.

5. Muslim educational ideals - Presidential address to the Punjab Muslim Educational Conference, 1923.

6. *Who was Who*, 1951-1961, London 1962.

7. *The Holy Qur'an-text, translation and commentary*, third edition (1938). The reference to travel is in the preface to the first edition.

8. In the preface of the Progressive Islam Series pamphlet No. 5, *Moral Education* Yusuf Ali provides some information on his contribution: "My address on that occasion attracted a good deal of attention, and won the interest and approval of many schools of thought...some friends of the Progressive Islam Association have since asked me if I would issue this address as a pamphlet, and I am doing so accordingly."

9. *The Times*, 20 May 1931.

10. Jauhar's deathbed instructions were that he should not be buried in 'occupied India' but near the Dome of the Rock in Jerusalem.

11. *Letters of Mian Fazli-i-Husain*, in particular pp.173-203. This section includes his detailed letters to the Aga Khan, Shafaat Ahmed Khan, Zafrullah Khan and even one to the Viceroy Irwin.

12. See K.K. Aziz, *Britain & Muslim India*, for a full discussion. Laski's remarks are on p.127.

13. *Hindustan ki tamaddun ki tarikh* was translated into English as *A Cultural History of India during the British Period* and published by D.B.Taraporevala Sons & Co., Bombay, 1940. The quotation is from the English edition's preface. An Urdu reprint was published by Karimsons, Pakistan in 1967.

14. Muhammad Rafiq Afzal (ed.), *Guftar-i-Iqbal*, pp. 245-247, citing *Inqilab* newspaper, Lahore, 21 November 1931.

15. Muhammad Abdullah Chughtai, *Iqbal kay suhbat mai*, pp. 250-261

16. Abdul Raoof Urooj, *Rijal-i Iqbal*, p.328. The phrase in Urdu *qaum ki himmat barhai* has been translated as 'revitalised his people'.

17. *Statesman* (Calcutta), 30 January 1937 (YA: 185). The dinner took place on 29 December 1931 after Indian students met at the University Union Hall, Torrington Square for the first gathering of 'Indian students abroad'. The conference was opened by the vice- chancellor of London University. There were two speakers, Dr. F: K. Sircar, convenor of the conference, and Yusuf Ali, who spoke on 'The Indian University'. His message that universities in India were poorly adapted to students' needs was probably a popular one.

18. J.F.Bruce, *A History of the University of the Punjab*; pp.177-178.

19. An account of the All-India Muslim Conference is given by K.K. Aziz (ed), *The All-India Muslim Conference 1928-1935 - A documentary record*. Aziz notes, "The outstanding achievement of the Conference was that it saved the Muslims from a far from improbable organisational disaster," p.15. See Batalvi, *Iqbal kay akhri do saal*, pp.211-215 for a more critical assessment, in particular Jinnah's refusal to participate.

20. *Letters of Mian Fazli-i-Husain*, pp. 240-241. Fazli Husain's concern for the Conference is indicated in the instructions he gave to Abdullah Haroon to contribute 700 rupees to the Conference. "I think it is necessary that you should be present, and present a few days before the actual meeting so that you may contribute towards the success of the gathering. The fact that you have been in England and Ottawa renders this all the more necessary." Fazli Husain also extracted a promise from the Nawab of Dacca to attend. Little is known of Yusuf Ali's role in the proceedings.

21. *The Religious Polity of Islam* would be the seventh pamphlet of his 'Progressive Islam' series. Its only reference to a topical matter is a passing comment on the election process based on universal franchise.

22. M.H. Faruqi's *Hayat-i-Iqbal kay chand makhfi goshay*, reproduces a news item from *Inqilab*, Vol. 7, p.243. This is a report of a tea party organised in Lahore's town hall on 1 March 1933, to welcome Iqbal on his return from the Third Round Table Conference.

23. Report, *The Times*, 2 June 1933.

24.ibid.

25. *The All-India Muslim Conference 1928-1933 - A documentary record*. ibid. Dr. Aziz has reproduced the Joint Committee questions and responses pp.137-281. The other four members of the delegation were Maulana Muhammad Yakub, H. S. Suhrawardy, Khalifa Shujauddin and Haji Rashid Ahmed.

26. Sir Annepu Patro, a member of the Madras Legislative Council, put Yusuf Ali through the wringer:

> *A.P*: Will you tell me whether you have had any electoral experience in the last 12 years? Have you contested any seats for the Provincial Council or the Central Legislature?

> *Y.A*: I did not actually contest a seat, but I have been in touch all the time, and I was a candidate for a little while in the United Provinces.

> *A.P*: You were defeated.

> *Y.A*: No, I did not go to the poll.

> *A.P*: So you have had no experience of the working of the Legislatures, either Central or Provincial.

> *Y.A*: Not as a member.

> *A.P*: I mean as a member.

> *Y.A*: But I have been fairly in touch with political questions.

> *A.P*: I do not want all extra answers. Say Yes or No. Will you please tell me how long it is since you retired.

> *Y.A*: I retired in 1914.

> *A.P*: You retired in 1914?

> *Y.A*: Yes.

> *A.P*: Since then you have been spending all your time in England.

> *Y.A*: Not all my time.

> *A.P*: Most of your time.

> *Y.A*: I have been domiciled in England, but I have been in India fairly frequently. May I just add one word [referring to the discussion on direct election to a central legislature]. The opinions that I have expressed are not my personal opinions. They are the opinions of the Association [Muslim Conference].

> *A.P*:I have not asked that question.

*The All-India Muslim Conference 1928-1933 - A documentary record.*ibid. pp. 156-157. K.K. Aziz holds that the Muslim Conference delegation was inexperienced: "The witnesses...lacked political ability as well as argumentative skill...the Muslim case did not gain by their advocacy. They fumbled for arguments, they did not have all facts at their fingertips, they were neither ready of wit nor rich in repartee. Sometimes they were tied up in knots and Muslim delegates sitting on the Joint Committee rescued them from awkward questions."

It is interesting to note that Yusuf Ali's inquisitor was a good friend of Jinnah; Wolpert, ibid., p. 190

27. *The All-India Muslim Conference* ibid., p. 170.

Wolpert believes that Jinnah too was unaware of the Pakistan proposal at this stage: "If Jinnah knew about the Pakistan scheme at this date, there was no indication in his papers of such knowledge or of any personal interest expressed in it." *Jinnah of Pakistan*, p. 132. Wolpert refers to the Craddock questioning but is inaccurate in describing Abdullah Yusuf Ali's origins as being from "the North-West Frontier Province."

28. The most prominent of these students was Rahmat Ali. See K.K. Aziz, *Britain & Muslim India* and also his *Complete works of Rahmat Ali*. In the former Aziz notes that "His conception, however, differed radically from Iqbal's, in that he demanded the creation of three sovereign Muslim states in India: Pakistan, consisting of Punjab, Kashmir, the North-West Frontier Province, Sind and Baluchistan; Bangistan, comprising Bengal and Assam; and Osmanistan, containing Hyderabad Daccan and Berar. In 1947 when Jinnah accepted the present borders of Pakistan, Rahmat Ali resented this betrayal of the Nation." p.144. Rahmat Ali was more or less exiled from Pakistan and died in Cambridge in 1948 where he is buried.

29. *The All-India Muslim Conference*, ibid., p.194.

30. Obituary note on Sir Frederic Lely; *The Times*, 26 November 1934.

31. *The Holy Qur'an-text, translation and commentary*, third Edition (1938). The quote is from the Preface to the First edition.

32. Yusuf Ali would also complete his manuscript on 4 April, 1937, as noted in *L'Envoi*, the concluding note in *The Holy Qur'an*, ibid. Meticulous in everything he did, the project was initiated and completed on his birthday anniversaries. This may be a coincidence or merely Yusuf Ali playing on a sense of literary destiny.

33. The cover title was *The Holy Qur'an: An introduction in English, with the original Text in parallel columns, a running rhythmic commentary in English and full explanatory Notes.* There was no reference to copyright, though the phrase on the cover 'Reserved by A. Yusuf Ali' suggests that the copyright was retained by Yusuf Ali. Printing was carried out at the Ripon Printing Press, Lahore, 'by Mirza Muhammad Sadiq, proprietor'.

The size was about A4. All the thirty instalments were bound in the same light blue vellum except for the fifth, which was in pink.

34.AHI: Volume for period 1/7/1934 - 28/4/1937.

The letters, in English, were pasted on to pages of the register book. They are reproduced below because of the light they throw on an institution with which Yusuf Ali was closely associated and also for their wider historical interest.

Letter 1 - From Muhammad Asad to Iqbal

July 12 1934

Dear Dr. Iqbal Sahib

Your letter of 10th. inst. has afforded me great pleasure. Your suggestion - teaching Theology at the Islamia College - is indeed a very good one, and I am in principle prepared to accept such a post if it is offered to me. The thing I imagine is not a simple teaching of Fikh as usually done by Maulvis, but a full and systematic course on the origin, the philosophy and the development of Islam since the first revelation of the Qur'an till the final collection of Hadis. Of course, matters of Fikh would automatically come in, but they would not form the only goal of my teaching. I feel certain that I will be able to accomplish the most necessary thing:- to infuse into young Muslims, at least into some of them, that feeling of intellectual pleasure and satisfaction without which no tuition of religious matters can be of any use. I have no doubt whatever - provided of course, that I am free to build up the things as I wish them - that within a very short time, say two or three years, the Islamia College would become leading in Northern India as regards a philosophical tuition of Islamic theology. I am sure that you could help me with your advice. I have given you the outline of my ideas concerning your suggestion, but I think it would be better if I come to Lahore and discuss the whole directly with you. I intended to go to some hill for a fortnight, as I have to write certain things now and the summer climate of Delhi exerts a paralysing influence on me. So I have thought I could go as well to Dalhousie; thus I would have the opportunity of seeing you within the next few days. With the best wishes for your health.

Yours faithfully

Mohammed Asad

P.S. I should be obliged if you would write me as soon as possible so that I might be able to arrange my plans accordingly as I have told you, I must go to the hills in these days, but I would postpone my departure until I get your answer.

(The Anjuman Proceedings then note that Asad should be informed that the college was now closed for the summer and that he should not postpone his trip)

Letter 2 - From Muhammad Asad to Iqbal

31st July 1934

I have just received your letter of yesterday's date.

I thank you heartily for your endeavour in my matter. As to the proposed pay of Rs 250/-for the probationary period of six months, I shall accept if provided the Anjuman fixes, after that period, a salary on a graduated scale, like that of other professors of the college, as you suggested yourself; and that the salary should be in the beginning (that is after the probation) not less than Rs. 300. Do not think that I am trying to strike a bargain, I only desire to work efficiently and to form my future lectures and courses as an original scientific effort, as is done in European Universities and for this purpose I used (*sic*) a certain minimum of comfort which ensures complete mental rest. And also I would have to give up - as mentioned by me in previous letters - my connection with the continental newspapers who desire me to act, from next autumn, as their correspondent in the Near East. But on the other hand, I regard my appointment at the Islamia College as a basis of a more extensive work in the service of Islam, and this is well worth to me.

I intend going to Kashmir after a few days, and I shall stop at Lahore to see you and discuss the matter finally. But if you could write me in the meantime about the definite view of the college committee, I would be very much obliged to you.

Thanking you once more, and hoping for a permanent improvement in your health.

(signed - Mohammed Asad)

(The Anjuman Proceedings have the note 'Committee accepted'; however for some reason this appointment never materialised. The position was taken up by Maulana Mawdudi on an honorary basis in 1939.)

35. AHI: ibid., entry for 14 July 1934. The phrase 'life of the community' is a translation of *qaumi zindigi*.

36. Yusuf Ali's work at *The Eastern Times* is mentioned in two sources: Abdussalaam Khurshid, *Way Suratain Ilahi*, p.269; Abdul Raoof Urooj, *Rijal-e-Iqbal*, p.329.

37. Abul-Laith Siddiqui, *Malfuzat-i-Iqbal*, p.71.

38. AHI: ibid., entry for 15 April 1935.

39. Iqbal severely criticised Fazli Husain: "It is really unfortunate that this urban-rural question should have received the support of Sir Fazli Husain, who obtained power in

the first instance not as a rural leader but as a Muslim of the Province, but unfortunately clung to power by accentuating rural-urban differences. In this way, he secured as his colleagues some third class men with no title to Government power." From D.C. Verma, *Sir Chotu Ram - Life and Times*, p. 108.

40. *The All-India Muslim Conference*, ibid., p.194.

41. Muhammad Abdullah Chughtai, *Iqbal kay suhbat mai*, p. 401.

42. *Guftar-i-Iqbal*, ibid. pp.204-205, citing a public appeal made by Iqbal and co-signatories on 8 May 1936.

43. *Crescent*, magazine of Islamia College, Lahore; October 1936; article by Yusuf Ali, 'Principal to the Students' (YA 146).

44. *The Civil & Military Gazette*, Lahore, 19 July 1936 (YA 115). The British press also reported Yusuf Ali's tribute: "At a meeting of the World Congress of Faiths at the Great Hall, University College, Gower Street, London, yesterday Mr A. Yusuf Ali referred to the death of Sir Fazli Husain and said that the Punjab had lost a capable son and India an able leader." 11 July 1936, *The Times*.

It is a measure of Fazli Husain's intellectual calibre that he earned these plaudits from Yusuf Ali, normally sparing in his praise of Indian Muslim contemporaries.

45. Report, *The Times*, 29 July 1936.

46. Interview with author, Lahore, January 1989.

47. *The Civil & Military Gazette*, Lahore, 17 May 1935 carried a report of Yusuf Ali's address to the Lahore Rotary Club on 'Educational Reform'(YA111).

The Sussex Daily News of 7 October 1937, in a report on a talk given by Yusuf Ali on Palestine to the Brighton Rotary Club, refers to Yusuf Ali as past president of the Lahore Rotary Club, but the word 'president' has been pencilled out and overwritten 'member' (YA 70).

48. Letter from Professor Hamidullah to the author, 6 March 1988: "...I met the late Prof. Muhammad Shafi in Lahore and he recalled that Abdullah Yusuf Ali was known in the Punjab as a scholar, writer of articles in journals, and was astonished that he was in Hyderabad as a minister of Land Revenues."

Professor Shafi was principal of the Oriental College, Lahore, and Yusuf Ali acknowledges his help in the preface to the third edition, *The Holy Qur'an*, ibid.

49. *Way Suratain Ilahi*, ibid. p. 268; *Rijal-e-Iqbal*, ibid., p.329.

50. "My own position is perfectly clear. I came under a special engagement, reserving the right to stand for legislatures," *Eastern Times*, Lahore; 17/11/1936 (YA 153).

"I never agreed to any condition barring me from politics. On the contrary I expressly repudiated any such condition." *Eastern Times*, Lahore; 27/12/1936 (YA 167).

51. *Eastern Times*, Lahore; 17 November 1936 (YA 153).

52. *Paisa Akhbar* (Urdu), Lahore; 14 January 1937 (YA 179).

53. *Eastern Times*, Lahore; 27 December 1936 (YA 167).

54. ibid.

55. *The Light*, Lahore; 24 December 1936 (YA 168).

56. ibid.

> The criticisms of Yusuf Ali's salary and proficiency in Arabic were made by a Mr Durrani. *The Light* attributed Durrani's attacks to a personal vendetta: "The reason is that Mr Yusuf Ali had the misfortune to have once acceded to a request of Mr Durrani to write a Foreword for one of the latter's publications. In that Foreword Mr Yusuf Ali expressed disagreement with certain views of the writer and Mr Durrani is not a man to forget or forgive."
>
> Dr K. K. Aziz has suggested to the author that Mr Durrani referred to by *The Light* might have been one Gazi Karim Durrani.

57. *Paisa Akhbar*, Lahore: 14 January 1937 (YA179).

58. *The Civil & Military Gazette*, Lahore; 7 January 1937 (YA 170).

59. Baidar Malik, *Yaran-i-Maktab: Tehrik-i-Pakistan aur Islamia College*, p. 215.

60. *The Civil & Military Gazette*, Lahore; 13 January 1937 (YA 175).

61. *Way Suratain Ilahi*, ibid., p.268-269.

62. Letter, *The Times*, 11 June 1937 (YA 39).

63. In a 'letter to the Editor' Muhammad Shafi wrote to *The New Times*, Lahore, 21 December 1936 in his capacity as Secretary of the influential Inter-Collegiate Muslim Brotherhood: "...our relations with Allama Abdullah Yusuf Ali have been most cordial, and we are indebted to him for his sympathetic support and genuine guidance from time to time." (YA163).

64. *Tribune*, Lahore, 4 December 1936 (YA156).

65. *Eastern Times*, Lahore, 2 March 1937 (YA187); Yusuf Ali also composed the following paean:

> "The occasion of the Silver Jubilee of His Exalted Highness should be celebrated with special rejoicings not only in the Hyderabad State, in which I include the Berars, but throughout India. His Exalted Highness's noble qualities of head and heart have endeared him to all qualities of people. We rejoice that his rule has been fruitful of blessings for so many millions, and we pray that he may long be spared to us, for his personality sheds lustre on the Princely Order and on the Muslim name in India."
>
> *Pilot* (Weekly), Amritsar, (undated) February 1937 (YA189).

66. *Yaran-i-Maktab: Tehrik-i-Pakistan aur Islamia College*, ibid. p. 191-192.

On one occasion there was some confusion over which verses were to be discussed and after commencing Yusuf Ali realised that his commentary was not related to what had been read out in Arabic. He quickly rose and left the meeting but later apologised to the staff member.

67. *Masjid* (Urdu), Lahore, 16 April 1937; article titled *Sayyid Shaheed Hadrat Imam Husain alaihis salaam.*

68. *The Civil & Military Gazette*, Lahore, 22 April 1937. Yusuf Ali's laudatory remarks were made at a dinner of the International Fellowship Society, Lahore.

69. *The Holy Qur'an*, ibid. *L'Envoi.*

6

UNQUIET SPIRIT

During 1936 and 1937 it was not just India that was lurching into crisis. The whole world seemed to be teetering on the brink of catastrophe. The very institutions which Yusuf Ali looked on for order and good sense, the British monarchy and the League of Nations, stood battered. The Edwardian world he knew and loved was like an ocean liner proceeding full speed for a fateful encounter with a massive iceberg. The Spanish Civil War (1936-39), the Muslim revolt in Palestine (April 1936), Italy's invasion of Ethiopia (Abyssinia, 1935-36), Hitler's reassertion in the Rhineland (March 1936) – there was a full catalogue of portents that charged the political atmosphere with a sense of expectation.

Even the British monarchy was not what it used to be. George V died in January 1935 leaving unresolved the problem of the Prince of Wales's infatuation with Wallis Simpson, the wife of an American businessman. She began to feature on state occasions at the new King's side, even though the Simpsons would not divorce till October of the following year. The British press kept a craven silence on the affair till December 1936 but then the story broke. The Royals' romantic scandals were now out in the open. Edward VIII's insistence on marriage with a divorcee prompted a constitutional crisis in Britain and amid much personal bitterness he was forced to abdicate in favour of his younger brother, crowned George VI in May 1937. Indian public opinion stood bemused, particularly as plans had been afoot to entertain Edward in India for the traditional Coronation Durbar.[1]

The reputation of the British monarchy stood tarnished. Yusuf Ali had long been an ardent royalist and his speeches and articles in the 1914-18 war displayed a fervent adoration of George V and Queen Mary. He introduced the Urdu phrase *chahra-e-mubarak* (auspicious face) to a London audience as a means of referring to the King.[2] In 1937 he was still in awe, as if nothing had changed in nearly twenty five years. He addressed a meeting of the Monarchist League held in Kensington in July 1937, which offered the royal family as 'precious examples of virtue and purity'.[3] His sense of loyalty blinded him to obvious inconsistencies. Yusuf Ali's other blind spot, even after the recent troubles at Islamia College, was the strength of the Indian independence movement. He clung to a political vision that belonged to bygone Edwardian England:

> India as an integral part of the Empire shares in all the advantages and dignity associated with our Monarchy...We may have our own fears about some features in the unfolding political life of the country. But there can be no doubt whatever that Monarchy is a source of strength and stability for India, and the title: 'Emperor of India' borne by our Sovereign reflects a lustre and dignity on the country which she may not otherwise enjoy...I feel convinced that we have already in the present fact of Monarchy a strong bulwark against hasty revolution, a historic link between diverse peoples and a promising symbol of stability and union.[4]

The only Indian political group ready to give credence to such views were the Unionists of Punjab, whose former minister, Sir Feroz Khan Noon, chaired this Monarchist League meeting in his capacity as Indian High Commissioner. Yusuf Ali was becoming hopelessly out of touch with events in India. Even as he spoke India was undergoing dramatic change. In the elections of 1937 Sir Sikander and his Unionist Party had won in Muslim-majority Punjab, but eight other provinces with Muslim minorities were taken by the Congress Party, including the UP. Congress's refusal to share any power with the Muslim League proved an eye-opener for Muslims. Even in the Punjab an alliance was being forged between the Unionists and the Muslim League, a closing of ranks that gave the Muslims of India a far greater sense of security than any faith in a distant and foreign monarch.

Yusuf Ali's support of the Empire and monarchy drew him to the activities of Sir Francis Younghusband, an Englishman of the old school who believed there was a mysterious, spiritual purpose underpinning

Britain's imperial ambition.[5] Sir Francis enthusiastically espoused the idea for a 'Congress of Faiths' after contact with an Indian *swami*.[6] He created a seventeen-member 'British National Council' to plan the first 'International Council of the World Fellowship' which was held at University College, London in July 1936 and opened with a personal message from Edward VIII. The one Muslim representative on the Council was Shaikh Abdul Qader, another former Unionist now in London as adviser to the Secretary of State for India – it is as if the British Government did not wish to go beyond a narrow circle of loyalists for information on India - who perhaps arranged for Yusuf Ali's participation.[7] Yusuf Ali was again invited as the Muslim representative in the next annual 'Congress of Faiths' conference held in Oxford in July 1937, at which distinguished speakers included the Buddhist Maung Aye Maung and William Sperry, Dean of the Divinity School at Harvard University. The chairman was Herbert Samuel, now Lord Samuel, also serving as representative of Judaism at the proceedings. The esoteric discussions at the Congress were in strange contrast to the political realities of the day. Like Sir Francis, Yusuf Ali was also a great enthusiast of the notion of a spiritual fellowship, which blended well with his world view of harmony between Britain and India. He soldiered on with his visionary aspiration that 'religion, rightly understood, should make for Peace by supporting Righteousness, Justice and Fair-dealing among men'.[8] The same sense of mission took him in early September to a conference in Geneva on 'Peace through Religion' sponsored by the League of Nations, where he was acclaimed as '*le grand chef Musulman*'.[9]

Throughout the 1920s Yusuf Ali spoke in defence of the League of Nations as the pre-eminent institution for achieving international cooperation and world harmony. He had even served as a spirited member of the Indian delegation to its Conference in 1928. The League was one of the few contemporary institutions referred to in the Qur'anic commentary, the first occasion being in the instalment published in October 1936 which contained the translation of *Surah Nur*.[10] However the League's inability to take steps against Italy for her aggression in Abyssinia shook his faith. In the instalment published in July 1937, he would refer to the League as a 'failure'.[11] It was an ideal which had proved flawed. His address at the

'Peace through Religion' conference in Geneva would pin hope for world peace and harmony on the collaboration of the USA and the British Empire. Their common language, English, was the key for achieving political understanding.[12]

On his way back to London from Geneva, Yusuf Ali stopped at the French capital to attend the Paris Exhibition. He was thunderstruck to find the Palestine Pavilion with its banner 'The Land of the Jews'. It was a moment of revelation. He lost no time in speaking out in London on the Palestine issue. From October 1937 to the end of the year he attended numerous meetings to express the Muslim point of view. The proposals of the Peel Commission to partition Palestine and create a Jewish state in the more fertile areas touched a raw nerve in Yusuf Ali. Palestine was under British mandate and he felt let down. The venues at which Yusuf Ali spoke out against the Peel proposals included the Near and Middle East Association in London, the New Peace Movement at Cambridge and the Rotary Club of Brighton. Jauhar, had he been alive, would have warmed to Yusuf Ali's controlled passion and perhaps even been surprised that a leaf was being taken out of the Khilafatists' book: Yusuf Ali declared that Palestine was part of the *jazirat ul-arab* and no Muslim would willingly see it given to people of another religion. In the same address he went on to deplore the steps taken against the Arab revolt, such as the introduction of 'Star Chamber' methods, the alteration of the law to allow the validity of uncorroborated evidence and the ban on the Mufti of Jerusalem.[13] Such strength of feeling perhaps arose from a sense that his trust had been misplaced, not just in the League of Nations but with cynical politicians like Herbert Samuel who espoused grand ideals of spiritual fellowship while at the same time remaining silent on the injustices being committed against the Palestinians.[14]

Yusuf Ali's arguments on the Palestine question were carefully constructed with the skill of a barrister. He based his case on the terms of the mandates and first-hand knowledge of the circumstances at the Paris Peace Conference. His expositions commenced with an explanation that the League of Nations did not give the country holding the mandates – Britain in the case of Palestine – any proprietary rights:

Palestine was held under an 'A' mandate, which had been especially framed with the idea that the people in the mandated country were equally civilised, but being in this case a broken-off section of the Turkish Empire, they were in need of governmental experience. But this was only until they could stand on their own legs. The mandatory's duty was to advise and prepare them for self-administration. They were an independent people. Both Iraq and Syria, held under similar mandates, had their independence recognised so why not Palestine? Lord Balfour went out of his way to say that England would use her influence to enable the Jewish people to have a home in Palestine provided that the rights of the non-Jewish people were in no way affected.[15]

Yusuf Ali let the British audiences clearly know that the partition of Palestine was an injustice. The Khilafatists would have wondered why it had taken Yusuf Ali eighteen years to register his protest on the broken pledges to Muslims, but he redeemed himself, speaking up when there was neither a Jauhar or Ameer Ali alive to publicise the cause. His eloquence and grasp of the situation led to him standing in as a substitute speaker for the Palestinian leader Jamal Husseini on one occasion in Cambridge.[16]

The League of Nations was an ideal Yusuf Ali had been able to abandon; love of monarch and loyalty to Britain and Empire were in the fabric of his personality and could not be disposed off in the same manner. He was restrained in criticising the authorities, not venturing beyond the statement: 'The Imperial Government's acceptance of the principle of partition [of Palestine] had surprised and pained Muslims.'[17] His poem 'Palestine' possessed an ethereal quality in keeping with his determination not to be blunt:

> What joys and sorrows – laughter, tears –
> Are woven in thy web of life?
> What thrills of mingled hopes and fears?
> What tragic dreams of love and strife?
> What statecraft plots have scarred thy brow?
> O Holy Land of Palestine!

O Land of Peace! say when and how,
In these strange days, can peace be thine?
One way alone can bring thee peace:
That ancient rights be not suppressed,
That aliens from encroachments cease,
And Quds be given its rightful rest.[18]

Jinnah by contrast had no hesitation in expressing his disgust in most unpoetic terms: 'During the recent times Great Britain has thrown her friends to the wolves and broken her solemn promises. Only those succeed with the British people who possess force and power and who are in a position to bully them...I am sure that there will be no peace in the Near East unless they give an honest and square deal to the Arabs in Palestine.'[19] The worldwide Muslim protests of 1937 were successful in placing the Peel proposals in temporary abeyance till 1943, when Zionist lobbying in the United States resurrected the idea of a Jewish state in Palestine.

Yusuf Ali celebrated *'id-ul-fitr* in Lahore in December 1937. He had prepared an index for the complete translation of the Qur'an, which he gave to Muhammad Ashraf, and checked preparations for the new edition. Yusuf Ali also used the opportunity to mend bridges with the *Anjuman-Himayat-ul-Islam* and spoke at a meeting to publicise their recent publication of the Qur'an.[20] There were numerous prize-givings to attend and meetings to chair, in which he had the company of Abdul Qader. Both participated in the 'Iqbal Day' activities organised by the Inter-Collegiate Muslim Brotherhood. There was also a public meeting in the YMCA hall at which Abdul Qader presided and Yusuf Ali spoke on the theme of privileges and responsibilities of student life. He resumed contact with the Lahore Art Circle and spoke on the French artist Millet, using material he had collected in France the preceding year. Yusuf Ali had prepared 'lantern slides' depicting Millet's home and studio, and his major works.[21]

Yusuf Ali also met Iqbal for the last time. Together they visited an exhibition by an artist called Kazmi, to whom Iqbal later wrote a letter of appreciation. It contained a reference to Yusuf Ali: 'I and Allama Yusuf Ali saw your art work *shikwa* and *jawab-i-shikwa* at Maulana Hali's commemoration. The view held by me and the erudite [Urdu: *mubassir-i-zamana*] Abdullah Yusuf Ali Sahib is that if through further hard work and application you master this field and present your work to the world of Islam, you will add to the styles of drawing and create a new school.'[22] The letter was sent a few days prior to Iqbal's death on 21 April 1938. Their mutual politeness and courtesy was to be unfailing, notwithstanding political differences that ran very deep. On Iqbal's death Yusuf Ali wrote an obituary note to *The Times*:

> The death of Sir Muhammad Iqbal removes from the Indian scene one of its two leading poets, both philosophers. But while the philosophy of Sir Rabindranath Tagore is contemplative and mystical, that of Iqbal was, if the term may be allowed, a mystical protest against mysticism. He looked upon the cult of Sufi mysticism as one of the causes of the downfall of political Islam - an opinion that is historically indefensible, though point is lent to it by the latter-day degradation of Sufism itself. His shrewd thrusts at the many weak points in modern Western life would have been more effective if he could have supplied a constructive basis for the evolution of the Indian Muslims as an important factor in the evolution of a united modern India.[23]

Yusuf Ali travelled from Lahore to UP in February 1938. He visited Aligarh to attend to matters at the Court of the University. He also visited Government House on 10 February 1938 and later called on the Congress president Jawaharlal Nehru. Yusuf Ali urged him not to be in such a hurry for Independence; his shining optimism still found something commendable in a province strained by communal tensions: 'Certain forces [the policies of a Congress government] have been set in motion which will make for a fuller social and political life and a more equitable economic life for India'.[24] Jinnah was also in UP at the time but there is no record of their having met. Jinnah's message to the students at Aligarh was starkly opposite: one hundred and fifty years of slavery under the British could be followed by further humiliation under a Hindu government. For Iqbal the Hindu-Muslim riots of 1937-38 were civil war by another name for which there was only one way out. He had a vision of the Muslims of India as a political unit guided by the *shariah*.[25] In Yusuf Ali's estimation neither Iqbal or Jinnah held out 'constructive' proposals for India.

When Yusuf Ali returned to London in April it was by air for the first time. The trip from Karachi took him two and a half days – his first journey from Bombay in 1893 would have lasted four weeks. The British government continued to regard him as their pre-eminent representative of Muslims – *le grand chef Musulman*. He could be trusted to dwell on India's bonds with Empire at various public meetings. He was selected to be in attendance on the arrival of Emir Saud, son of Abdul Aziz ibn Saud, in August. The reception committee at Victoria Station included Lord Fredrick Cambridge, the Egyptian Charge d'Affaires and the Afghan Minister.

Yusuf Ali was a great performer, and his confident public face as a champion of Muslim causes and eminent man of letters masked inner crises. The National Liberal Club in Pall Mall would be his base rather than the family home in Wimbledon. He remained estranged from the children of his first marriage and was soon to draw up a will condemning them in the harshest terms. It was not long before he would be estranged from Masuma as well, even though without her patient support and willingness to care for Rashid he could never have pursued so single-mindedly the years of scholarship on the Qur'an. Yusuf Ali could write and speak about human emotions and yet found it difficult to sustain long-term relationships. 'I always beg you to remember,' Yusuf Ali once addressed a group of students, 'that supreme above all questions of employment is the question of character. I test an educated man not by what he knows but by his capacity to love, understand and appreciate other people, and by his capacity to inspire confidence in himself because he has to some degree realised himself.'[26] Yusuf Ali was a brilliant communicator in writing and speech, but there was something unbending in his personality which came in the way of family relationships. The connection between self-knowledge and a capacity to love others was a beautiful intellectual notion, but that is what it remained. He sought out intimacy – 'intimacy' was a word he used frequently – as if it were a poetic ideal. The intimacy of family inter-relationships would elude Yusuf Ali in childhood and old age. Rashid, now sixteen, had seen little of his distinguished father in recent years.

Yusuf Ali would be confronted by feelings of isolation and despair. It was not a sort of despair which arose because of the conditions of Muslims or the warmongering of Hitler. It was an internally felt ennui which even the completion of his Qur'anic translation-cum-commentary had not been able to salve. He voiced his anxieties in a paper read before the London Society for the Study of Religion in November 1938. 'Our soul is encased in flesh and our mind can only form material pictures,' he said in dramatic style. 'Our will is constantly being attacked by temptations. There is so much that is evanescent, ugly, and false around us. There seems to be so much discord and injustice, pain and suffering, sorrow and disappoint-ment. Man sometimes feels as if he were Lord of all Creation, but with ever-increasing knowledge he realises what an infinitesimal dot he is in the stupendous forces around him. He then feels as if he were a helpless, restless, homeless, friendless creature in a universe of infinite dimensions, of which he can barely grasp three! The riddle of the universe oppresses him, and he cries: 'Vanity of vanities! All is vanity!' and includes his own life in the indictment.'[27] Yusuf Ali's brooding introspection was part of the same psychological make-up which found appeal in an idealised image of the self.

On 9 November 1938, Yusuf Ali addressed the Royal Society of Lit-erature in which he appeared to contrast his own philosophy of life with Iqbal's:

> In Iqbal's world we are to seek struggle and tension, not peace and calm. Life, to use his own words in illustration of his poetical philosophy, is ever 'a forward assimilative movement.' Personality is 'a state of tension,' and it is the state of tension that 'tends to make us immortal'. The struggle which we should make is to maintain this tension, to absorb the whole world into ourselves, not to be absorbed. 'Love is the desire to assimilate, to absorb', not to lose ourselves in the object of our love. He would dissent from Tennyson's lines:

Love took up the harp of life,
And smote on all the chords with might,
Smote the chord of self, that trembling
Passed in music out of sight.

Nor would he approve of the Sufi ideal, to be lost in God. For he uncompromisingly attacks the Sufi mystics, especially Hafiz and Saadi, for preaching the renunciation of the Self in order to reach God.[28]

Yusuf Ali interpreted the 'Sufi ideal' as self-denial – renunciation of the self. Perhaps such an interpretation of Sufism was essential to preserve the balance in a personality that was also egoistical and possessed a strong sense of destiny. In happier times he had offered a more rounded view of Sufis: 'They go about and mix in society. They are merchants, governors, travellers and follow other professions...their ideal is to help others and maintain contact with the rest of mankind.'[29] Nevertheless there was a nihilistic strand in his complex personality that sought to submerge itself in some greater whole – the first indication of this tendency was the hero-worship of George V in 1914.

Travel was the best therapy to shake Yusuf Ali out of his melancholy. In 1938 his reputation as an Islamic scholar crossed the Atlantic when the Qur'an translation and commentary was published by both Hafner in New York and Murray in Cambridge, Massachusetts. He left London on 12 November 1938 on a tour of Canada sponsored by the National Council of Education of Canada, the body which had also organised his visit in 1932. He was greeted at Winnipeg by the Deputy Minister of Education and over the next three months gave numerous lectures and press and radio interviews mainly on Indian affairs, though there were many opportunities to speak on Islam and issues like Palestine. He also discussed the threats being posed to the British Empire by Germany and Japan, and addressed meetings of the Canadian Institute of International Affairs. The mosque of Edmonton, reported to be the first in Canada, was also formally opened by Yusuf Ali in December 1938. Yusuf Ali was to name it and he chose Rashid Mosque, perhaps after his son. His itinerary was packed: he spoke on 'The Tenets of Islam' in Montreal, on 'India under the New Regime' at

Lennoxville and many other cities, and on 'The place of Islam in the Modern World' at Fort William. By December 1938 Yusuf Ali was in the Canadian heartland in the height of winter, addressing audiences on 'Moral Progress versus Scientific and Material Progress' at places like Manitoba and Saskatchewan. The press reports were glowing: 'He's of medium height, stocky of build. His hair is white and crisp and getting sparse. His manner is nervous, quick, superbly polite but direct. His English, although it is not his native tongue, is beautiful, precise, eloquent. His knowledge of English literature is profound; he himself has contributed much to it apart from his translation of the Koran and his commentary.'[30]

He was a superb Indian ambassador of the Empire. His charming public persona and oratorical skills prompted a fan mail from all types of organisations. The President of Acadia University, Nova Scotia, wrote to him: 'Few, if any, addresses have been more greatly enjoyed by those in attendance'. An institute in Toronto sent him its annual magazine which described his visit: 'He was charming. We fell in love with him at the very first when he smiled at us from the platform. But it was not until he began to speak that we realised how great was the personality and deep understanding of the man who stood before us, so simple and unassuming.' Yusuf Ali revelled in the adulation and kept newspaper cuttings describing his tour. He loved Canada, replying to one organisation: 'What I am so impressed with in Canada is the freshness and youthful vigour...we are all members of the same Empire. Let us hope that our respective countries will feel and act in as friendly a manner as we do act individually.'[31] The paradox was that crowds could feel his personality and he made strangers feel at ease, yet it was a conviviality limited to the public occasion. When alone he was truly alone.

Yusuf Ali had not lost interest in India. He wrote a series of articles for *Eastern Times* of Lahore on his experiences in Canada and compared what appeared to him as the harmonious French-English divide with the fractious state of Muslim-Hindu relations in India. Muslims had many lessons to learn in how to deport themselves as a minority: the French Canadians were well organised 'both in church and state' while 'our Muslims are disorganised and individualistic'.[32]

When Yusuf Ali returned to London in February 1939 it was more like a migratory bird on a transitory stop. Within six months he would be on the seas again. Following the pattern prior to his Canadian trip, he lived part of the time at the National Liberal Club in Central London rather than 3 Mansel Road, Wimbledon. In May the Muslim Society in Great Britain celebrated the Prophet's Birthday at the Portman Rooms, Baker Street. It was a well attended affair with Yusuf Ali as guest speaker.[33] Yusuf Ali's restlessness had reached a point where he could not bear to remain at one place for more than a few months. He left London in September, two days before Britain declared war on Germany. He was sixty-seven but still ready for adventure. The ship he travelled on, the S.S *Stratheden*, spent every night under blackout till reaching the Indian Ocean. For many days the passengers did not know what ports they were making for or whether the route would be through Suez or via the Cape. They came across submarines on more than one occasion.[34] He composed a poem on the crossing that shows how much his own spirits had become raised:

> We knew not the harbour for which we were bound;
> We knew not the route by which we should go;
> We sailed in the midst of a darkness profound,
> Prepared for a lurking insidious foe.
> We carried our life-belts ever and anon,
> Walking & sitting, at meals & at play;
> We manned our solitary nine-pounder gun;
> and we watched fore & aft, by night & by day.
> For a week we were lost to the world in a cloud,
> a thousand poor souls, women, men, young and old,
> In a sea bereft of ships, which we stealthily ploughed
> Without lights, without plans, with our story untold.
> With a breath of relief, in the Fortunate Port
> We anchored, & slowly with lights did we sail
> Through the channel that links East & West in a short
> Silver stream, with old Sinai well within hail.
> So here's to the ship with her fine gallant crew
> and here's to the captain that prudently dared!

For we reach sunny shores, and we humbly renew
Our vow to our Flag, - to be true and prepared.[35]

Yusuf Ali's last perilous sea voyage had been made during the Great War
en route to Scandinavia at the request of the Foreign Office. It is unlikely
he would have received permission to travel on the eve of war unless it was
to do with recruitment and propaganda work. One of his meetings in Delhi
was with Sir Sikander Hayat Khan, still serving as the Unionist premier of
the Punjab. Sikander was in close touch with Churchill over Indian
recruitment, even flying out to Cairo for discussions with him.

World War II, like the Great War twenty-five years earlier, had a gal-
vanising effect on Yusuf Ali and he was ready to stand and be counted. He
visited Aligarh and also spoke at the Anglo-Arabic College in Delhi on 14
October, where he stressed the need for India's cooperation with Britain
in the war effort.[36] He arrived in Lahore on 16 October, where he spent
ten days before departing for Bombay and then sailing back to Britain.

On his return Yusuf Ali wrote two pieces for use in the propaganda
effort directed by the Ministry of Information, 'The Muslims of India
stand by the Democracies' and 'India's attitude to the War'. The latter
contained an anecdote drawn from his recent trip. 'I was in Punjab in
October 1939,' he wrote, 'and was greatly impressed by a little incident that
came within my personal experience.' An ex-pupil had taken him to his
agricultural estate and said, 'Sir, these are stirring times! I have made some
improvements. But they can wait. This time I have come to see you and get
your blessings, in case I may be killed in battle before you come again this
way. I am going to join the Army with my fellow-villagers, to uphold the
Flag, and those principles of honour, liberty and fidelity in word and deed,
which you tried to instil into us....do you not approve?'. 'I gave my hearty
blessing. This is the spirit which animates great masses of people and goes
some way to explain India's attitude to the War.'[37] Another of his articles,
'India and the War', was published the following year by the British
Embassy in Tokyo as part of the 'British Information Series'.

On 8 December 1939, Yusuf Ali addressed a meeting of the East India
Association in Caxton Hall, Westminster, the same venue at which he had
spoken in 1914 calling on India to rally around the Union Jack. In exactly

the same manner as in World War I, he urged Indians to show restraint in their demands for political change: 'My plea, therefore, is that, whatever our individual views may be, we should for the present concentrate on the one great thing that we are all out to achieve, and with a strengthened and saved Empire, we shall then be able to achieve the very best of our ideals, both for India and the Empire.'[38]

During the Great War Yusuf Ali's call for patience might have had some support from groups seeking reform through constitutional changes, but the situation now was too far gone for such respectful compliance. At the outset of the Second World War Britain suspended constitutional discussions in India and, though Gandhi was prepared to accept this, the Congress leadership refused. The Congress ministries in the Indian provinces resigned in November 1939. The Muslim League, with strong support from the 'Untouchables' – a section of Indian society spurned by caste-conscious Hindus – in turn declared 2 December 1939 as a 'Day of Deliverance' from Congress dictatorship in provinces like UP. There was a war between Nehru and Jinnah just as intense as between the Germans and the Allies. Yusuf Ali lamented what was happening: 'The correspondence between Pandit Jawaharlal Nehru and Mr Subhas Chandra Bhose as representing the Congress on the one hand, and Mr Muhammad Ali Jinnah, President of the Muslim League on the other reveals a hopeless impasse from which it is difficult to see a way out without a radical alteration in the points of view of our communal leaders.'[39]

It is against this background that Yusuf Ali addressed another meeting at Caxton Hall in February 1940, on 'The Muslims of India, the War and the Political Field'.[40] He used this event as an opportunity to present a possible 'constructive' solution. Yusuf Ali rejected the notion of mutually exclusive zones for Hindus and Muslims on the ground that it would require 'impossible exchanges of populations', and sought an alternative which would prevent minorities from being swamped. His approach was the creation of a 'composite' party, which would be an alliance of Muslims, Hindus opposed to the Congress and other groups such as the Untouchables. Such a composite party would be large enough to form an effective counterweight against the Congress and lead to a two-party system in India. It was a restatement of ideas presented to the Joint Committee for

Indian Constitutional Reform in 1933. 'Other lines of cleavage which sometimes make a sort of timid appearance in Provincial Legislatures are: Town versus Country, or Agriculturists versus Non-agriculturists, or Capital versus Labour. These lines of cleavage can also be utilised in forming composite parties.' He also called on Muslims to take the lead and 'help India out of the impasse of fixed communal parties and perpetual impotent minorities'. He continued to hold the premise that India was a nation and Muslims should cooperate in 'composite' party schemes which transcended religious differences. There were no takers for Yusuf Ali's scheme.[41] In any case the times when the politics of India could be shaped by a quiet word in the ear of the Secretary of State for India were over.

The Muslim League met in March 1940 in Lahore and passed the famous 'Pakistan' resolution. The speed with which events were unfolding in India forced Yusuf Ali to reappraise his stand. While still not in favour of Indian independence he came to accept the Muslim League's analysis of the threat posed to Muslims by the Congress. In May 1940, two years short of seventy, he took on Nehru's man in London, Krishna Menon, in a debate organised at Southampton University. The motion was 'That it is in the interests of both the peoples of this country and of India that India be given complete independence forthwith', with Yusuf Ali predictably arguing against it. In the debate he accepted the Muslim League as representative of Muslim opinion and warned that the Hindus could not be given domination over the minorities.[42]

In the summer and autumn of 1940 the skies of Britain thundered with the sounds of war. German bombing raids were an everyday occurrence. The steadfast convenors of the World Congress of Faiths managed to organise their annual event in July, at which Yusuf Ali spoke. The Royal Society of Arts, too, defied the circumstances and invited Yusuf Ali to present a paper on adult education in India. One meeting of the East India Association chaired by the Secretary of State continued while an air raid was in progress. Excitement occasionally erupted from an unexpected corner. At another meeting of the East India Association, Yusuf Ali witnessed the assassination of a former Governor of the Punjab, Sir Michael O'Dwyer, shot dead at short range by a Sikh. His dramatic account was quoted by the press: 'In the front row, near where I was standing, I saw Sir Louis Dane, who is a friend of mine, collapse. I rushed to his side and he said "I'm hurt." He looked bewildered and I, of course, was stunned. I helped him to his feet and noticed he was bleeding from the arm. I helped him as much as I could. It was an incredible ending to a meeting which had been extremely friendly. There had been no interruption and everybody at the meeting received Sir Percy Syke's address with enthusiasm.'[43]

The dangerous times may have prompted Yusuf Ali to draw up his will in September 1940. Seven years earlier he had transferred ownership of 3 Mansel Road to Masuma. His will was not generous to any of his children, including Rashid. The children from his first marriage were specifically ruled out: 'These children by their continued ill-will towards me have alienated my affection for them, so much so that I confer no benefit on them by this my will'. He then directed that the bulk of his estate went not to Masuma or Rashid but to a fund to be set up in his name by the Court of the University of London for the benefit of 'Indian students at the University'. Masuma was left the household furnishings, his writings and papers and any books she liked from his collection and £40 every quarter 'until she remarries'. Rashid would inherit £40 every quarter for life and a lump sum of £3000. Any books left over were to be despatched to the library of Islamia College, Lahore, while there were very particular instructions for the handling of his diaries.

He and Masuma separated the following year. Their relationship may have been strained since 1940, because for most of that year Yusuf Ali preferred to stay at the National Liberal Club. He continued to receive his ICS pension of £800 till he died in 1953 and would leave an estate worth £20,578, which even after death duties was a sizeable figure.

In the autumn of 1940 he was still a tough old man willing to weather the Blitz over London. His heart was in the propaganda work. He described a Nazi victory as being a disaster of the greatest magnitude – greater than any which has ever befallen Islam and the progress of humanity.[44] He travelled afar from London to deliver the message, speaking at places like Hartlepool, Bristol and Hull. In Bristol in October he spoke twice on one day, to the Bristol Round Tablers and the local branch of the Royal Empire Society. The Ministry of Information briefed the organisers well on Yusuf Ali, in comparison with the botched-up efforts during the Great War when at times they were not sure whether he was a Hindu or a Muslim. At Hartlepool he was correctly introduced as a former president of the All-India Muslim Conference.[45] His message was one of reassurance: 'India and Islam' were loyal. One of his Bristol lectures had the title 'Islam and the War'. With no mandate but from himself he declared, 'As for India, the Muslims were entirely at one with the Allies because they knew that not the peace of India but of the whole world depended upon those free institutions which were associated with the name of Great Britain. The British Empire is the one solid factor all over the world and the Muslims are going to support it through thick and thin.'[46]

Yusuf Ali maintained his pattern of activities – propaganda work, diverse literary activity and comments on political developments in India – through into 1941. His literary output included a chapter on 'Muslim Culture and Religious Thought' for a publication of the Royal Institute of International Affairs, *Modern India and the West*. The foreword was written by Lord Meston – their association had lasted four decades – and this was the last collaboration. Meston was almost blind and died in 1943. Yusuf Ali also wrote several full-length articles and shorter book reviews for the magazine *Religions*. On the political front he was sufficiently aware of the increasing popularity of the Muslim League to write to *The Times* in defence of Jinnah, 'You cannot win over a people's good will by constantly abusing their leader.' He also was now reconciled to the demise of the 'one nation' theory: 'The sooner people realise that India is like the whole of Europe and not a small country like Czecho-Slovakia, the sooner will they understand the real problem'.[47] He still hoped for the emergence of a spirit of compromise and understanding between the Congress and the Muslim League, and its absence 'forebodes evil not only for that great country but also for the Empire'. Yusuf Ali would also regularly attend meetings of the South Place Ethical Society at Conway Hall, tucked away in a square in Holborn. This was a lively forum of non-conforming Christians, humanists and kindred spirits. At a meeting in May 1941, Yusuf Ali presented a paper on 'Ethics and Totalitarianism' that set out to show that the British Empire held superior ethics to Nazism and Bolshevism. 'The whole object of the Imperial system,' he proposed, 'is to provide a number of self-governing nations with a link by means of which they can combine their resources for purposes common to the whole of the Empire. That furnishes a basis for the future organisation of mankind, for if all nations could agree to federate in the sense that the British Empire of the future could federate there would be an end to war.'[48] His vision of religion had little to do with the 'outer world' of governance or organisation of society.

He was unwell for a while in the summer of 1941, perhaps marking the point he and Masuma separated. She moved out of 3 Mansel Road to live elsewhere in Wimbledon even though the property was legally her own. Yusuf Ali spent some time in Bristol where he received a letter from the Ministry of Information to discuss an offer:

31st July 1941

A. Yusuf Ali Esq. CBE
2 St Edwards Road
Clifton
Bristol 8

Dear Yusuf Ali,
The S/S [Secretary of State for India] tells me that when he saw you the other day you raised the question whether, now that you are quite well again, you should revive the idea of a visit to the USA or whether there was any other way in which your services could now be utilised. Would it be possible for you to call here one day next week, say on Wednesday, to discuss the question with me.

Yours sincerely
A.H. Joyce[49]

It is extraordinary that the Ministry of Information continued to look towards Yusuf Ali for advice when he was so out of touch with the state of affairs in India.

Much of Yusuf Ali's activities for the rest of the War are a mystery. He did speak at the 1941 World Congress of Faiths held in Oxford in October and also attended meetings of the Royal Society of Arts. Sometime in 1942 he prepared a further feature article against Nazism with the title 'Oppression in Muslim Countries'. His file in the records of the India Office has a note written on its front, 'See also P&J (S) file'. However the 'S' files were removed in 1982 from the India Office Records by the Sensitivity Review Unit of the Foreign Office. The full story of these years may lie somewhere in these missing papers.[50] He was certainly fit and well in February 1943 because he led the *'Id-ul-fitr* prayers at Shah Jahan Mosque in Woking, of which he was a trustee. The *khutba* was a sombre one: 'This year there are not many facts over which we can rejoice, either in the Muslim world or the world at large. But the great merit of our religious festival is that it is independent of the condition of the outer world. Religion deals with an inner world, whether in the individual or among mankind. If we order our lives wisely that inner world will not be obscured by the clouds outside but will rather send forth powerful rays to penetrate the gloom, doubts and uncertainty without.'[51] On a personal front all that is known is that by 1944 twenty-two year old Rashid had been commissioned in the 7th Rajput Regiment of the Indian Army.[52] Such news would have undoubtedly gladdened Yusuf Ali but it is likely that father and son were no longer in contact.

When the War ended in 1945 Yusuf Ali was still living at 3 Mansel Road, Wimbledon. Separated from his wife and without any children around him, the twilight years had begun. Long-standing friends like Akbar Hydari, Lamington, Meston and Younghusband were dead. Others like Shaikh Abdul Qader had returned to the sub-continent. Yusuf Ali was not given due credit after Partition in 1947, though his great contributions to Muslim political and educational causes, particularly in the Punjab, had been notable. The Unionist leadership which had conveniently flocked to the Muslim League knew of this work but kept silent. Jinnah, never a man to forget earlier slights, remained aloof from his Bombay *Anjuman-e-Islam* schoolfellow. There was a glimmer of recognition from the Pakistan High Commission in London, whose staff kept in touch. The High Commission also circulated details of an 'Iqbal Association' which had been established with him as President.[53] In November 1948 Masuma sold 3 Mansel Road for £4000, either because she needed the money or because Yusuf Ali had moved out of his own accord. He lived for a while at 2 Maunsell Street, Stratton Ground, a run-down district of Westminster in central London. It is not known what fate befell his vast collection of books or the black steel box containing the diaries. The possession he did hold on to was a scrapbook containing newspaper cuttings about himself and some other personal papers. He prepared a meticulous index for this collection, probably whiling away many a solitary hour in remembrance of past distinctions. In his diminishing circle of acquaintances was Dr Ali Hassan Abdel Kader, director of the London Islamic Cultural Centre, to whom he must have presented even this last possession. The scrapbook was uncovered many years later in the library of the Centre.

A remarkably well informed obituary in The *Times* noted that 'In advancing age he seemed to have a sense of frustration to find that so much of what he had done was vanity and vexation of spirit...Unhappily Yusuf Ali's last years were clouded by mental aberration. He entirely neglected his family duties and avoided financial responsibilities for his nominal home. In addition to his proportionate ICS pension he had private means; but he sank to a level of apparent poverty and lack of cleanliness which brought concern to old friends. He wandered about at the end, an unquiet spirit with no fixed abode.'[54]

A young Muslim scholar from the Comoros, Omar Abdullah, tried to locate him in 1951 through the help of Mr Majid, editor of the *Islamic Review*. He was advised to go to the Empire Club near Trafalgar Square.[55] This was part of the Royal Empire Society, Northumberland Avenue. Omar Abdullah remembered the reaction when he asked staff at the Club about Yusuf Ali: 'Are you looking for that old man who just sits there alone doing nothing? The one who never talks to anyone?'[56] Abdullah managed to conduct a few conversations with Yusuf Ali, one about the Qur'an: 'That translation!' was the retort. 'It took me three years and I wrote it in all the continents. I visited each and every place mentioned in the Qur'an.' Yusuf Ali was correct in recalling that thirty instalments were published in three years (1934-37) but this was the result of labours that commenced in the 1920s. He was in a confused state and had problems remembering details of the past. The two met once more in 1953, the year of Yusuf Ali's death. Omar Abdullah remarked that Lahore had once been a very ideal place for a

Muslim to live in. 'But it is no longer,' Yusuf Ali replied. 'And I'm quite happy here, I'm satisfied.' Abdullah left him, retaining in his mind the memory of a Muslim who had reached the highest of spiritual levels. In fact poor Yusuf Ali was mentally ill and badly in need of care.

The first week of December 1953 was desperately cold in London. A thick fog hung over the city and it was barely possible to move about. The headlines of the day were dominated by the Korean War. Masuma, or Mrs Gertrude Ali as she preferred to be called, remarked at his inquest that to her knowledge he spent days at the Royal Empire Society but after twelve years of living apart, she had no idea where he lodged. On the evening of Wednesday 9 December the police found Yusuf Ali sitting on the steps of a house in Westminster. He was taken to Westminster Hospital where he spent the night. The next day the casualty officer discharged him and a police constable left Yusuf Ali in a nearby London County Council institution for the elderly in Dovehouse Street, Chelsea. Perhaps as a result of a phone call from the hospital or the administrator of the old people's home, Mr G.M. Mumtaz, education officer at the Pakistan High Commission visited Yusuf Ali, "His condition was deplorable. I had known him in the days when he was a great man. I don't know what had caused it, because he was a wealthy man and had excellent friends in this country. Some of them are members of the House of Lords."[57] News of Yusuf Ali's plight travelled up the High Commission hierarchy, gaining some embellishment in the process. The culmination was an urgent despatch from the High Commissioner, Mirza Abul Hassan Ispahani, to Prime Minister M.A.Bogra:

> "My dear Mohammed Ali:
> I write to you in connection with a person known to me and respected not only by Muslim youth of my time, but by Muslims the world over for the great services he has rendered to Islam during his lifetime and for his translation of the Holy Qur'an into English. His name is Abdullah Yusuf Ali who was born 81 years ago. In the "Who's Who" of 1953, on page 36, one whole column is devoted to his qualifications, activities and achievements. I have just now learned that this venerable old man is in financial straits. He has been found sitting in

Trafalgar Square in tattered clothes on a suitcase having no money in his pocket. He has been taken to the London County Council Poor Home and we have been informed of his condition. Although, as you know, Government does not place a cent at the disposal of Heads of Missions to meet any emergent and deserving case, I have, on my own responsibility, asked Hyder, my Counsellor, to render such assistance as is necessary in providing him with a cheap room and food.

I appeal to you to consider this case with the sympathy it deserves and have Government sanction a small allowance which should be sufficient to keep him in a cheap boarding house and let him live the few years of his life that still remain unexpended, in reasonable comfort. He also needs, of course, some clothes. You will agree that the grant of an allowance of a few pounds, say 20 per month, by Government should not be a financial burden. Allama Yusuf Ali has rendered great service to Islam and Muslims and it is in the light of this service that Government should show its generosity. If a precedent is required, I may cite the case of poet Nasrul Islam of East Pakistan who has, for some years, been receiving a substantial pension from Government for the service he has rendered to poetry and literature. It is absolutely clear that Yusuf Ali has neither money nor anyone who is willing tu support him.

As the request is urgent, I shall be most grateful if sanction is conveyed to me, if possible by return of bag."[58]

Yusuf Ali's situation was deteriorating by the hour. He was taken ill again and died in St Stephen's Hospital in Fulham on 10 December. Ispahani despatched another message to Karachi with the precise time:

11 December 1953

My dear Mohammed Ali:
In continuation of my letter of yesterday regarding Allama Abdulla Yusuf Ali, I write to advise you with regret that the poor man died in hospital at eight last night. It pains me to think that so able and

eminent a gentleman should have met with so pathetic an end. May his soul rest in peace.[59]

The full circle was completed of a life which had spent much of its youth in institutions and, cruelly, so much of its final years as well. The tired and old Commander of the British Empire slipped away. "If his case had been so bad," M.A.Bogra wrote regretfully, "I wish someone would have reported it earlier so that [the Pakistan] Government could have taken some action to see that his last days were spent in some kind of decent comfort."[60]

An inquest was conducted by the Coroner of the County of London on 14 and 16 December 'in fairness to the widow and the hospitals'.[61] The coroner concluded that he was perfectly satisfied that everything that could be done for Yusuf Ali had been done. A death certificate was issued noting 'senile myocardial degeneration' as cause of death. Staff at the Pakistan High Commission arranged the funeral and he lies buried in Brookwood Cemetery, Surrey, not far from the Woking Mosque. The grave is near that of Marmaduke Pickthall, another distinguished scholar of the Qur'an.

Yusuf Ali had appointed as the trustees and executors of his will, prepared in 1940, Lloyds Bank, his son Rashid and his solicitor, Harold Syms.[62] Acting on its terms, Lloyds Bank duly notified London University of the bequest that had been left to them for a fund for the benefit of Indian students. Yusuf Ali had specifically asked that it should be 'called after my name'. However a meeting of the Court in 1954 deemed it part of the Vice-Chancellor's Discretionary Fund for Indian Students.[63] Yusuf Ali also left instructions for his diaries: 'I bequeath to the Muslim University of Aligore [*sic*] (United Provinces, India) free of duty all my diaries (now kept in a black steel box locked), and I direct that such diaries shall be deposited by the University in its Library and shall not be opened until the expiration of 30 years from my death.' These were never sent to Aligarh and their fate is perhaps one of the secrets which Masuma carried to her grave in 1962.[64]

Notes to Chapter 6

1. Edward VIII had planned a visit to India in the winter of 1937. His first trip as Prince of Wales took place in 1921; on that occasion his letters home were filled with denunciation of reform-minded politicians like Montagu who had 'given in and pandered to the natives'. See Philip Ziegler, King *Edward VIII*, p.139. Of Edward VIII's three brothers, the one selected to take his place was the Duke of York. The Duke of Kent had been tainted with a blackmail scandal involving a young man in France and the Duke of Gloucester was also deemed unreliable.

2. Speech at Caxton Hall, London; 23 November 1914. An extract is provided in Chapter 3.

3. Yusuf Ali's speech to the Monarchist League, reported in The *Kensington News*, London, 23 July 1937 (YA56).

4. ibid.

5. "We cannot help feeling that we are contemplating the development of one vast world-movement...I have described the efforts which Government, driven by the force of public opinion in Great Britain, made to bring justice to the people of India, to educate them, and to improve their lot in every way. And, besides these Government endeavours, there have been the immense missionary efforts which the peoples of the West have been called upon to make. We have clearly been working under some mighty spiritual impulse. And in India herself we can observe an uprising of a desire to enhance her material and spiritual welfare...Europeans and Indians alike are striving after the highest spiritual things. The ultimate object seems to be the final spiritualisation of India." From Francis Younghusband's *Dawn in India*, p.317.

Sir Francis was Yusuf Ali's quintessential Englishman. The Younghusband family had done service in the Indian colonial administration for generations and took to leadership in the manner born. Francis himself was born in Murree, North West India in 1863 and in 1903 became a celebrity in Edwardian England for his adventures as an emissary of the Empire in Tibet. The family were friends of the Royal Family. Francis Younghusband was later the Resident (chief representative of the Raj) in Kashmir and at some point in his Indian career went through a process of conversion to become a Christian mystic. He also emerged as one of the official experts on the Muslim world and wrote a report on the Caliphate for the India Office's Political and Secret department after World War I (IOL:L/P&S/11/119). Yusuf Ali's obituary note on Sir Francis was printed in *The Times* on 4 August 1942: "While he was true to his English heritage, he so completely understood all that is best in Eastern thought that he was a true link between East and West. He will be missed for his many private virtues as well as for the splendid public work which he was doing to consolidate the bonds between India and England."

6. IOL:MSS Eur F197/119. Francis Younghusband's papers contain the history of the World Congress of Faiths. The Indian *swami* providing the inspiration was Kedernath Das Gupta, who had organised an 'International Conference of Faiths' in Chicago in 1933. Younghusband was invited to speak at the second conference in New York in May 1934 and also in the following year. In 1935 he became chairman of the British Committee of an association known as the 'Threefold Movement' - Union of East and West, League of Neighbours and Fellowship of Faiths.

7. In the preceding year's conference the only Muslim speakers were Abdul Qader and Yusuf Ali. Shaikh Al-Maraghi of Al-Azhar had been invited but could not attend. In his speech Abdul Qader referred to Yusuf Ali's Qur'anic scholarship in glowing terms. Yusuf Ali was able to reciprocate this goodwill by describing Abdul Qader as 'an embodiment of modern Muslim thought'. See Younghusband, *A Venture of Faith*, p. 145.

8. Quotation from *The World's Need of Religion*, World Congress of Faiths, 1937.

9. *Journal des Nations*, Geneva, 2 September 1937 (YA 65). Many of the members of Younghusband's 'British National Council' were associated with the League of Nations: Alfred Zimmern, Lord Allen of Hurtwood, Dame Elizabeth Cadbury and Dame Edith Lyttleton.

10. The *Holy Qur'an - text, translation and commentary*, third edition (1938); note 2992: "While modern nations have abolished ordinary slavery, the 'White Slave Traffic' is still a big social problem in individual states and before the League of Nations."

11. ibid., note 4927:

> "Individual quarrels are easier to compose than group quarrels, or in the modern world, national quarrels. But the collective community of Islam should be supreme over groups or nations. It would be expected to act justly and try to compose the quarrel, for peace is better than fighting. But if one party is determined to be the aggressor, the whole force of the world community is brought to bear on it. The essential condition of course is that there should be perfect fairness and justice and respect for the highest principles....the League of Nations fails because these essentials are absent."

12. *Journal des Nations*, Geneva; 5 September 1937 (YA 65):

> "*Il y a deux grands blocs de territoires et de populations dont le rapprochment de plus en plus etroit signifie un immense apport de forces a la cause de la paix mondiale. Ce sont les Etats-Unis d'Amerique et l'Empire britannique....l'anglais est la langue dominante de l'adminstration chez eux. C'est un immense avantage pour la propagation et la consolidation d'idees politiques et de comprehension politique.*"

13. Report in *Great Britain and the East*, 4 November, 1937 (YA79). Yusuf Ali was supported by Waris Ali, the son of Justice Ameer Ali. The two had much in common: ICS service in the UP under Lord Meston; both were twice married to English women.

14.Herbert Samuel, former British High Commissioner of Palestine and leader of the Liberal Party, was a Zionist yet sufficiently prominent in the 'Congress of Faiths' to take charge of this body after Younghusband's death. Like Lord Reading (Rufus Isaacs) he served as chairman of the Palestinian Electric Corporation, founded specifically for electrification of projects in the 'Jewish Homeland'. "The names of the dynamic four who will go down in history in the rebuilding of Zion will be Theodore Herzl, who saw the vision; Chaim Weizmann, who grasped the occasion; Arthur Balfour, who caused the world to renew the ancient Promise in a modern Covenant; and Herbert Samuel, who turned principle into practice, word into fact." From Ronald Storrs's memoirs, *Orientations*, p. 437. Samuel supported the idea of a Jewish state in Palestine but opposed the Indian Muslims' campaign for Pakistan because 'there were already too many sovereign states in the world for international peace'. See K.K. Aziz, *Britain and Muslim India*, p.147.

15. Based on reports of Yusuf Ali's speeches taken from *The Sussex Daily News*, 7 October 1937 (YA70) and *The Brighton & Hove Herald*, 9 October 1937 (YA72).

16.*Cambridge Review*, 12 November 1937 (YA80).

17.*International Affairs*, Sept-Oct. 1937, p.779 (YA62).

18.*The Mussalman*, Calcutta, 28 January 1938 (YA95).

19.M.H.Saiyid, Mo*hammad Ali Jinnah - A political study*, p.205.

20.Baidar Malik, Te*hrik-i-Pakistan aur Islamia College*, p. 296.

21.*The Civil & Military Gazette*, Lahore; 18 January 1938. (YA93).

22.Muhammad Abdullah Chughtai, *Iqbal kay suhbat mai*, p.489.

Iqbal's choice of adjective *mubassir-i-zamana* - translated here as 'erudite' – is significant. The Urdu phrase also implies perspicacity.

23.*The Times, 25 Ap*ril 1938.

24.*The Civil & Military Gazette*, Lahore; 12 May 1938 (YA105).

25.Iqbal wrote many letters to Jinnah to explain his concepts of a   Muslim nation. In one letter in 1937 he advised Jinnah,

"How is it possible to solve the problem of Muslim poverty? ...if the [Muslim] League can give no such promises I am sure the Muslim masses will remain indifferent to it as before. Happily there is a solution in the enforcement of the Law of Islam and its further development in the light of modern ideas. After a long and careful study of Islamic Law I have come to the conclusion that if this system of Law is properly understood and applied, at least the right to subsistence is secured to everybody. But the endorsement and development of the *Shariat* of Islam is impossible in this country without a free Muslim State or States...if such a thing is impossible in India the only other alternative is a civil war which as a matter of fact has been going on for some time

144

in the shape of Hindu-Muslim riots." Quoted from M.H. Saiyid, *Mohammad Ali Jinnah*, p.183.

26. Yusuf Ali addressed a group of Indian students attending a scout jamboree in Britain. Reported in S*outhport Visitor*, 21 October 1937 (YA73).

27. Its title was the 'Idea of Salvation in Islam', later published as the fourteenth and last pamphlet in the 'Progressive Islam' series.

28. From Yusuf Ali's 'Doctrine of Human Personality in Iqbal's Poetry' published in *The Transactions of the Royal Society of Literature*, New Series, Vol. XVIII, 1940.

29. *Crescent*, magazine of Islamia College, Lahore, October 1936. The quotation is from Yusuf Ali's article 'Social Equality in Islam - a summary of Principal's sermon on 31 May 1936' (YA147).

30. *Edmonton Journal*; 8 December 1938 (YA 239).

31. *Oakwood Oracle*, 1939, magazine of the Oakwood Collegiate Institute, Toronto (YA300).

32. *Eastern Times*, Lahore; 'My Canadian Tour -III'; 7 April 1937 (YA297).

33. The Muslim Society of Great Britain resembled a club of eccentric Englishmen. Prominent members included Sir Ernest Bennet, who was present at the Battle of Omdurman in 1898 and listed 'investigating haunted houses' as a hobby in *Who's Who*. Other titled persona active in its affairs were Lady Headley and Lord Harrington. Lord Lamington owned 12,000 acres in Scotland and when serving as Governor of Bombay from 1903-1907 also held the office of 'Most Worshipful Grand Master of all Scottish Freemasonry in India'. (Source: *The Freemason & Masonic Illustrated*, 23 February 1907). The chairman of the May 1937 meeting was Ismail de Yorke, the Society's president. The event was reported in *Eastern Times*, Lahore; 26 May 1939 (YA 304).

34. In an interview with the Lahore *Tribune* of 17 October 1939, Yusuf Ali recounted the adventure of his outward journey from Britain to India.

35. The poem is handwritten, signed 'AYA' and dated 10 October 1939. A note explains that the 'fortunate port' was Port Said. The third line of the third quatrain contains an illegible word which the author has interpreted as 'bereft'(YA360).

36. *Statesman*, Delhi, 14 October 1939.

37. IOL:L/I/1/1268 file Number 1. This is Yusuf Ali's personal file and includes correspondence between the Ministry of Information and the India Office relating to his propaganda services. 'British Democracy as seen by a Muslim' is in this file and dated December 1939.

One letter in the file, dated 18 August 1941, is from D. Cliffe of the India Section of the Ministry of Information to H.J. Fells of the India Office. This letter lists five feature articles prepared by Yusuf Ali:

p74   The Muslims of India stand by the Democracies.

p104   India's Attitude to the War.

p4035 Islam & the Nazis.

p4036 British Democracy as seen by a Muslim.

p4068 British Rule in India.

Cliffe wrote, "There was some question as to whether or not he employed a pen name but it was decided he does not...I am sending the articles off in the meantime to avoid delay."

38. *The Asiatic Review*, Vol. XXXVI, 1940; p.74-75(YA316).

39. From *A Cultural history of India during the British Period*, the quotation describes the 1937-38 period. The Urdu version of this book was completed in September 1931; the English edition, published in Bombay in 1940, contains additional detail on developments since 1931.

40. *The Asiatic Review*, Vol. XXXVI, 1940, pp. 226-239. Yusuf Ali presented his scheme at a meeting of the East India Association, held at Caxton Hall on 6 February, 1940. The meeting was chaired by Sir Harold Wilberforce-Bell, and was also reported in *The Times* of the following day.

41. K.K.Aziz comments on Yusuf Ali's proposal for a 'composite' political party: "At the best of times his plan would have been difficult of fulfilment; at this hour it was painfully irrelevant." See: K.K.Aziz, *A History of the Idea of Pakistan*, pp. 609-612.

42. *Wessex News*, Southampton; 28 May 1940 (YA331).

43. *Daily Mail*, London; 13 March 1940 (YA325). O'Dwyer was killed by a Sikh in revenge for the notorious Jallianwala Bagh massacre in Amritsar that took place during his governership. However the officer responsible for the 1919 tragedy was General Dyer.

44. IOL:L/I/1/1268 file Number 1. Article 'Islam and the Nazis'.

45. *Northern Daily Mail*, West Hartlepool, 25 September 1940 (YA343).

46. *Western Daily Press*, Bristol, 2 October 1940 (YA346).

47. Letter, *The Times*, 15 January 1941 (YA352).

48. *South Place Ethical Society Monthly Recorder*, July 1941 (YA361).

49. IOL:L/I/1/1268, ibid.

50. ibid. The note is on the cover of the file. The author raised the issue with staff of the India Office Library in 1989 but was informed that the Foreign Office had not been known to relent on the 'S' series of papers that were taken away in 1982. The sensitivity may be related to the role of some Indian Muslims in London, with whom Yusuf Ali had long-standing associations. These included Sir Feroz Khan Noon, the High

Commissioner for India in 1941, and Waris Ali, his war adviser. The former may have been involved in proposing the creation of a Zionist State in Palestine. See *Impact International*, Vol. 21:3&4, 1991. Sir Feroz was later a prime minister of Pakistan.

51. *The Islamic Review*, Woking. Vol. 31, No. 2, February 1943, pp. 100-101. An obituary notice on Yusuf Ali in this journal (February 1954) stated that he had been a trustee of the mosque.

52. Indian Army List, October 1944. His son's full name is stated as 'Rashid Yusuf-Ali'.

53. The existence of a six-page cyclostyled document on an Iqbal Association, issued by the Pakistan High Commission, London is mentioned in S.A. Durrani's *Iqbal Europe Mai*, p.65.

54. *The Times*, 15 December 1953. Yusuf Ali's obituary was two-thirds of a column long in the first edition. It was removed entirely from later editions of the day.

55. Yusuf Ali was a long-standing member of the Royal Empire Society, elected a Fellow on 11 March 1929 on the nomination of a churchman, the Reverend Stewart Gordon Ponsonby, at the time Rector of St Mary-le-Bow in the City of London and seconded by Sir George Boughey, a former member of the Indian Civil Service in the United Provinces. The Society possessed a fine library near Trafalgar Square and also rooms which members could book for an overnight stay.

56. *Africa Events*, London, November 1985.

57. *The Daily Telegraph*, London, 17 December 1953.

58. Ispahani's letter to Mohammed Ali Bogra, 10 December 1953. Mohammed Ali Bogra papers, International Centre for Islamic Studies, London.

59. ibid. Ispahani's letter to Mohammed Ali Bogra, 11 December 1953.

60. ibid. Bogra's letter to Ispahani, 14 December 1953.

61. The inquest number was 86 and it was recorded in the register for the Western District of London (covering Westminster) but the coroner's case papers have not survived.

62. The firm of solicitors Henry, Massop and Syms, of 11 Lincoln's Inn Fields, placed a notice in *Wimbledon Borough News*, 22 January 1954. It invited 'all persons having claims against the estate of the deceased person' to contact them or Lloyds Bank Ltd, Executor and Trustee Department, West End Branch. The absence of Rashid's name suggests he was not resident in Britain.

A Grant of Probate was issued to the Bank out of the Principal Probate Registry on 2 April 1954. In the terms of the complex will, Yusuf Ali's wife and son would receive some income from the trust capital: "Out of the income of my residuary estate my trustees shall pay every quarter in advance the sum of £40 to my wife Masuma Gertrude

Yusuf Ali during her life or if she remarries until her remarriage, and every quarter in advance the sum of £40 to my son Rashid for life; the remaining income (if any) to be added to the capital and invested on the 1st of April in each year; the first of each such quarterly payments in advance to be paid as soon as possible after the date of my death and the next of each such quarterly payments three months thereafter, and until the income of my residuary estate shall be ascertained and received by my Trustees, such quarterly payments may be raised and paid out of capital."

Contacted by the author in 1991, the bank was unwilling to disclose any details concerning Yusuf Ali's family. The author believes Rashid took up employment in the Hyderabad Police force after World War II.

63. At its meeting in 1954, the Court of the University discussed how much of the £20,000 estate had to be put aside to guarantee the quarterly payments to Masuma and Rashid. After allowing £3000 for death duties, it was proposed that £6,000 could be made immediately available for the Vice-Chancellor's Discretionary Fund. The balance of £11,000 would be retained by the executors as a trust fund to satisfy the income clause for Yusuf Ali's family in their lifetime.

64. Gertrude Masuma Ali (nee Mawbey) died at the age of sixty-seven in Liverpool. Yusuf Ali's first wife, Teresa Shalders, died in Bournemouth in 1956 at the age of eighty-four.

Part II

Endeavours

7

EDUCATIONAL CAUSES

Yusuf Ali's reputation deservedly rests on the translation and interpretation of the Qur'an, but his other great accomplishment was in the field of education. He played a leading role in numerous educational conferences and was a fellow and member of the executive committee of the senate of the University of Punjab. He also served on the Court of the University of Aligarh. He was an academic who had lectured at London University, worked as principal of Islamia College, Lahore, on two occasions and had written school text books. He was a practical educationalist, at ease discussing the preparation of secondary school timetables, teachers' pay and adult literacy campaigns. His advice was sought by the Unionist government of the Punjab in pre-partition India of the 1930s, and in this way he contributed to a far-reaching educational programme which was to benefit Pakistan. These activities made him a leading educationalist of the Indian sub-continent from the turn of the century. His writing and speeches on educational matters frequently touched on three themes which warrant further elaboration: religious instruction and denominational schools; policies and projects in secondary, university and adult education; and the language question.

Yusuf Ali's own early education was in Bombay's first Muslim primary school set up to provide both religious and a modern, British curriculum-based education. From the age of about ten he spent a further seven years in Bombay, attending a school and college run by Scottish missionaries. This was followed by three years in Cambridge. He cherished academic life and left instructions for his estate to be used to create a fund for the benefit of Indian students at London University. He had the unique experience of meeting distinguished and varied educational luminaries such as Sir

Sayyid Ahmed Khan and Madame Montessori. Though not an innovatory educationalist himself, Yusuf Ali had an approach marked by a sense of the practical and the achievable. He worked in an unobtrusive way, strengthening the institutions with which he came to be associated. His emphasis on educational issues made him swim against the tide of the time because the Muslim leadership which mattered – the Ali Brothers, Jinnah, Iqbal – believed that the struggle for political independence was overriding. Yusuf Ali eschewed 'controversial politics', a term of opprobrium for political activity which embarrassed or discredited the British. He held that such 'controversial politics' were detrimental to the progress of India and detracted from her real problems. He remained unswerving in this belief in defiance of circumstances. Speaking at the Anglo-Arabic College in Delhi in October 1939, Yusuf Ali called the student audience's attention to the important work required to be done in education, sanitation, and housing – 'problems which must claim the immediate attention of the youth of the country'.[1] It was a statement made at a time of high political drama when the Congress, Muslim League and the Viceroy each manoeuvred to turn the war situation to their advantage. This difference did not make him any less sensitive to the aspirations for Muslim dignity and self-respect. Muhammad Iqbal singled him out as the best candidate for the principalship of Islamia College in 1935, in full knowledge of the divergence in their political beliefs. It was a trust not betrayed. A student once entered Yusuf Ali's office at Islamia College in an obsequious manner. This behaviour earned the following admonishment: 'A Muslim youth does not scrape and bow; stand upright and speak.'[2] It is a small anecdote which speaks volumes about Yusuf Ali's hopes for the next generation.

Yusuf Ali was very guarded in his support of denominational schools in India, in spite, or perhaps because, of his experiences as a student and principal in such institutions. His first objection was a pedagogical one. Even at Aligarh 'religious instructors had been appointed to teach on the old lines which did not appeal to the students but which appealed to their parents and to the community generally'.[3] Whenever committees were appointed to give greater definition to religious instruction, their members often held opposite views and even the compromise reports which they presented were in most cases merely recorded and then forgotten. Yusuf

Ali was scathing about 'the greybeards' who imparted religious education in antiquated forms and 'our teachers as a class who have not shown any great aptitude for religious education of one kind or another'.[4]

Apart from differences among Muslims on the content of religious instruction and a lack of inspiring teachers, Yusuf Ali had a deeper, philosophical reservation on religious education as a formal subject at the primary or secondary level. Speaking at the All-Ceylon Muslim Educational Conference in September 1938 he outlined his concern that such teaching might grasp the letter but not the spirit of religion, saying, 'I have been asked many times, and I am being asked now, to help in the preparation of a syllabus or curriculum of religious instruction. In my opinion a syllabus or curriculum of religious instruction is of very little use. Such a curriculum is possible for theological studies, for those who wish to prepare for religious ministry. It would involve a deep study of religious history, philosophy, and literature, and a scholarly knowledge of the Arabic language and literature. This would involve a life-long study for specialists. It is not for everyday working folk. But every child should be taught life and behaviour, which for a universal religion like Islam, should be the same as religion. Our religious instruction should make our children better men and women – not more angular and less adapted to take their part honourably in the life of the nation.' Then, perhaps recalling his own upbringing, Yusuf Ali added, 'The best age for such instruction is in early childhood, and the best place is the home.'[5] Yusuf Ali's political views led him to brand denominational schools as divisive but he was also well aware that Muslim parents did not want 'a godless and soulless education'. 'It has been seen that denominational education if pushed too far tends to strengthen and perpetuate denominationalism in religion, that denominationalism flows into social life and tends to permeate it and that it embitters politics and hampers political progress.' He was writing this in 1925 as an advocate of Indian unity. However, 'where two communities like the Hindu and the Muslim are organised in opposite camps, and have a separate consciousness which is not only religious but also racial, economic and social, and where they are not equally matched in numbers and resources, a number of compromises have to be made. Fortunately, the state schools being undenominational the experiment of denominational schools on a limited scale can be tried without undue encroachment on the national edifice.'[6] It was with this clarification that Yusuf Ali took up the principalship of the Muslim denominational Islamia College in 1925. Over a decade later at the All-India Muslim Conference in 1936, when principal of Islamia College for a second tenure, he reiterated his long-held view that the Muslim community should accept a broad-based educational policy rather than seeking 'special corners of isolation'. He went on to warn the conference, 'Any community afraid to swim in midstream of its sister communities would find nothing but disappointment and disillusion in the final verdict of History.'[7]

Yusuf Ali did not propose to leave state schools without religious education. He envisaged the emergence of an eclectic curriculum in which denominationalism was minimised. At the Punjab Educational Conference in 1937 he outlined this proposal: 'Cannot the more liberal-minded religious men of the various communities make a provision for the training of competent teachers for religious instruction – those who would, on the one hand avoid too much formalism and, on the other, lay as much stress as possible on ethical ideals, the formation of character, and the need for co-operation and unity amongst the various sections of our people?'[8] These were very much the sentiments of the World Congress of Faiths conferences held each summer in Britain and regularly attended by Yusuf Ali.

Notwithstanding his reservations about denominational colleges, Yusuf Ali brought a positive attitude to Islamia College. He believed that the 'whole justification' of a communal college was that 'its standard should be equally high with that of other colleges, and at the same time should provide for the special needs of the community concerned.'[9] He was able to demonstrate success: seventy percent of his English Honours class passed, with one of the students coming second in the whole province. Conforming to his concept of religious instruction, Yusuf Ali initiated Sunday 'sermon period addresses' delivered by staff on a rota basis 'dealing with some religious aspect from the point of view of science, literature, philosophy, mathematics or other subject on which the speaker is specially competent to speak'.[10] By all accounts Yusuf Ali was a popular principal, since it was the students who asked for his reinstatement after the bitter disputes with a faction of the *Anjuman-Himayat-ul-Islam* in the winter of

1936. He was not past taking part in College sports days, on one occasion winning the staff race. His commitment was utterly sincere:

> How can I ever forget you,
> Dear young men of Lahore!
> My dreams were entwined in your future;
> Yours was my love evermore!
>
> Did you not lend me your heart-throbs?
> Was not your happiness mine?
> Shared we not, working and playing,
> A joy like a breeze from the brine?
>
> When youth, in its freshness and glory,
> Can be comrade to age that has faced
> The chastening rod of experience,
> Life yields of its most precious taste.
>
> Through books and through nature we wandered;
> We laboured together, with zest;
> Together we laughed when we captured
> A truth that was wrapped in a jest.
>
> Then here's to the days we look back to!
> Truly a rich varied store!
> Oh, how can I ever forget you,
> Dear young men of Lahore![11]

Yusuf Ali made professional contributions to educational policies in secondary, tertiary and adult education. Though they were at different ends of the educational spectrum, he believed secondary and adult education were interconnected because 'if we want to educate our children well, it is a good principle to insist upon it that we should also educate the parents. Parents can be a great help or hindrance to teachers.'[12] He held that secondary education was the weakest link in the Indian educational system. Its aim seemed merely a stepping stone to a university education, while in reality it should also provide vocational and craft-related skills for those not proceeding to higher studies. The larger part of the population was agricultural, and good agricultural education would help to prevent 'the depopulation of the countryside or its denudation of its best brains in favour of the towns'.[13] Even in the mid-1930s Yusuf Ali was alert to the issue of migration from the rural areas to the urban centres. He put a sound modern education based on economic geography 'first in order of importance'. Yusuf Ali's second priority was in craft education because 'industrialism as understood in the 19th century is finding more critics than defenders'. Large-scale industrialism was not suitable but instead steps should be taken to recover the manual and manipulative skills 'which we have been in danger of losing for the last two or three generations, but which we can still recover under a proper system of education'. Yusuf Ali was an important intellectual asset to the Unionist government of the Punjab during a period of rapid expansion of state secondary schools in the province.

In Yusuf Ali's sonorous phrase, universities were 'corporations for comprehending truth'.[14] He served on the Punjab University Enquiry Committee (October 1932-March 1933) which undertook a wide-ranging policy study of the University's finances and development plans. He argued against plans for promoting existing degree colleges into universities in their own right because 'even the present University has been unable to secure a firm financial foundation or attract large endowments. The prospect of multiplying universities increases the weakness of our one university.'[15] It was an unpopular opinion to hold, as 1931-32 was a period of particular communal tension in the Punjab and there was popular demand from the Muslim groups for the elevation of one of their colleges to university status. Yusuf Ali responded by saying that it was not a matter of 'loaves and fishes' – an allusion to the employment a new university would provide to Muslims of the province – but of preserving the quality and character of the Province's academic and intellectual development.[16] Yusuf Ali was a critic of the Indian university system, frequently arguing that it was unsuited to Indian conditions and had to be completely overhauled.[17] His concept of a university was very much in the Oxbridge mould: 'The universities are meant for a select class of people who can think independently and act according to reason.'[18] Yusuf Ali's reputation led to suggestions in the press in 1936 that he be considered by the Governor for the position of vice-chancellor of Punjab University.[19] The 'Indianisation' of vice-chancellorships was unfortunately still some time away and Yusuf Ali was not one to flatter others for personal advantage. He accepted British overlordship but without servility.

He was a pioneer in attempts at popularising adult education in India. He disagreed strongly with the view that universities should be stretched to cater for the 'old and effete'. The rest of society had a right to be educated, but through other institutions. He himself participated in several adult education experiments in the Punjab, one with the Society for the Promotion of Scientific Knowledge of which he had been vice-president in 1936. At a conference held in Britain in 1937, Yusuf Ali discussed his various experiences and projects.[20] One of these concerned a group of his college students who undertook to run night classes for literacy in their local wards in Lahore. A weekly class was started but this could not continue for long, because the members of the class said they were not only too old to learn but also had to work during the day which tired them for study at night. Yusuf Ali described another experiment where he and his friends arranged for the use of school buildings for a nightly class. The teachers were professionals employed in day schools but the strain was too much for them and some became ill from overwork. Yusuf Ali's conclusions were that concentration on literacy alone was not sufficient for adult education and that there should be creative manual activities. 'Literacy by itself does not quicken our faculties, purify our emotions, or promote that inner feeling of moral and spiritual satisfaction in ourselves which is the essence of a health and rational life.' A third project started under Yusuf Ali's supervision was a free adult school at Mughalpura, an industrial suburb of Lahore. He worked with a group called 'The Young Friends, Punjab' which imparted instruction not only to illiterates but also to literate adults, and included games, picnics, lectures and other activities in its programme. The motto of this group was 'Youth organised on a non-communal basis alone can bring about India's emancipation'.[21] Yusuf Ali genuinely disliked communalism in the field of education.

The question of a common language was a great issue of debate in which Yusuf Ali aligned himself firmly on the side of English as the only practical option for India. The educational system had 'enthroned English as the common language of culture'.[22] He identified several disadvantages in adopting Urdu. It was 'as nearly beyond the comprehension of the artisan or the ploughman as would be a simplified form of English. A Hindustani language suitable for the man in the street all over India would require to be created. And the creation would involve the coining of a large number of technical terms in the arts and sciences, as well as modern terms to express the results of new inventions like the cinema and broadcasting etc.'[23] English on the other hand was a standard language with a worldwide circulation. Through it and its literature contacts are established not only between different communities in India but between its provinces and with the whole of the outside world.[24] With the growth of provincial autonomy Yusuf Ali feared that 'provincial vernaculars may be pushed up even in the universities, as is being done in Bengal' leading to further divisive influences.[25] In 1937 he warned a Muslim audience at Aligarh, 'It would be a mistake on the part of the Muslim community to slacken in their study of English, which is the administrative language of India now and will remain so for as long as we can at present foresee.'[26]

Yusuf Ali possessed that gift of a brilliant man which enables him to clothe drab and hackneyed ideas in fresh plumage. Even when analysing mundane issues he had something fresh to say. In many cases the inspiration was his belief that human potentialities must be addressed, a perspective so important for an educationalist. On one occasion in 1938 he wrote: 'In all our work, administrative and literary, the human element should be kept always prominently in our view. Otherwise our work becomes lifeless and meaningless.'[27] Yusuf Ali's sense of caring comes across well in the way he discussed rural education. It was not enough to provide a basic level of technical competence; the boys and girls should be made to realise the beauty of the countryside. 'If only we could make the young educated villager feel a thrill for the beauty of the countryside and a pride in the higher forms of agriculture, we should enrich village life instead of impoverishing it, and at the same time we should prevent a drift to the towns.'[28] Another example which illustrates his insight as an educationalist is this remark on the role of the teacher, 'The child is nearest to the mould in which God fashions us...what a wonderful privilege it is, therefore, for the teacher to approach such a nature, to study its inborn instincts before they are perverted by questionable motives and to give it the direction which will imbue our earthly life with something of a spark drawn from Heaven.'[29]

The best example of Yusuf Ali's flair as an educationalist lies in the increased morale and heightened confidence he brought about at Islamia College in his second tenure as principal. His last speech-day address to the College contained a testament of his educational approach:

> I should like to close with a few words to my students. My dear students! You and I have worked together in accord, understanding and affection. Some of you are intellectually gifted and have won prizes and distinctions. May you win more, in academic work and in life, and attend to the finer niceties of character. Some of you have shone in sports. May you build up healthy bodies but not neglect your intellectual and spiritual interests. Some of you have not shone at all, but have plodded on as average students. Be not discouraged. The world consists of average men, and it is by integrity, sincerity and truth that you will be judged. Some of you may be failures. So long as your hearts are true and your minds not invaded by roots of evil, there is no cause for despair. A failure in one field may turn out a success in another. Discover your own tastes and aptitudes and try to follow the paths indicated by them instead of battering your heads against the stone walls of a hard world. We seniors are ready to help you, but the initiative, the choice and the responsibility must rest with you. Some of you there may be who may have done wrong and perhaps have suffered punishment. If you take your punishment in the right spirit, it may be a blessing for you. For our punishments are meant to be ameliorative, not vindictive.
>
> My dear, dear students! You are all dear to me, whether brilliant or stupid, dull or average, good or below the standard of goodness which I want and expect. In many ways, known and unknown to you, I have

tried to shape your character and thoughts. Try to take a more cultivated intellect, a large heart, a fuller hope, a stronger will, and truer instincts as the legacies of your College life.[30]

His Islamia College graduates were to form an important section of the intelligentsia of Pakistan for the next three decades. There is a debt owed to this inspired educationalist.

Notes to Chapter 7

1. *Statesman*, Delhi, 14 October 1939.

2. Yusuf Ali's remark was in Urdu. Quoted in Baidar Malik's *Yaran-i-Maktab: Tehrik-i-Pakistan aur Islamia College*, Lahore, p.216.

3. From the chapter 'Muslim Culture and Religious Thought' in *Modern India & the West*, p.399.

4. Address to the Punjab Educational Conference, reported in *The Civil & Military Gazette*, Lahore, 25 April 19377 (YA34).

5. *Eastern Times*, Lahore, 15 September 1936 (YA133).

6. From Yusuf Ali's *India and Europe*; p.103-104.

7. From Yusuf Ali's presidential address to the Secondary Education Section of the All-India Muslim Educational Conference, Rampur, 1936. This was published in the *Indian Journal of Education*, Volume 1, No. 5-6; May-June 1936; pp.1-10 (YA23).

8. *The Civil & Military Gazette*, Lahore, 25 April 1937 (YA34).

9. *The Civil & Military Gazette*, Lahore, 12 May 1938 (YA105).

10. *Eastern Times*, Lahore, 9 March 1937 (YA198).

11. Yusuf Ali's poem 'Memories - dedicated to the students of Islamia College, Lahore'; *Eastern Times*, Lahore, 4 October 1940 (YA348); it was written while he was staying at the National Liberal Club in Pall Mall, London. The poem belongs to a sad period in his life - by 1940 he was irrevocably estranged from the first children of his first marriage, about to be separated from his second wife and soon to lose contact with their son Rashid.

12. From Yusuf Ali's presidential address to the Punjab Muslim Educational Conference, Lahore, 1923; published as a pamphlet by *Muslim Outlook*, Lahore.

13. ibid., *Indian Journal of Education*, Volume 1.

14. Yusuf Ali's address 'The University in a changing world', weekend conference held at F.C. College, Lahore, 7 September, 1936 (Typed note of proceedings, YA25).

15. Ghulam Husain Zulfikar, *Tarikh-i-Jam'a-i-Punjab*, pp. 173-191.

16. ibid.

17. Yusuf Ali called for 'a complete coordination of the whole system of education from beginning to end', in an address to the Lahore Rotary Club, reported in *The Civil & Military Gazette*, Lahore, 17 May 1936 (YA111); his letter to The Times, 24 August 1937 argued for educational policy to be set at a national rather than provincial level, to rescue India from 'the stranglehold of out-of-date traditions and local or communal interests' (YA60).

18. 'The University in a changing world', ibid.

19. *Eastern Times*, Lahore, 23 December 1936 (YA164).

20. The three accounts of Yusuf Ali's adult education ventures are included in his article 'Adult Education-II' in *Hindustan Review*, April-May 1938. (YA76).

21. *Tribune*, Lahore, 19 January 1938 (YA96).

22. *The Holy Qur'an - text, translation and commentary*, third edition (1938), note on 'Translations of the Qur'an'.

23. 'Adult Education -II', *Hindustan Review*, Patna, April-May 1938 (YA76).

24. ibid.

25. Yusuf Ali's presidential address to the University Section of the All-India Muslim Educational Conference, Golden Jubilee Session, Aligarh, 27 March, 1937; pamphlet (YA201).

26. ibid.

27. Obituary note on W. H. Moreland, *The Times*, 4 October 1938.

28. From Yusuf Ali's lecture at the Ram Sukh Das College, Ferozpur, on 9 October 1936 (YA23).

29. From Yusuf Ali's presidential address to the History and Civics Section of the Punjab Educational Conference, December 1926. A copy of the proceedings is held at the Punjab Public Library, Lahore.

30. From Yusuf Ali's speech at the Annual Prize Distribution, Islamia College on 7 March 1937.

8

A WELL ORDERED WORLD

In 1896 the capital city of the mother country of the British Empire was astir with preparations for the diamond jubilee of Queen Victoria's accession. It was being said with satisfaction that no sovereign since the fall of Rome had been able to muster subjects from so many and such distant countries all over the world. Britain stood as the unassailable world power, with her ruling classes convinced of their racial and intellectual superiority. It was in this milieu that Yusuf Ali was completing his studies in London. Like other young middle-class Indians who had won their passage to Britain on merit rather than rank or riches, he was now part of the Indian elite that could easily find a comfortable niche on their return home, lead a life untroubled with the world around them, swim with the tide, and if all went well, collect a knighthood at the end. It required courage to be different.

A type of Muslim personality emerged in the colonial period that saw its main goal to be the creation of a synthesis that would, in some mystical union, reconcile the rulers and the ruled. Yusuf Ali was driven by a deep-seated psychological urge to build a bridge between East and West. It affected his life at all levels, from the public to the most personal. It led to his choice of an English wife, not once but twice. An inner voice urged Yusuf Ali to reconcile opposites, a venture always fraught with tragedy. He had many critics who regarded his Empire-Loyalism and espousal of institutions like the League of Nations as mere opportunism. His actions, however, stemmed from a far more profound attitude of mind. His was the courage of being prepared to be an idealist.

Yusuf Ali's Passmore lectures delivered in London in 1906 were the first occasion when he spoke about his quest for a harmony between East and West. He saw himself as one of those 'University men in India', referring to the Oxbridge-returned graduates 'whose minds are still seeking an adjustment between Western ideals and Eastern traditions'.[1] The book emerging from these lectures was dedicated to George Birdwood, who possessed 'special insight of the inner consciousness of the East'. The 'East' as an entity always meant something significant to Yusuf Ali. The unity of the best of East and West was a life aim, and his fertile mind identified two routes to the pinnacle – Art and Fellowship.

Yusuf Ali's choice of art arose from his academic training as a classicist. He retained a love of Hellenic artifacts through to old age.[2] There is a reference to the higher role of art in a pamphlet published in 1916. Describing the exhibitions of Rodin and Mestrovic held at that time in London, he observed how the sculptors 'cemented the highest thought of the Allied nations by means of their art.'[3] He added, 'Such is the power of art; while it lays emphasis on national characteristics, its truth illuminates dark places and serves to brings nations together.' Yusuf Ali's own artistic temperament found expression in poetry, which he used in describing his feelings about the Great War and his aspirations for the future in a poem composed in 1918:

If East and West thou couldst survey,
And North and South in Art unite, -
Why is the human spirit's sway
Less potent now, why dimmed its light?
Have faith:these birth-throes but presage
For all humanity a Great New Age![4]

Of course the 'New Age' did not emerge after the war, but his optimism for world harmony was not dimmed. In 1925 he affirmed, 'The best possibilities for building up international brotherhood lie open through the medium of Art.'[5]

Apart from art, the other means for achieving a harmony of East and West could be through the recognition of shared spiritual ideals: 'In my view, the religion of all thinking men is the same, however different may be the philosophy by which they explain their spiritual instincts, or the moulds in which they cast their spiritual hopes.'[6] Yusuf Ali's vision of international cooperation through the common language of art and fellowship grounded on shared spiritual ideals drew him to a variety of organisations. He founded the Lahore Art Circle and was its chairman in 1937. He was very active in the World Congress of Faiths from 1936 to 1941 and participated in the Ethical Union, a similar body. He was a member of the Lahore Rotary Club and spoke at Round Table and Rotary Club meetings in Britain. He supported the League of Nations, believing that it might be a forum to 'further the progress of mankind', and also participated in its 'Peace through Religion' programme.

The pursuit of world fellowship even led him to commend Freemasonry in India. A reviewer of his *A Cultural History of India during the British Period* could not help commenting, 'One of the best chapters in the book is that which treats of the effects of the legal, social, literary, philosophical, and scientific ideas of the West on Indian cultural institutions. The importance of Freemasonry as a factor bridging the racial and social gulf is duly stressed.'[7]

His belief in world co-operation persisted during World War II. In May 1941 he was writing in the same vein as during the Great War of 1914-18, 'When the war is over things will not go back to where they have been. Everyone will face a situation in which the best efforts of all will be necessary to rebuild a new world.'[8]

In Yusuf Ali's intellectual schema, the quest for international harmony and fellowship between East and West naturally led to the need for cooperation between India on the one hand and Europe and Britain on the other. He wrote a book with the title *India and Europe* that expressed his rationale thus: 'Modernism in thought and action, in spiritual and material outlook, as evolved in Europe, is a natural stage of evolution in which the whole of mankind has contributed.'[9] India should take the best from Europe and in turn 'the religious experiences and spiritual cravings of India have much in them that will help the thought of modern Europe, as it has helped its thought in the past.'[10] In his view it was eminently reasonable for East and West to seek harmony when two of their most representative elements – India and Europe – had so much to offer to each other.

Yusuf Ali was capable of expressing this dependency in far more specific terms. He was well aware of the way India had helped Britain to achieve greatness. 'She provides a splendid training ground for British soldiers, civilians, administrators and educationalists. She supplies a practically unlimited field for the investment of British capital, which explores new possibilities and remains under British control. For most of Britain's manufactures, she furnishes an ever expanding market, and she feeds Britain's industries with raw materials of all kinds. British shipping does her carrying trade, and British machinery works her industries. Her central position in Asia enables Britain to hold a dominant position in the East.'[11] In return, 'the *pax Britannica* has enabled India to develop her moral and material resources. Membership of a great liberal Empire has expanded her vision and brought her into intimate touch with the greatest thought and the most practical movements of the world. Her social organisation is moving gradually from an archaic or medieval base to a democratic basis. There is no department of her life which has not been vivified by the Anglo-Saxon love of order and organisation.' These sentiments, expressed in 1918, were a refrain in much of Yusuf Ali's subsequent writing and political associations. He collaborated extensively in the inter-war years with the monarchist Unionist governments of the Punjab. He expended considerable intellectual effort in explaining his Empire-Loyalism and held on to it even in the face of the Indian Independence struggle. Though grieved by the racial arrogance of the English, he was tied to them by too many bonds of fellowship – of education, marriage, employment and friendship.

There was a further final tier to Yusuf Ali's intellectual schema. The interdependency between India and Europe required the cooperation of the Muslim world and the Muslims of India with the British. In the Great War the Muslims had fulfilled their pledges, 'for the sake of British interests and the peace of the world'.[12] In World War II as well, Yusuf Ali would declare, 'The British policy in the Middle East is in the interests of the Muslim states and the Muslims of India.'[13] He was himself an exemplary Muslim propagandist for the British in both of these periods. Britain too had much in which to instruct Muslims. Writing in 1941 at the age of sixty-nine, when there could be no question of his craving for a knighthood or personal wealth, he presented this compliment, 'The British do not flaunt their spirituality. They practice it in a quiet homely way. In this they appeal to the Muslims, whose ancient tradition – although perhaps obscured at the present day - was of the same character.'[14]

The commonality of interests that he perceived between India and Empire and between East and West were two sides of the same coin. The enemies of the Empire were also responsible for preventing the unity of East and West.'The machinations of the Hohenzollerns,' he wrote soon after the end of World War I, castigating the German royal family, '[had] rudely disturbed .... [the] happier union and solidarity between East and West which we hope to see re-established not only within our Empire, but in the world at large.'[15] This was the well-spring of his passionate propaganda on behalf of Britain. He risked his life and reputation on the mission to Scandinavia in 1918 because of this moral imperative. A few months later a letter he wrote to *The Times Literary Supplement* explained why it had been so important for him to act. 'The enemy's game is to sow mischief by developing a further argument. The East cultivated the gifts of the Soul; the West is busy with mundane matters - fighting, government, law and commercial traffic. Obviously the East must despise the West and is justified (they blandly insinuate) in doing so.' The 'enemy' in this particular case was not Germany but members of the Indian National Committee confronting him in Sweden. His letter continued, 'My plea is that these lines of reasoning are fallacious. The East is not passive and disdainful. The West has a soul to save, its own and others' as much as the East. They have both contributed and are contributing their powers to the spiritual development of mankind. Each must work on the only principle that will justify us to history - "the faith that is in us". Britain's work in India must not be judged merely on its material side, splendid though it is. It is even greater in the intellectual and moral sphere.'[16]

His personal contribution to this great confluence - 'the great movement', a favourite term of his - of Muslims and Britain, India and Empire, East and West, would be 'the most marvellous Book in the world'.[17] It was a book that belonged to 'Eastern literature'.[18] His service was to present it 'in a fitting garb in English...I want to make English itself an Islamic language.'[19] He performed this task because it was in his very being that the polarities of East and West had come to be focused: 'I have explored Western lands, Western manners and the depths of Western thought and

Western learning, which has rarely fallen to the lot of an Eastern mortal. But I have never lost touch with my Eastern heritage.' Yusuf Ali's remarks on the death of Justice Ameer Ali dwell on a role that would now be his to emulate: 'sincere devotion to the cause of progressive Islam...[and] a true bond of union between the best traditions of the East and the West.'[20] Yusuf Ali too took up the cause of 'progressive Islam' and through his scholarship of the Qur'an offered to the West the best of 'Eastern' traditions.

At the 1940 World Congress of Faiths held at Bedford College, London, Yusuf Ali described the importance of men sharing each others' spiritual visions, an allusion to his own endeavour to promote that aim, saying, 'Those who are not afraid rejoice that there are others seeking the light; and if they catch the rays other than their own, their faith and hope are strengthened in ever-widening circles.'[21] He did not bring any deep Arabic scholarship to his task or any formal training in the Islamic sciences but a passionately held belief in his destiny to bridge East and West and make the message of Islam more accessible.

At a personal level Yusuf Ali lived piously, prayed in congregation and led Friday and *'id* prayers, visited Karbala and performed the *Hajj*, fasted in *Ramadhan* and wrote articles on the Prophet referring to him as 'My *Mahbub*'(Beloved).[22] He admired the nineteenth-century Shaikh Karamat Ali of Djwanpur, and also Sufism based on a *tariqa* (mystic order) was close to his heart. '[But] these people do not arrogate to themselves the rights of an exclusive church. They do not acquire large secular properties; they do not live idle lives of luxury.'[23]

It was within such a well ordered world view of shared spiritual visions between East and West and interests in *tassawuf*(mysticism) that Yusuf Ali sought to find a place for Islam as a 'world religion', an expression he used in *India and Europe*. It was an Islam that was confident and outward-looking, free of sectarian prejudices. He knew enough of scientific developments to defend his point of view, and did not feel compelled to explain away supernatural phenomena in the language of science. The modern sciences, he believed, were not hostile to spiritual concerns and as their area of knowledge and experience enlarged they were becoming less and less material.

The spirit of the medieval Islamic treatise, the *Rasail* of *Ikhwan-us-Safa*, which expounded all the new sciences of its day, was deeply religious. Newton, who may be claimed as a father of modern physics and modern science, was a deeply religious man. Who could read the wonderful astronomical expositions of Jeans and Eddington or contemplate the forces of radio-activity and atomic structure or come into the remotest touch with the Quantum theory or the problems of Energy and Relativity without feeling that matter itself now appeared in a more complex light to modern science than was postulated by the materialists of even a generation ago? In a sense matter itself had become spiritualised by modern science.[24]

Yusuf Ali presented a confident and outward-looking Islam, but shorn of some essential elements. The aspect most curtailed was its message in the socio-political arena and the relevance of the *shariah* in affairs of state. The well-ordered world could only accommodate a cut-down Islam. Perhaps because of the Indian setting in which Muslims were a minority or his acquiescence to British domination, Yusuf Ali had come to accept that government was now divorced from religion, or in his words, 'The fight between Church and State is – for most of us – a matter of past history'.[25] The requirement now relevant was to take sides in the battle 'between cynicism and faith, between apathy and well-doing, between international rivalry and jealousy and personal integrity and independence'. He sought to justify this point of view through the construction of elaborate arguments, considered in the next chapter. From his earliest years, Yusuf Ali had been witness to awe-inspiring displays of British organisation and discipline. Unable to foresee its imminent decline, he saw the Empire's pre-eminence ordained. If his religious vision led him to appreciate the unity and harmony of Nature, then the flourishing of the British Empire too must have appeared part of God's plan on earth.

Notes to chapter 8

1. Preface to *Life and Labour of the People of India*, 1907.

2. The evidence is in an article Yusuf Ali wrote for *Religions*, January 1941, on 'Hellenic Culture and the Modern World'. It includes the following, "The Greek love of beauty took concrete form in all departments of life...in painting, what would we not give for a painting of Zeuxis or Apelles if we could but have a glimpse now?" (YA351).

3. In his *Mestrovic and Serbian Sculpture*, 1916.

4. Poem 'To Thorvaldsen' in his *Traek af Indien Kultur* (Danish), 1918.

5. *India and Europe*, 1925, p.123.

6. ibid, p.97.

7. 'A Cultural History of India during the British Period', reviewed in *The Asiatic Review*, January 1941 by C. Colin Davies (YA353). This book was an Urdu translation of *Hindustan ki tamaddun ki tarikh*, completed by Yusuf Ali in September 1931.

   Yusuf Ali's awareness of the role of Freemasonry may explain a passage in his *Life and Labour in India*, "in private and public life the influences that go furthest are not those that are most talked about." His article 'Goethe's Orientalism' published in *Contemporary Review*, August 1906 also contains several references to the cult. The Qur'anic commentary too uses the term to imply a tacit agreement "...Finding encouragement from their passion and their fellow-feeling, she openly avows as a woman amongst women (by a sort of freemasonry) what she would have been ashamed to acknowledge to others before." See *The Holy Qur'an*, third edition, note 1680.

   In the eighteenth century, the Freemasonry movement adopted many symbols of pre-Christian Hellenic thought to lure intellectuals who were abandoning the Church. The neo-platonic strand continued into the nineteenth century; Indian Muslims with a European classical education would have felt a degree of affinity to it. The masonic symbol of the 'Great Architect' would have been quite compatible with monotheistic belief. Yusuf Ali's commentary note No.1066 is interesting in this context.

8. *South Place Ethical Society Monthly Recorder*, July 1941 (YA361).

9. *India and Europe*, p.97.

10. ibid.

11. Yusuf Ali's article in *Overseas*, the monthly journal of the Overseas Club and the Patriotic Club of Britons Overseas, Vol.III, No. 25, February 1918.

12. *The Civil & Military Gazette*, Lahore, 10 November 1937.

13. Transcript of Yusuf Ali's article 'Oppression in Muslim Countries', written in 1942 (YA unnumbered). Yusuf Ali was quoting in approval a remark by Sikander Hayat Khan.

14. IOL:L/I/1/1268 File No.1. The extract is from an article 'British Democracy as seen by a Muslim', dated 9th May 1941.

15. Letter, *The Times*, 29 November 1918.

16. *The Times Literary Supplement*, 19 September 1918.

17. *Eastern Times*, Lahore, 15 September 1936 (YA133).

18. *The Holy Qur'an* ibid., note 5982: "In Eastern literature, especially in religious allegory, there are usually more meanings than one, enfolded in each other. They must be understood, if the reader wishes to get the full sense out of the passage. This applies specially to the Qur'an."

19. ibid., preface to the First Edition; also the following quotation.

20. *Obituary note, The Times*, 6 August 1928.

21. Proceedings of the World Congress of Faiths, 1940. Yusuf Ali's address was given on 6 July 1940 (YA340).

22. *Eastern Times*, Lahore, 28 April 1939 (YA301).

23. *Crescent*, magazine of Islamia College, Lahore, October 1936 (YA147).

24. Pamphlet of the World Congress of Faiths, *The World's Need of Religion*, Oxford, 24th July, 1937; p. 4. Yusuf Ali also observed, "Einstein is right in plumbing the depths of Relativity in the world of physical science. It points more and more to the need of Unity in God in the spiritual world." See *The Holy Qur'an*, ibid., note 762.

25. 'The World's Need of Religion', World Congress of Faiths, Oxford, 24 July 1937, p.7. Also the following quotation.

9

QUR'AN AS GUIDANCE

Yusuf Ali's scholarship on the Qur'an was published in instalments between 1934 and 1937. Though he continued to write articles and reviews on a variety of topics for at least seven more years, this was to be his best known work. It has made his name instantly recognisable in the English-speaking Muslim world. The commentary took the form of over six thousand footnotes to the translation, numerous appendices and a running interpretation written in the style of blank verse.[1] It was a monumental effort that records the encounter of an intelligent and con-templative mind with the majesty of the Qur'an. Its hallmark is its emphasis on the spiritual dimension of Islam and message of moral revival. The origins for this orientation can be traced back to Yusuf Ali's life experiences, aspirations and ideological commitments. A troubled domes-tic life, early academic specialisations and employment as a college princi-pal were experiences which intertwined with his vision of the meaning of the Qur'an.

By the time Yusuf Ali was thirty years old the young Bombay scholar of modest means had become transformed into a self-assured Edwardian gentleman, one of the first Indian Muslims to attain executive rank in the elite Indian Civil Service. The plight of the Ottomans in the Balkans or North Africa prior to the Great War did not move him in the way it did contemporaries like Muhammad Ali Jauhar or Iqbal. At first he analysed religious practices in India as a social historian, in the tradition of the officer-scholar of the ICS pursuing an extra-curricular interest. The next decade of his life brought rude shocks to one unaccustomed to failure. The first was the infidelity of his wife Teresa Shalders in 1911, while the second occurred around 1920 when the children of this union turned against him with a vengeance. These emotional traumas in mid-life altered Yusuf Ali's perceptions and, though he never fully went back on his Empire-Loyalism, there was a rekindling of religious sentiment. Yusuf Ali's bond with the Qur'an was forged in these times of anguish when searching for solace. This made the study deeply personal. He even cast a veil over his years of private research so that the eight pamphlets published in the 'Progressive Islam' Series between 1925 and 1933 would make no reference to a work of Qur'anic exegesis in the making. The Qur'an's message of succour and hope to the individual appealed most to Yusuf Ali. It provided his scholarship with a distinct orientation that was retained when publication in 1934 brought the results of his labour into the public domain.

Yusuf Ali's discovery of the Qur'an in times of distress is not only referred to directly in the Preface of *The Holy Qur'an — text, translation and commentary*[2,] but also indirectly at various points in the commentary. There is a description of how 'many violent settlements of the spirit are but heralds of the refreshing showers of spiritual understanding that come in their wake. They purify our souls and produce spiritual life where there was a parched spiritual desert before.'[3] Elsewhere there is a biographical ring to a comment on children whose 'conflict with your ideals may vex your spirit,' but this behaviour 'may at the same time search out your fidelity to God'.[4] Yusuf Ali's sense of hurt ran deep and surfaced as late as 1940 when he castigated his estranged children for maintaining an attitude of ill will and hostility 'in spite of all I have done for them'.[5] The question raised in the commentary, 'If there were no Hereafter, how could you reconcile the inequalities of this world?'[6] ceases to be an abstract one against the backdrop of his own sense of betrayal and disappointment. The Book's oft-repeated reminder on the transient nature of worldly existence became all-absorbing to him. It gave his commentary a sense of detachment from the affairs of this world: 'Where is the bravery and beauty of yesterday? All that is left is dust and ashes! What more can we get from this physical material life?'[7] In the same vein he quoted his favourite English poet Longfellow: 'All the world's a fleeting show for man's illusion given.'[8] The story of Zulaikha and the Prophet Yusuf in which the princess 'had learnt much in sorrow, pain and humiliation' took up many pages of his commentary. He could identify with Zulaikha, because as with his humiliation at the hands of Mary Teresa, the princess too 'had learnt the vanity of carnal love'.[9] Yusuf Ali's self-revelation was not dissimilar to Zulaikha's: true love was 'pure surrender of self, which has no earthly stain on it'.[10] Worldly life acquired a shabby quality, 'our carnal life is sustained with carnal food, and its joys and pleasures at the best are those which are projected in the screen of this material world. Their real life is sustained from the ineffable Presence and Nearness of God.'[11]

Together with this personalised and other-worldly orientation, the second factor affecting Yusuf Ali's Qur'anic scholarship was his academic training. He lectured in Greek history immediately after graduation and retained a lifelong love of Hellenic culture. An article he wrote in 1941 depicts his undiminished enthusiasm even after completion of the commentary:

> The beauty of Hellenic architecture we can see in some measure on the Acropolis today. The beauty consists not only in its forms and proportions but in its setting and in the marvellous way in which it uses the beauties of nature around it. In pottery and in the arts of daily life we are conscious of the Hellenic love of beauty and its ingrained capacity for full expression. But the beauty of the Hellenic language and the literature enshrined in it defies all analysis. It has been well said that if the gods came to the West, they would speak the language of Plato.[12]

Yusuf Ali's fascination with Hellenic heroes led him to dwell at length in the commentary on Zul-qarnain and the possibility of this historical character being Alexander the Great. Yusuf Ali noted of his research, 'I have studied the details of Alexander's extraordinary personality in Greek historians as well as in modern writers...few readers of Qur'anic literature have had the same privilege of studying the details of his career.'[13]

Yusuf Ali also identified closely with the search for the mysterious and unseen in Hellenic thought: 'Each verse is but a Sign or Symbol: what it represents is something immediately applicable, and something eternal and independent of time and space – the "Forms of Ideas" in Plato's Philosophy. The wise man will understand that there is an "essence" and an illustrative clothing given to the essence, throughout the Book;'[14] 'The original form or Idea or pattern, according to Plato's mystic doctrine as developed in his 'Republic', may also be compared with the "names" or nature and quality of things which God taught Adam;'[15] 'the whole phenomenal world is a symbol. The reality lies behind it, like the real light behind the Cave, in Plato's Theory of Ideas.'[16] Such intellectual preoccupations led Yusuf Ali to a heavy-handed search for symbols in the verses of the Qur'an. The fish became a symbol of secular knowledge,[17] the shin 'a symbol for the most hidden mystery'[18] and the sun a mystic reference to intelligence.[19] There are frequent elaborations on the Qur'an's references to water and light,[20] and the abbreviated letters or *muqatta'at*.[21] This esoteric approach was not unrewarding and his desire to read the Qur'an intelligently opened doorways to profound truths, for example: 'The postures in prayer are symbolical of attitudes of mind, and behaviour in life generally, and the 'movements' may refer also to vicissitudes, in which a man's soul is tried and tested just as the body is exercised in standing, bowing, kneeling and prostration in prayer.'[22] His commentary contains eloquent passages inviting the reader to recognise in 'the Book of Nature', the phenomenal world, 'the hand of the powerful and beneficent God'. The signs of God were many, 'in His great world, in nature, in the heart of man, in revelation'.[23] 'If we study such signs in the right spirit, we learn the highest lessons for our spiritual life.'[24] The conclusion would be that 'God's Creation is not without a higher serious purpose. It is not in vain, or for mere play or sport.'[25]

While Yusuf Ali generally put his Hellenic influences to good use, it did bequeath to his scholarship a suggestion that the 'mysteries' were only accessible to the select. There is a touch of exclusiveness in the comment, 'A crowd mentality is not best for the perception of the final spiritual truths.'[26] He has references to the select who possess 'inner knowledge' or 'mystic knowledge' and appreciate 'the inner world'.[27] Such sentiments were in keeping with an interpretation of the Qur'an as a guide for the spiritual development of the individual. Yusuf Ali's quest for 'inner knowledge' was not to be restricted to Qur'anic studies and his distrust of the 'crowd' would also shape his educational philosophy and political beliefs.[28]

The third factor exerting an influence on both the style and content of his commentary was his employment as principal of Islamia College,

Lahore, through the 1935-37 period which saw publication of the work in monthly instalments. By all accounts Yusuf Ali was a well-liked and conscientious headmaster, who mixed with the boys in class and on the sports field. He had an empathy with the young, whose 'glory is enthusiasm without self-interest'.[29] There was a great display of support in his favour when he offered to resign in January 1937 in protest against a faction of the *Anjuman-Himayat-ul-Islam*. Yusuf Ali lectured an English Honours class three times a week, obtaining exceptional results.[30] In such a classroom milieu his command of English literature became even more finely honed. The commentary is replete with quotations from luminaries like Shakespeare, Milton, Tennyson and the like.[31] Occasionally a headmaster's touch has found its way into a Qur'anic footnote: '*Sartor Resartus* [a work by Carlyle]...is strong meat to the novice in literature.'[32]

Yusuf Ali's natural instincts were to wish the best moral character for Islamia's students. In this he led by personal example. During his tenure as principal, one of the teachers at Islamia College, Professor Ghulam Hussain, organised a reception in honour of Dr Taseer, a distinguished Lahore intellectual. Yusuf Ali did not attend but was offered some titbits by another member of staff designed to cast Professor Hussain in a poor light. Yusuf Ali's response was to summon Professor Hussain and ask the gossip-monger to repeat his story. Such severe treatment worked marvels and staff were henceforth careful in his presence.[33]

The commentary reflects a principal's urge to instruct and impart: 'In all things be moderate. Do not go the pace, and do not be stationary or slow. Do not be talkative and do not be silent. Do not be loud and do not be timid or halfhearted. Do not be too confident and do not be cowed down.'[34] Similar guidelines for good conduct are to be found in other notes: 'We must not speak unseasonably and when we do speak we must not beat about the bush, but go straight to that which is right, in deed as well as in word'[35] and 'Islam aims at making every Muslim man or woman, however humble in station, a refined gentleman or lady.'[36] These were uplifting sentiments inspired by the immediacy of contact with the young provided by Islamia College. The commentary reaches its most eloquent in such accounts of upright character: 'The true Muslim must be pure in body, mind and heart. His motives should always be sincere and his religion without any alloy of worldly gain.'[37]   Yusuf Ali's employment as a college principal offered him another doorway to absorb the spirit of the Qur'an.

Like Sir Sayyid Ahmed Khan before him, Yusuf Ali did not consider his lack of training in the formal Islamic disciplines any bar to writing a Qur'anic commentary. If the traditional scholars had not risen to the challenge of explaining the message of Islam to the new educated classes, 'the younger generation that is pressing in upon us well demand that our interpretation is consonant with the best knowledge that we possess.'[38] Yusuf Ali responded to the challenge in a practical way, deploying his erudition and command of English to great effect. It was good that 'qualified Muslims should attempt to present the picture which their own mental and spiritual vision presents to themselves.'[39] However, he was also careful to note that this re-interpretation must proceed 'in a spirit of reverence and fidelity to the real and original traditions of the best period of our history'.[40] Yusuf Ali bypassed the traditional *ulema* but retained at all times an inherent conservatism, so that his commentary would never be unduly provocative or earn the type of odium which befell Sir Sayyid's work. The furthest Yusuf Ali would venture in criticism of traditional scholarship was in warnings of 'deadening formalism'[41] and 'excesses in doctrine'.[42] The publication of the commentary passed without much comment from *ulema* circles because too few were conversant with English. Sayyid Sulaiman Nadwi's glowing testimony may have silenced any doubters: 'The Muslim litterateurs have with unanimity spoken very highly of the beauty, eloquence and grandeur of the Translation.'[43] Questions were raised on Yusuf Ali's reliance on secondary sources, but the quality of the commentary and obvious sincerity disarmed criticism.[44] Yusuf Ali possessed a grasp of the written Arabic and its grammar and had passed an Indian Civil Service examination in the language in 1895 with a mark of 340 out of 400. He made no attempt to disguise the fact that his command of Arabic was grammatical rather than conversational.[45]

Yusuf Ali's close contact with students, both in Lahore and at meetings of the Progressive Islam Association in London, led to an awareness of the doubts and sense of scepticism that coloured the new generation's attitudes towards religion. He was aware that Indian Muslim youth were in intellectual crisis, unsure where they stood on great questions - whether religion was holding them back from 'progress', or if religious faith could be reconciled with science. He was prepared to engage in the debate between religion and modern attitudes, unlike many of the traditional *ulema* who were hopelessly out of touch. In his own lifetime he had witnessed a scientific and technological revolution in the west and understood perfectly the new hope that Indian society too should move with the times: 'The scientist now holds in his hands the key to every kind of future advance in human culture.'[46] The publication of his commentary was a boon to educated Indian Muslims because it assured them Islam had nothing to fear from science. In Yusuf Ali they had a scholar who not only quoted from scientific textbooks but was able to relate the latest scientific observations to verses in the Qur'an with enthralling brilliance:

> As man's intellectual gaze over the physical world expands, he sees more and more how Unity is the dominating note in God's wonderful Universe. Taking the solar system alone, we know that the maximum intensity of sun-spots corresponds with the maximum intensity of magnetic storms on this earth. The universal law of gravitation seems to bind all mass together. Physical facts point to the throwing off of planets from vast quantities of diffused nebular matter, of which the central condensed core is a sun.[47]

The students of Islamia College had before them a religious man not baffled by physics. Yusuf Ali's reassuring message was that science offered a path to faith. Though the languages of science and religion were different, the two domains of knowledge did not belong to separate, watertight compartments. 'I believe in progressive interpretation [of the Qur'an],' he wrote in an introductory note to his translation, 'in the need for understanding and explaining spiritual matters from different angles.'[48] Islam welcomed scientific enquiry: 'In the application of spiritual truths to our own times and our own lives, we must use every kind of knowledge, science, and experience which we possess.'[49] His was an important and positive contribution through which a generation of college-going Indian Muslims was able to reconcile science and religion. Though Yusuf Ali believed that scientific discoveries could help in arriving at religious truths, he was no crude rationalist. Unlike Sir Sayyid, he did not feel compelled to explain away miracles mentioned in the Qur'an through some scientific explanation. For example the light which Moses saw on the mountain was a spiritual light, not one caused by a traveller's fire, as Sir Sayyid proposed.[50] Yusuf Ali was above this sort of apologia.

His creative impulses were fired not just by a sense of public service but by the need to make Muslims good citizens of the Empire and less susceptible to the siren song of the anti-British freedom movements. In retrospect the one aspect of Yusuf Ali's interpretation of the Qur'an that was, and remains, deeply controversial has to do with his ambivalence towards the socio-political role of Islam in contemporary society. His Qur'anic commentary shows an awareness that Islam 'makes no sharp division between sacred and secular affairs'.[51] It acknowledges that religion 'takes account of every just and legitimate interest without separating spiritual from temporal affairs'.[52] The appreciation of Islam as a comprehensive way of life can be found in Yusuf Ali's other writings: 'The Muslim concept of state was theocratic';[53] 'The Muslim state never acknowledged that finance was not part of morals.'[54]

Such occasional references, however, are peripheral in comparision with the dominant themes in the commentary – a philosophy of other-worldliness, significance of an 'inner world' and pursuit of moral excellence. Yusuf Ali was far more in his element presenting the message of the Qur'an as a message of individual hope rather than a source of guidance for the governance and management of society. Piety was personal worship rather than seeking to apply the spirit of Islam to address sociopolitical issues. Islam *was* comprehensive – 'spiritual and temporal' – but Yusuf Ali offered the reader of his commentary a number of arguments to lessen the practical implications of such a belief. The only social movement in the name of religion he could consider feasible was some form of ecumenical association of spiritual fellowship.

Yusuf Ali's first justification for the separation of Islam from day-to-day matters of governance was that politics had become an activity demeaning for pious and religious men: 'The seeking of worldly Power, even if intended to be used for God's service, has a little of Self in it.'[55] Politics involved 'log-rolling' or betrayals, making it no better than sin and wickedness.[56] This comment is to be found in the instalment published in January 1937, the time of the bitter controversy with Barkat Ali, the anti-Unionist politician. Though Yusuf Ali had been sufficiently interested in politics to stand as candidate in two election campaigns, the experience had clearly been a distasteful one. He gained only a long-standing distrust of politics. His attack on Indian *Wahhabism* in 1906 included a warning that nothing could be more damaging than 'the thoughtless admission of the foul and tainted exhalations of rough-and-tumble politics to what should be the pure and serene atmosphere of religious peace and freedom'.[57] Yusuf Ali's attitude to religion and politics were formed at the turn of the century when many Indian Muslims, keen to demonstrate their loyalty to Empire, associated politics with agitation and anti-British sentiment.

A second strand to his thinking on the subject was support for the view that Muslims must obey, as a religious duty, the ruler of the day. The commentary contains a careful statement of this position:

> All ultimate authority rests in God. Men of God derive their authority from Him. As Islam makes no sharp division between sacred and secular affairs, it expects ordinary governments to be imbued with righteousness and stand in the place of the righteous Imam, and we must respect and obey such authority; otherwise there will be no order and discipline. Where, in actual fact, there is a sharp division between law and morality, between secular and religious affairs, as is the case in most countries at the present day, Islam still expects secular authority to be exercised in righteousness, and on that condition, enjoins obedience to such authority.[58]

This too was a long-established opinion in Indian Muslim circles, and was invoked at the outset of World War I to justify continued loyalty to Britain when she declared war against Turkey. Yusuf Ali's Empire-Loyalism led him to accept British rule as righteous: 'British civilisation presents an object lesson of incalculable value to the Muslims. Not only is there unity, but there is dogged perseverance.'[59] Such a point of view deemed political struggle to establish the *shariah* as an irrelevance. Islamic institutions to do with governance and management of society could be held in abeyance. *Jihad* in particular was relegated to theory because 'a most important condition' was that it should be sanctioned by a 'righteous Imam', 'such as Muhammad was par excellence.'[60]

Yusuf Ali's third justification for distancing Islam from the political realm can be found in a theory of history based on the evolution of society. This process of evolution possessed an inevitability, 'The Western Church has since [the eighth century] worked on definitely new lines, and its offshoots among the Protestant Churches, have, consciously or unconsciously, been influenced by the broad principles of Islam. What the course of future religions may be and how God will unfold His All-Wise Plan it is not given to us mortals to know.'[61] Ideas from one society diffused to another and processes of assimilation were at work. His mind worked off a broad tableau in which 'culture must assimilate culture or human evolution would be stopped for ever'.[62] In *Religious Polity of Islam*, a book referred to in the commentary, he observes that it is setting 'too narrow bounds to Islam to identify it with any particular set of concrete customs or institutions, however wise and reasonable they may have been in origin'.[63] The suggestion is that Muslims may be marching against the tide of history by insisting on implementing Islam in sociopolitical terms. The Righteous State, like the Righteous Imam, was an ideal to which Muslims could attach the greatest spiritual value, but on practical issues, 'the trend has decidedly set, in circles that count, in the direction of the usages of the West.'[64] In response to the apprehension that the best Islamic ideals might be lost in this truncation, Yusuf Ali offered this assurance: 'Many modern institutions follow logically from them, even though they seem so new.'[65] Perhaps he could be so sanguine because of the conviction that the twentieth century had irrevocably altered the world. It was not possible for Muslims to unhitch themselves from the West and in calling for a return to the pristine Islam of the first Muslims the Islamic revivalist movements were being dangerously simplistic.

If the logic of the Qur'an obliged him to accept that no sharp distinction existed between the 'spiritual and temporal', his political beliefs propelled him in a separate direction. He lived with this contradiction, assuaging his conscience with such prescriptions as 'His [man's] work may be on earth but his heart is in Heaven.'[66] Religion ruled the personal, 'inner', mental realm rather than affairs of state. The only collective action in the name of religion that made sense to him was a spiritual fellowship. Yusuf Ali paid lip service to the concept of Islam as ideology and a comprehensive way of life and deemed it necessary to present it in apolitical terms. Paradoxically this was a political gesture affirming his own allegiance to Empire. By limiting religion to the spiritual 'inner' realm he was free to choose other masters for affairs of the 'outer' world. From 1936 he became a keen participant in the World Congress of Faiths. It embodied an idea, expressed in the commentary, of an organisation in which 'persons of diverse talents may unite in the spiritual world for their own highest good and in the service of God'.[67] World War II put an end to such dreams. The war also brought the demise of Empire and so the curtain descended on Yusuf Ali's elaborate world-view.

Notes to Chapter 9

1. *The Holy Qur'an - text, translation and commentary*, third edition (1938), contains 6,310 commentary notes and fourteen appendices. All subsequent references in this chapter are to this edition. Readers should note that other editions, for example those published by Amana Corporation/IIIT (1989, 1992) or the King Fahd Holy Qur'an Printing Complex (1990) have made significant amendments to Yusuf Ali's original work (see note 27 below).

2. *The Holy Qur'an*, ibid. The preface to the first edition contains the following biographical reference, "A man's life is subject to inner storms far more devastating than those in the physical world around him. In such a storm, in the bitter anguish of personal sorrow which nearly unseated my reason and made life seem meaningless, a new hope was born out of a systematic pursuit of my long-cherished project."

3. ibid., note 3107.

4. ibid., note 5496.

5. From Yusuf Ali's will.

6. *The Holy Qur'an*, ibid., note 4180.

7. ibid. note 1412.

8. ibid. note 492. Longfellow is also referred to in notes 2950, 4063 and 4071. Yusuf Ali described Longfellow as one of the most masterly English poets to the Lahore advocate

Mr Aziz, father of the historian K.K.Aziz.(Dr K.K. Aziz's private communication with the author).

9. *The Holy Qur'an*, ibid., note 1711.

10. ibid.

11. ibid., note 477.

12. Hellenic Culture and the Modern World, *Religions*, January 1941 (YA351).

13. *The Holy Qur'an*, ibid., Appendix VII, 'Who was Zul-qarnain?'

14. ibid., note 347.

15. ibid., note 996.

16. ibid., Appendix VI. For another reference to Plato see note 1584.

17. ibid, note 2408.

18. ibid, note 5622.

19. ibid, note 1827.

20. For references to water see note 3107. References to the symbolic meaning of light are to be found in Appendix VIII ('Mystic Interpretation of the Verse of Light') and notes 2997 and 3001.

21. References to the *muqatta'at* can be found in *The Holy Qur'an*, ibid., Appendix I, the introduction to Surah X (Yunus) and note 2455.

22. ibid., note 3235.

23. ibid., note 3993.

24. ibid., note 4573.

25. ibid., note 2950.

26. ibid., note 3857.

27. ibid., note 3913; note 5349. Evidence of Yusuf Ali's *tasawwuf* inclinations have been largely removed in the Amana/IIIT and Ifta/King Fahd Holy Qur'an Complex editions. Any phrases with terms like 'mystic' or allusions to a deeper layer of meaning in the Qur'an only accessible to the select have been expunged, e.g. 58:11 and commentary notes 3226, 3943, 4560, 5526, 5778, 5793, 5795. Moreover three appendices have been dropped: Allegorical interpretation of the story of Joseph; Mystic interpretation of the Verse of Light; The Muslim Heaven. The editors of the Ifta edition have also deleted Yusuf Ali's use of the word 'mysteries', e.g. 67:14 and commentary note 5749.

28. Yusuf Ali believed in the exclusivity of university education - 'the universities are meant for a select class of people who can think independently and act according to

reason'. From Yusuf Ali's speech 'The University in a changing World', weekend conference held at F.C. College, Lahore, 7 September, 1936. ('Typed note of proceedings in the Yusuf Ali scrap book, YA25).

His distrust of mass involvement in politics surfaced on numerous occasions. In *The Religious Polity of Islam* he notes "the tendency in modern undiluted democracies is to chance everything on a stake of universal suffrage" (p.18). His 1940 essay, 'Muslim Culture and Religious Thought', also expressed great scepticism for the voting process in the selection of political leadership through adult suffrage.

29. *The Holy Qur'an*, ibid., note 5058.

30. Seventy per cent of Islamia College's English Honours class passed in 1936-37. One of his students came second in English in the whole province. *Eastern Times*, 24 December 1936 (YA166).

31. Some references in *The Holy Qur'an*, ibid., are:

    Bunyan: note 581

    Burns: Appendix VI, and note 181

    Carlyle: note 1008

    Coleridge: notes 4572, 5498

    Dickens: note 862

    Kipling: note 1694

    Milton: notes 1343, 1881, 4035,4203, 4440

    Shakespeare: notes 47, 284, 439, 1308, 1662, 1663, 3354, 3866, 3987, 5202, 5919, 6262

    Shelley: notes 2514, 3196

    Spenser: note 3271

    Tennyson: notes 456, 1021, 2481

    Wordsworth: notes 68, 298, 4865

    Wolfe: note 2352

32. ibid., note 1008.

33. This anecdote is taken from *Yaran-i-Maktab*, p.191.

34. *The Holy Qur'an*, ibid., note 3604.

35. ibid., note 3775.

36. ibid., note 3036.

37. ibid., note 1358.

38. From Yusuf Ali's presidential address at the University Section of the All-India Muslim Educational conference, reported in *Eastern Times*, 6-7 April 1937 (YA201).

39. *The Holy Qur'an*, ibid., Translations of the Qur'an.

40. All-India Muslim Educational conference, ibid.

41. *The Holy Qur'an*, ibid., note 177.

42. ibid., note 675.

43. Sulaiman Nadwi's quotation continues, "One is gratified to see that the Allama has absolutely avoided the misleading construction of the verses and has not made the question of miracles the plaything of mental gymnastics. In understanding the meaning of the verses, the Allama has taken the help of commentators of Arabia. The printing is of very high order and in outward appearance can be compared with the printing executed in London." The remarks were reproduced in the inside cover pages of the fifth instalment of Yusuf Ali's Qur'anic translation-cum-commentary published in July 1935.

44. *The Light*, Lahore, 24 December 1936, castigates a Mr Durrani for his 'uncharitable diatribe' against Yusuf Ali. See Chapter 5, note 56. An admirer of Yusuf Ali noted a reliance on "Shah Abdul Qadir Sahib Dehlawi's standard translation," see *Islamic Culture*, Hyderabad, Vol. XXVIII, No. 1, January 1954.

45. Professor Hamidullah has a recollection of meeting Yusuf Ali 'early in 1935' while travelling by ship from France to Bombay: "He told me that he was translating the Holy Qur'an, and we discussed certain points which I do not remember now. He also told me he was a descendant of Hajjaj ibn Yusuf. By chance there was a group of Moroccans, I think, in the same boat, going apparently for Hajj. I had the honour of serving as translator, and the late Yusuf Ali told me that he understood Arabic well when he hears it, but is himself unable to reply, to talk." Letter from Professor Hamidullah to the author, March 1988.

    The reference to Hajjaj ibn Yusuf is bizarre. Hajjaj (died AD 714) is remembered in Muslim history as a ruthless but able Ummayad viceroy who campaigned against the Kharijites.

46. Presidential address to the University Section, All-India Muslim Educational Conference, Golden Jubilee Session, Aligarh, March 1937.

47. *The Holy Qur'an*, ibid., note 2690; for a reference to scientific text books see note 3021.

48. ibid., Note on 'Commentaries on the Qur'an'.

49. ibid.

50. From S. A. Ashraf, 'Isam and modern scientific attitudes', *The Islamic Quarterly*, Vol. XXIII, No. 3 (1979).

51. *The Holy Qur'an*, ibid., note 580.

52. ibid., note 4927.

53. From *Indian Muhammadans*; speech presented at the Royal Society of Literature, December 1906.

54. *Religious Polity of Islam*, 1933.

55. *The Holy Qur'an*, ibid., note 4190.

56. ibid., note 3445.

57. From *Indian Muhammadans*, ibid.

58. *The Holy Qur'an*, ibid., note 580.

59. IOL: L/I/1268 File No.1. Transcript of World War II speech for Ministry of Information, 'British Democracy as seen by a Muslim'.

60. *The Holy Qur'an*, ibid., note 205. References in the commentary to *jihad* and fighting are invariably accompanied with mention of a 'righteous Imam' to sanction such action. See notes 205, 236, 1209, 1234, 1320, 1373.

61. ibid., Appendix V, 'Egyptian Religion and its steps towards Islam'.

62. See Yusuf Ali's *A Cultural History of India during the British Period*, 1931, p.179.

63. *The Holy Qur'an*, ibid., note 4579, refers to his *Religious Polity of Islam*.

64. From 'Muslim Culture and Religious Thought', Yusuf Ali's contribution to L.S.S. O'Malley (ed.) *Modern India and the West*, 1941.

65. *Religious Polity of Islam*, 1933.

66. *The Holy Qur'an*, ibid., note 5759.

67. ibid., note 3114

10

CONCLUSION

In the United Provinces around 1897 or early 1898 there was a moment of transition when an old patriarch, who had pioneered the adoption of the higher English education for Muslims, met a young, academically minded ICS officer. Sir Sayyid Ahmed Khan with his great white beard and Yusuf Ali, impeccably attired in an Edwardian suit, were the changing faces of Muslim India. It was a transition in style as well as substance. The generation that had witnessed the physical might of British colonialism in the aftermath of the 1857 insurrection was replaced by one that had to come to terms with an intellectual and cultural onslaught. Sir Sayyid and like-minded peers resolved to be loyal to the Empire because that was the only realistic option; Yusuf Ali and those of a similar mind-set accepted British superiority from inner conviction. Nevertheless Yusuf Ali was accomplished, loyal to Islam and imbued with a sense of public duty – the very qualities to which Sir Sayyid aspired for the next generation and for which he founded Aligarh.

In his background and upbringing Yusuf Ali was not very different from many of his well known contemporaries. Much of his early schooling was at missionary institutions, but this was an experience shared with Iqbal, Jinnah and Jauhar. Like them too, he proceeded to further studies in England. Yet Yusuf Ali acquired a Britishness that was untypical. It was rare for a young Indian Muslim to marry an English woman in a Church of England ceremony; it was rarer still for an educated Indian to adore British royalty. Why did Yusuf Ali's Britishness not run skin-deep but penetrate the core of his being? As he would himself no doubt point out, 'Do not forget or undervalue the human element.' Part of the answer may lie in his father's own allegiance to the British and the great kindness shown to the family by Sir Charles Lely, Collector of Surat. While at school and university, Yusuf Ali was also befriended by inspiring and eminent British mentors. He was grateful for their affection and concern and offered in return an emotional and undying trust. Other factors no doubt contributed to this Anglo-Saxon bond, including perhaps the need to prove to his children that he was a true-blooded patriot like any man in the parish.

Yusuf Ali once concluded a speech at the Royal Society of Arts in London by declaring his four mottoes, 'Staunch loyalty to our Sovereign; Patriotism for our Country; Friendliness to neighbours; and the sum and substance of them all, Absolute truth to ourselves.'[1] It was a carefully worded testament connecting individual conduct, civic duties, 'responsible' nationalism and Empire-Loyalism. The chairman of the meeting was a former Viceroy who added, 'The Mohammedans of India are true to everyone of those mottoes except the last.' Yusuf Ali did not protest – it is difficult to imagine a Jinnah or Jauhar putting up with such insufferable arrogance. He lived his life in a state of tension, one part accepting British superiority, the other searching for something through which Indian Muslim self-respect could be restored. All this is said not to belittle the man but to understand the conditions of his life. It is one hundred years since he first arrived in Britain to study and Muslims continue to experience the very same feelings of attraction and revulsion in their relationship with the west. Yusuf Ali was a prototype British Muslim who through his exegetical masterpiece was able to salvage something great and precious from the experience.

Yusuf Ali possessed a brilliant intellect and extraordinary industry, but his life was a sorry story of misplaced trust. Those he looked upon as friends in the ICS were glad to see him leave because a native Indian was a block on promotions and did not fit in. He abetted Serbian nationalism when this was merely one ploy to dismember the Ottoman world. The Empire that he trusted would play fair with India because of her sacrifices in the Great War stalled political reforms. The terms of the mandates of the League of Nations were not honoured. Yusuf Ali was a well-meaning Muslim intellectual co-opted by the British establishment. He belonged to a certain class of Muslim intelligentsia that considered it terribly important to be well thought of by the British. This class was ever willing to cede ground in order to appear reasonable and 'non-controversial', but without obtaining any concessions in return. The effect of this misplaced trust was to prevent it from reacting in a shrewd political manner when the interests of Muslims were under threat. In stark contrast, those such as Rufus Isaacs and Herbert Samuel also served the Empire and supported idealistic ventures such as the Congress of Faiths, but at every turn they made sure that the strategic interests of their co-religionists were preserved. When Yusuf Ali completed his Qur'anic work he did not enjoy the peace of mind to be expected. He remained a restless soul, with bouts of depression and self-doubt, his second marriage also turning sour. These domestic trag-edies mirrored the greater failure of the Empire in creating an equitable order. To the end he remained true to Monarch and Mother Country because, in a sad way, this was part of the fabric of his being.

The different outlooks of Yusuf Ali and his great contemporary Muhammad Iqbal represent two distinct Muslim identities. Yusuf Ali subscribed to an elaborate world view in which Britain and the West were enthroned as the dominant powers. Iqbal on the other hand was under no illusions that the West wished to exploit and divide Muslims. The quest to reconcile East and West was all-important for Yusuf Ali even though it did not prove a happy experience for him even at the personal level. Iqbal, in marked contrast, was uninterested in such a reconciliation. Yusuf Ali even thought that Iqbal had an 'obsession' in seeking out the spiritual and moral defects of the West.[2] Their differing perceptions on the League of Nations captures the gulf – a legitimate world organisation for Yusuf Ali, an assembly of 'grave robbers' for Iqbal. Yusuf Ali's apolitical Islam led to an acceptance of the ideal of an Indian nation, though by 1947 he was not in a fit state to live in either India or Pakistan. He accepted the notion of an Indian 'nation' even though all the signals warned of Muslim extinction under the wheels of a careering Hindu juggernaut. Iqbal's 'political Islam' alerted him to the hollowness of an all-encompassing Indian nationhood from an early stage.

When Pakistan came into existence Yusuf Ali was emulated by many an ambitious young bureaucrat who aspired to be Europeanised without losing touch with Islam. It was because of Iqbal's intellectual legacy, carried forward by leaders like Mawdudi, that a conception of Islam as a way of living – an ideology – could be held aloft. For Yusuf Ali religion became foremost personal piety. For Iqbal the logical consequence of religious belief was this and more – the Muslim as a man or woman of action and struggle. Yusuf Ali once wrote, 'Though Iqbal's literary genius and his philosophical interpretation of Islam brought him immense popularity, he was yet an isolated figure...In public affairs, and in building up the 'new temple' (*naya shiwala*, to use his term) his influence was negligible.'[3] Fortunately his prediction was inaccurate, but the gulf between these outlooks remains palpable. In spite of their differences Iqbal and Yusuf Ali shared many common ideals and worked hard for the sake of succeeding Muslim generations. Islamia College, Lahore, was witness to their passion for improving the educational standards of Muslims. It is not in Muslim interests for either Yusuf Ali or Iqbal to become isolated figures, just as there is need for a synthesis between an understanding of Islam as a great spiritual balm and an all-encompassing ideology. Such great men deserve more than becoming mere talismans whose names are invoked without a real comprehension of their struggles, intellectual contributions and aspirations.

Yusuf Ali's life began with promise, swung between moments of darkness and summits of achievement and ended in tragedy. In a sense it was like the history of British India.

Notes to Chapter 10

1. This and the following quotation are from Yusuf Ali's speech in December 1906 to the Royal Society of Arts, London, 'The Indian Muhammadans: their past, present and future', *Journal of the Royal Society of Arts*, No. 2824, Vol. LV, 4 January 1907.

2. Yusuf Ali's 'Doctrine of Human Personality in Iqbal's Poetry', a paper read on 9 November 1938 at the Royal Society of Literature. Published in the *Transactions of the Royal Society of Literature*, New Series, Vol. XVIII. In this address Yusuf Ali also noted that 'Iqbal delighted in such books as Spengler's *Decline of the West*.'

3. 'Muslim Culture and Religious Thought', Yusuf Ali's contribution to L.S.S. O'Malley (ed.) *Modern India and the West*, 1941.

Captions to documents and photographs

Civil Service of India.

Candidates selected in 1894.

Open Competition and Final Examination Combined

List resulting from the combined marks of the Open Competitive and Final Examinations.

Order of merit	Name.	Presidency or Division of Presidency to which Assigned.	Total m.a.		
			In Open Competition	In Final Examination	In Open Competition and Final Examination combined
1	Pim: Alan William	N.W. Provinces &c.	3114	1766	4880
2	Hailey: William Malcolm	N.W. Provinces &c.	2960	1397	4357
3	Sheepshanks: Richard	Bengal	2563	1589	4152
4	Percival: Philip Edward	Bombay.	2377	1516	3893
5	Dadachanji: Piroze K	Madras	2180	1684	3864
6	Bryant: John Forbes	Madras.	2453	1294	3747
7	Yusuf-Ali: Abdullah ibn Khan Bahadur	N.W. Provinces &c.	1911	1778	3689
8	Wood: Richard Boardman	Madras	2145	1415	3560
9	Clarke: Robert Thomas	N.W. Provinces &c.	2148	1389	3537
10	Coupland: Herbert	Bengal	2135	1330	3465
11	Ghosal: Jyotsnanath	Bombay	1902	1541	3443
12	Cunliffe: Arthur Jabot	Burma	2471	946	3417
13	Clarke: Geoffrey Rothe	N.W. Provinces &c.	2188	1216	3404
14	Leslie-Jones: Leycester Hudson	N.W. Provinces &c.	1715	1614	3329
15	Stephenson: Hugh Lansdown	Bengal	1916	1359	3275
16	Moore: Harry Christopher	Burma	1867	1406	3273
17	Bushell: William Done	Bombay	2362	890	3252
18	Willimott: Andrew Beauchamp	Madras	1836	1411	3247
19	Hart: Sidney George	Bengal	1768	1478	3246
20	Allen: Edward Cuthbert	N.W. Provinces &c.	2041	1126	3167
21	Chand: Duvan Teh	N.W. Provinces &c.	1493	1634	3127
22	Webb: Charles Morgan	Burma	2173	947	3120
23	Hodson: Thomas Callan	Bengal	1796	1299	3095
24	Tylet: Hector Granville Sutherland	N.W. Provinces &c.	1693	1396	3089

G 100125

1900. Marriage solemnized at St. Peter's **in the** parish **of** Bournemouth **in the** County Borough **of** Bournemouth

No.	When Married	Name and Surname	Age	Condition	Rank or Profession	Residence at the time of Marriage	Father's Name and Surname	Rank or Profession of Father
10	Sept 18th 1900	Abdullah ibn Yusuf-Ali	28	Bachelor	Joint Magistrate Indian Civil Service	Rajur N W Provinces India	Khan Bahadur Yusuf Ali Jan	Municipal Indian Commissioner
		Teresa Mary Shalders	27	Spinster	—	Bru Holme Wollstone Park Road Bournemouth West	Isaac Noah Shalders	Gentleman

Married in the Church of St Peter according to the Rites and Ceremonies of the Church of England by Licence by me.

This Marriage was solemnized between us, { Abdullah ibn Yusuf-Ali / Teresa Mary Shalders } in the Presence of us, { Alice Mary Shalders / W. Scott Evans }

Henry Slater curate of Newcastle on Tyne

350992

<u>IN THE HIGH COURT OF JUSTICE</u>

<u>Probate Divorce & Admiralty Divi-
sion</u>

<u>(DIVORCE)</u>

YUSUF ALI

- v -

Yusuf Ali

&

Thorne.

- - - - - - - - - - -

P E T I T I O N

for Divorce.

--- - - - - - - - - - - - - -

13 APR. 1911

Lewis & Lewis,

Ely Place,

Holborn. E.C.

With Compliments

[signature]

14 Race Course Rd,
Lahore. Mar. 23, 1929

205

63. Peace through Religion
64. Do
65. Do
66. Do
67. Board Teachers' Conference, 9 Apr. 1937
68. Immature marriages
69. Prince of Yemen
70. Palestine (British)
71. Do
72. Do
73. Character
74. Harper House Conference
75. Adult Education
76. Do
77. St. John's Gate
78. Do
79. Palestine
80. Do   also 88
81. Sir Jagadis Bose
82. } Wayfarer Guild;
83. } cause & other
84. Adult Education
85. Palestine
86. Ramadhan / 3554. Poem
87. See 74
88. Palestine, 79-80
89. Id message
1938
90. Iqbal Day, Lahore
91. Lahore Music Concert
92. Export Day
93. Millet's Art

94. Punjab
95. Palestine ; Poem
96. Free Adult
97. Do , Photo
98. Govt House, Lucknow
99. Struggle of Belief
100. Congress of Faiths
101. Adult Education
102.} New Ideas in Educa.
103. }   Oxford
104. Sir Mohd Iqbal, d.
105. Reform & Reaction
106. Afghan Reception
107. Oerleds
108. Adult Education, 28 &
109. Cheap Power Develop...
110. Do   19.7.38
Back again to 1956-7?
1936
111. Education & Reform, Rotary 17.5.
112. Unemployment & Social
113. Italy & Abyssinia
114. Palestine Delegation
115. Faith & Fellowship - Bro. ?
116.} Ceylon Muslim
117.} Trovial. Conference
118. }
119. }
120. Do. Civil. College, Religion
121. Do
122. Do - leading Article
123. Do. Zahira Old Boys
124. Do. Arrival Photo
125. Do. First Sermon

We knew not the harbour at which we were bound;
We knew not the route by which we should go;
We sailed in the middle of a darkness profound,
Prepared for a booking ...

We carried our life-belts ever & anon,
walking & sitting, at meals & at play;
We manned our solitary nine-pounder gun;
And we watched fore & aft, by night & by day.

For a week we were lost to the world in a cloud,
A thousand poor souls, women, men, young & old,
In a sea reft of ships, which we stealthily ploughed
Without lights, without steam, with our story untold.

With a breath of relief, in the Fortunate Port
We anchored, & slowly with lights we did sail
Through the channel that links, East & West in a short
Silver stream, with old Sinai well within hail.

So here's to the ship with her fine gallant crew,
And here's to the Captain that prudently dared!
For we reach sunny shores, & we humbly renew
Our vow to our Flag, — to be true & prepared.

208

PERSONAL

11th December 1953

P.O. 2/53/29

My dear Mohammed Ali:

In continuation of my letter of yesterday regarding Allama Abdulla Yusuf Ali, I write to advise you with regret that the poor man died in hospital at eight last night. It pains me to think that so able and emminent a gentleman should have met with so pathetic an end.' May his soul rest in peace.

Sincerely yours,

M. A. Hassan Ispahani

M. A. H. Ispahani

The Hon'ble Mr. Mohammed Ali,
Prime Minister of Pakistan,
Karachi.

Appendix I

Yusuf Ali Bibliography

APPENDIX I

YUSUF ALI BIBLIOGRAPHY

This bibliography is in five parts. The **first** presents a chronological bibliography of the books, pamphlets, journal articles, book reviews, formal addresses and other literary works. The **second** part lists the editions, reprints and revisions of Yusuf Ali's translation and commentary of the Qur'an. The **third** and **fourth** parts include some reviews and citations. The **fifth** and final part documents the obituary notices on his death.

Part 1 - Chronological Bibliography

1900

A Monograph on Silk Fabrics produced in the North-Western Provinces and Oudh. Allahabad: N.W. Provinces and Oudh Government Press, 124pp.

1906

Civic Life in India. *Imperial and Asiatic Quarterly Review*, January-April, pp.225-248.

Goethe's Orientalism. *The Contemporary Review*, Vol.XC, August, pp. 169-181.

1907

The Indian Muhammadans: Their Past, Present and Future. *Journal of the Royal Society of Arts*, No. 2824, Vol. LV, 4 January.

Life and Labour of the People of India. London: John Murray, 360pp. Dedicated to Sir George Birdwood. Reprinted Lahore: al-Biruni, 1977.

1914

Indian Troops and Moneylenders (letter), *The Times*, 5 October.

Indian Bazaar Rumours (letter), *The Times*, 17 November.

1915

Work for India (letter), *The Times*, 11 June.

India's Services in the War. *Contemporary Review*, Vol.108, No.598, pp.446-456.

India's Rally round the Flag. *Asiatic Review*, Vol. 6, No. 13, pp.26-33.

1916

Our Immediate Future. *Hindustan Review*, Vol. 33, No. 197, January.

Town life in India: As seen in Lucknow. *Hindustan Review*, Vol.33, No.198, February, pp.126-141.

Lord Hardinge's Viceroyalty. *Nineteenth Century & After*, Vol.79, No.409, March, pp.703-716.

Mestrovic and Serbian Sculpture. Foreword by His Excellency M.Jovan M.Jovanovitch. London: Elkin Mathews, 31pp. (The Vigo Cabinet Series).

1917

India's Effort: Is It Sufficiently Understood? *Nineteenth Century & After*, Vol.81, No.480, February, pp.348-365.

Muhammad - A Towering Personality. *Islamic Review* (Woking), Vol. 5, Nos.2-3, February-March, pp.60-61.

Indian Labour in Tropical Australia (letter), *The Times*, 25 September.

The Type of Elijah, *Islamic Review* (Woking), Vol. 5, No. 12, December, pp.515-520.

The Imperial War Conference. *Hindustan Review*, Vol. 34, No. 216, pp. 97-100.

The Modern Hindustani Drama. *Transactions of the Royal Society of Literature*, Second Series, Vol.35, pp.79-99.

The Importance of Hindustani. *Bulletin of the School of Oriental Studies*, 1917.

1918

The Rowlatt Report (letter), *The Times*, 6 August.

India in Denmark (letter), *The Times Literary Supplement*, 19 September.

On Constantinople (letter), *The Times*, 29 November.

*Traek af Indien Kultur.*David Grunbaum, (ed.). Copenhagen: V.Pios Bog Handel-Povl Branner, 66pp. (Danish translation by L.C. Marten and D. Grunbaum of Yusuf Ali's lecture 'Features of Indian Culture').

India and the Empire. *Overseas*, Vol. 3, No. 25, pp.37-40.

1919

Peacock Throne (letter), *The Times*, 10 September.

1920

India since 1713. In H.C. Barnard,(ed.), *The Expansion of the Anglo-Saxon Nations: A Short History of the British Empire and U.S.*, London: Black.

1921

India and the League of Nations. *Contemporary Review*, Vol. 119, No. 665, pp.633-641.

Anglo-Muhammadan Law. by R.K. Wilson. 5th edition revised by Abdullah Yusuf Ali. Calcutta: Thacker & Spink, 573pp.

1923

The Self-Revelation of Babar. Lucknow: United Provinces Historical Society. The copy in the British Library, London, includes Yusuf Ali's handwritten note: 1927, 14 Race Course Road, Lahore. This is perhaps the date of publication.

Muslim Educational Ideals. Lahore: Muslim Outlook. Presidential address delivered at the Punjab Muslim Educational Conference.

1925

India and Europe: A Study of Contrasts, with a view to discovering avenues of cultural cooperation. London: Drane, 132pp.

The Making of India: a brief history. London: Black, 318pp. maps

Greatest Need of the Age (Progressive Islam Pamphlets No.1). The Progressive Islam Pamphlets were published by Luzac & Co., London, as well as by other publishers.

Khutba-e-sadarat, All-India Tanzim Conference, 29 December 1925. Urdu pamphlet (not dated, publisher not known). Photocopy obtained from Quaid-e-Azam Library, Lahore.

1926

Islam as a World Force. (Progressive Islam Pamphlets No.2). 43pp. Lahore: Anjuman-Himayat-ul-Islam.

Civics in Education and Practical Life. In J. E. Parkinson & R. H. Whitehouse (eds.), Proceedings of the Punjab Educational Conference and Exhibition (copy in Punjab Public Library, Lahore).

1927

Glimpses of the Punjab: A souvenir of the 14th meeting of the Indian Science Congress, held at Lahore in January. Edited by Abdullah Yusuf Ali and Charles Herbert Rice. Lahore: Indian Science Congress, 98pp., maps.

Three travellers to India. Lahore: M. Gulab Singh, 89pp. Account of India as seen by Yuan Chwang, Ibn Batuta and Francois Bernier

Al-Biruni's India, *Islamic Culture* (Hyderabad Deccan), pp. 31-35 (January), 223-230 (April), 473-487.

Article on 'Karamat Ali', *The Encyclopaedia of Islam*, Vol. II, Leyden, 1927, pp.752-754.

Article on 'Khodja', *The Encyclopaedia of Islam*, Vol. II, Leyden, 1927, pp.960-962.

1928

Social and Economic Conditions during the Middle Ages of Indian History, *Islamic Culture* (Hyderabad Deccan), pp. 360-375 (July)

Ameer Ali (obituary note), *The Times*, 6 August.

Indian Reform (letter), *The Times*, 16 November.

Education in India: the new outlook. *Nineteenth Century & After*, Vol. 104, No. 622, pp.745-756.

Outlines of Indian History. Lahore: Uttar Chand Kapur & Sons, 399pp. For the use of matriculation students in Indian high schools.

1929

The Fundamentals of Islam. (Progressive Islam Pamphlets No.3). 11pp. Also published in Sufi Quarterly (Geneva).

Personality of Muhammad. (Progressive Islam Pamphlets No.4). 23pp. A speech delivered in London at the Festival of 'Id-ul-Adha. (2nd. edition Lahore: M.Feroz-ud-din, 1931).

1930

Sir Thomas Arnold (obituary note), *The Times*, 13 June.

Moral Education (Progressive Islam Pamphlets No.5). Speech at the 5th International Moral Education Congress at the Sorbonne in September 1930.

The Position of Women under Muslim Law in India. In A. R. Caton (ed.), *The Key of Progress*. London: Oxford University Press, pp.94-97.

Anglo-Muhammadan Law. R. K. Wilson, 5th edition revised and brought up to date by Abdullah Yusuf Ali. Calcutta: Thacker & Spink.

Social and Economic life in Medieval India. *Islamic Culture* (Hyderabad Deccan), Vol. iv, pp.199-222.

1931

Personality of Man. (Progressive Islam Pamphlets No.6). 15pp. Hyderabad Deccan: Islamic Cultural Office. Also published in *Islamic Culture*, Hyderabad, Vol. v, October.

Imam Husain and his Martyrdom. (Progressive Islam Pamphlets No.7). 41pp. Lahore: M. Feroz-ud-din.

Hindustan ki tamaddun ki tarikh (preface dated September 1931). Urdu edition reprinted by Karimsons, Pakistan, 1967. (Translated into English as *A Cultural History of India during the British Period*, 1940. Translator not specified but the publisher's note suggests that it may have been Yusuf Ali).

1932

Dr Mackichan (obituary note), *The Times*, 12 April.

Medieval India: Social and Economic Conditions. London: Oxford University Press, 55pp. English translation of lectures in Urdu delivered at the Hindustani Academy, Allahabad, 1928 (Urdu text published in 1939).

1933

King Faisal of Iraq (letter), *The Times*, 11 September.

Religious Polity of Islam. (Progressive Islam Pamphlets No.8). 21pp. Hyderabad Deccan: Islamic Cultural Office. Also published in *Islamic Culture*, Hyderabad, Vol. vii.

Indian Reactions to the White Paper. *Asiatic Review*, Vol. 29, No.99, pp.411-434.

1934

First instalment of *The Holy Qur'an: An Interpretation in English, with Arabic text in parallel columns, a running rhythmic commentary in English and full explanatory notes.* (June).

Sir Frederic Lely (obituary note), *The Times*, 26 November.

Muhammad in History. (Progressive Islam Pamphlets No.9). 22pp. Markaz-i-Ishaat-i-Seerat; Jullindur City; Punjab. A speech delivered to the Muslim Club of Simla.

Beauties of the Qur'an. (Progressive Islam Pamphlets No.10). 16pp. Lahore: Khaliq Ahmed Faruqi, 16pp. Muslim Brotherhood Series No.6.

1935

Two parables from the Qur'an. *Islamic Review* (Woking), Vol. 23, No. 1, (January), pp.6-7.

On a pilgrimage to Mecca (article), *The Times*, 7 June. (This appeared in the early edition only; the British Library and the newspaper's own archives have only retained the 'Royal Edition' for the day, from which this article is absent).

Some Aspects of Local Government in Foreign Lands. Lahore: Local Self-Government Institute, 16pp. Inaugural address delivered to the students at Local Self-Government Institute, Punjab, at the opening meeting held on 30th October.

The Religion of Rabindranath Tagore. *Transactions of the Royal Society of Literature*, New Series, Vol. IX, Chapter V. Also published in *Islamic Culture*, Hyderabad, Vol. iv, 1930.

1936

Religion and Social Equality. *Islamic Review* (Woking), Vol.24, No. 9, (September), pp.342-347.

Presidential address to the Secondary Education Section of the All-India Muslim Conference, Rampur. This was published in the *Indian Journal of Education*, Volume 1, No. 5-6; May-June, pp.1-10.

Mustapha Kemal Ata-Turk (article), *Eastern Times*, Lahore, 3 June.

The Indian Theatre (book review), *Journal of the Central Asian Society*, October, pp.687-89.

The Universities of India (book review), *Journal of the Central Asian Society*, October, pp.689-90.

Ramadhan 1355 H. (poem), *Eastern Times* (Lahore), 15 November.

The Essential Basis of Religion. (World Fellowship through Religion Pamphlet No.1). 15pp. London: World Congress of Faiths.

Religion and Social Equality (Progressive Islam Pamphlets No.11).

Life and Literature. (Progressive Islam Pamphlets No.12). 18pp. Lahore: M.Feroz-ud-din. Summary of Punjab University Extension Lectures.

1937

Presidential address to the University Section of the All-India Muslim Educational Conference, Golden Jubilee Session, Aligarh, 27 March, 1937; pamphlet.

Presidential speech at the Second Annual Session of the Punjab Board Teachers' Union, Lahore, 3 April. Pamphlet printed at the Ripon Printing Press, Lahore.

Sayyid Shaheed Hadrath Imam Husain alayhis-salaam (article) *Masjid*, Lahore (Urdu weekly), 16 April.

The New Constitution in India (letter), *The Times*, 11 June.

The World's Need of Religion. Pamphlet published by the World Congress of Faiths for its conference held at Oxford, July.

Reform of Indian Education (letter), *The Times*, 24 August.

Sir Jagadis Bose (obituary note), *The Times*, 27 November.

Thirtieth and final instalment of *The Holy Qur'an: An Interpretation in English, with Arabic text in parallel columns, a running rhythmic commentary in English and full explanatory notes*. (December).

The Idea of God in Islam. (Progressive Islam Pamphlets No.13). 18pp. Lahore: Abdus Salam Khurshid.

1938

Palestine (poem), *The Mussalman*, Calcutta, 28 January.

Problems of adult education in India. World Association of Adult Education, Second Series, No. XII, February.

Adult Education. Two articles in *Hindustan Review*, February and April-May issues.

Sir Muhammad Iqbal (obituary note), *The Times*, 25 April.

Dr C. J. Goldsmid-Montefiore (obituary note), *The Times*, 16 July.

W. H. Moreland (obituary note), *The Times*, 4 October.

1939

Averroes: Philosopher of East & West. *Religions*, January, pp. 30-36. Quarterly published by Luzac, London.

The Glorious Future of the Muslims (book review), *Asiatic Review*, January.

Review of Sayyid Tufail Ahmed Manglori's *Hindustan mai musulmano ka raushan mustaqbil* - Islam in the world (book review), *Journal of the Royal Asiatic Society*, January.

The Idea of Salvation in Islam. (Progressive Islam Pamphlets No. 14). 15pp. February. Read before the London Society for the Study of Religion, 1 November 1938.

The Muslim World and Palestine. *The British Union Quarterly*, January-April, pp.54-59.

My Canadian Tour (articles). Three instalments in *Eastern Times*, Lahore, 24 March, 31 March, 7 April.

My *Mahboob* – Holy Prophet of Islam (article), *Eastern Times*, Lahore, 28 April.

The Prophet's Services to the Cause of Human Morality. *Islamic Review* (Woking), Vol. 27, No. 7, July, pp.245-247.

Sir Reginald Glancy (obituary note), *The Times*, 21 December.

Tarikh-i-hind kay azmana wusta mai ma'ashri aur iqtisadi halaat, Allahabad: Urdu Academy, 109pp. Three lectures presented to the Urdu Academy, 2-4 March 1928. (An earlier Urdu edition may have been published).

1940

The Muslims of India, The War and the Political Field. *Asiatic Review*, Vol. 36, pp.226-250, Lecture delivered before the East India Association, Caxton Hall, London, 6th February.

Lord Lamington (obituary note), *The Times*, 24 September.

The Somalis & their Religious Ideas. *Religions*, October.

Memories (poem), *Eastern Times*, Lahore, 4 October.

Comments on a paper by Sir Alfred Watson on the political situation in India, made at a meeting of the East India Association. *Asiatic Review*, Vol. 36, pp.74-75. The meeting took place on 8 December.

The Message of Islam. London: John Murray. (Wisdom of the East Series). 127pp. Comprises the rhythmic commentary from *The Holy Qur'an*. Also published in the United States by E.P. Dutton & Co.Inc. (New York), 1940.

A Cultural History of India during the British Period. Bombay: D.B.Taraporevala, 334pp.

India and the War. (British Information Series No.7). 16pp. Tokyo: British Embassy.

Adult education in India. *Journal of the Royal Society of Arts*, Vol. 88, No.4558, pp.482-495.

Doctrine of Human Personality in Iqbal's Poetry. *Transactions of the Royal Society of Literature*, New Series, Vol.XVIII, pp.89-106. Based on a lecture at the Society, 9 November, 1938.

1941

Indian Moslems – lesson of the Sudeten Germans (letter), *The Times*, 15 January.

Hellenic Culture and the Modern World. *Religions*, January.

Ethics and Totalitarianism. *South Place Ethical Society Monthly Recorder*, Red Lion Square, London, July, pp.8-9.

The University of Bombay (book review), *Religions*, July.

Islam and Japan (book review), *Religions*, October.

German air raids on London (poem), *Eastern Times*, Lahore, 21 November.

Muslim Cultural and Religious Thought. In L.S.S. O'Malley, (ed.).

Modern India and the West. London: Oxford University Press, pp. 389-414.

1942

Sir Francis Younghusband (obituary note), *The Times*, 4 August.

1943

'Id-ul-Fitr sermon, Woking. *Islamic Review*, Vol. 31, No. 2, (February), pp.100–101.

1944

Note on 'Islam', *Religions*, October, p.27. This short note is the last known published work of Yusuf Ali:

> In the second Sura of the Qur'an occurs this passage: Many People of the Book desire you to be unbelievers....but forgive them and avoid them. This implies that we are to entertain no personal rancour against those who do wrong, but for our own perfection [crossed out and overwritten 'protection'], we should shun their company, lest their example should affect us, consciously or unconsciously. A phrase frequently repeated in the Qur'an is: Shame in this world and a grievous punishment. 'Shame in this world' obviously means a deterioration of our social relations, which may affect us in many ways, including our social and economic position. 'Grievous punishment' implies something more definitely tangible, such as a fine or imprisonment, or even the ultimate penalty of death. But this would be exacted, not by the individual concerned, but by or through the State where a State exists.

The above note is one of the cuttings in the Yusuf Ali scrapbook in the author's possession. The replacement of the word 'perfection' with 'protection' was handwritten by Yusuf Ali.

Part 2 - The Qur'an

First edition

The Holy Qur'an: An Interpretation in English, with Arabic text in parallel columns, a running rhythmic commentary in English and full explanatory notes. Lahore: Shaikh Muhammad Ashraf, 1934–1937 (30 instalments, index).

Second edition

The Holy Qur'an: Consolidation of the 30 instalments into three volumes, with the original instalment covers retained within the body of each volume (second edition not explicitly stated).

Third edition

The Holy Qur'an – text, translation and commentary. Two-volume edition, leather cover with gold embossed lettering. Lahore: Shaikh Muhammad Ashraf, 1938. 1862pp. 14 appendices, index. An inside page contains the note: 'All rights, including rights of translation and reproduction reserved by A. Yusuf Ali'. Contains 'Preface to the Third Edition'; numerous reprints by Ashraf including 1943, 1969, 1973, 1979.

The Holy Qur'an, New York: Hafner Publishing Co., 1938.

The Holy Qur'an, New York: Hafner Publishing Co. 1946. Printed at the Murray Printing Company, Cambridge, Mass. Copyrighted 'Khalil ul-Rawaf'. The following note is included: '*Bismillahir-rahmanir-Rahim.* I have undertaken the publication of this magnificent translation of the Holy ul-Qur'an as rendered into English by Allama Abdullah Yusuf Ali in commemoration of the visit to the United States of America of the Saudi Delegation headed by His Excellency Sheikh Abdulla Es-Sulaiman El-Hamdan, Treasurer of the Royal Saudi Arabian Kingdom. Khalil ul-Rawaf (signed)'. There have been numerous reprints citing the 'ul-Rawaf' copyright.

The Meaning of the Illustrious Qur'an, Ashraf: Lahore, 1957. Without Arabic text and appendices.

The Holy Qur'an, Mecca: The Muslim World League, 1965.

The Holy Qur'an, Riyadh: Dar ul-Liwaa, 1966(?). Includes Sayyid Abul 'Ala Mawdudi's 'Introduction to the study of the Qur'an' in English and Arabic. Distributed by the Kingdom of Saudi Arabia General Presidency for Scientific Research, Ifta, Islamic Propagation and Guidance.

The Holy Qur'an, Beirut: Dar ul-Arabia, 1963. Reprint 1968.

The Holy Qur'an, Delhi: Kitab Publishing House, 1973 (a three-volume publication, likely third edition).

The Glorious Qur'an, Leicester: The Islamic Foundation in cooperation with the Muslim Student Association of the United States and Canada, 1975.

The Holy Qur'an, Beirut: Dar ul-Kitab ul-Lubnani, 1979. 'Printed under the auspices of late King Khaled Abdul Aziz of Saudi Arabia.'

The Holy Qur'an, Beirut: Dar ul-Qur'an ul-Karim, 1983.

The Holy Qur'an, Brentwood; Maryland: Amana Corporation, 1983. Copyright claimed by Amana Corporation. Distributed by the al-Rajhi Company, Saudi Arabia.

The Holy Qur'an, New Delhi: Nusrat Ali Nasri for Kitab Bhavan, 1987. This is a variation of the third edition, containing no commentary but only the English translation, the Arabic text and an interposed column of Roman transliteration.

Roman transliteration of the Holy Qur'an, New Delhi: Taj, 1990. English translation with Arabic text, but not the commentary. Some changes have been made to the translation, e.g. 'God' replaced by 'Allah'.

Amana/IIIT editions

The Holy Qur'an - text, translation and commentary, 'New Revised Edition'. Brentwood, Maryland: Amana Corporation, 1989; in cooperation with the International Institute of Islamic Thought (IIIT), United States of America.

This edition differs from the third edition, as it contains amendments to both the translation and commentary. The annotation 'eds.' or 'R' (revised) has been employed to indicate changes to the commentary and introductions to *surahs*, though not the translation. The editors responsible for the revision are not named though the Publisher's Note (unsigned) states that 'a number of committees reviewed all the responses carefully, examined the text meticulously, updated the material and refined the commentaries. The last complete review was undertaken by the late Ismail

226

Raji Faruqi...Amana Corporation and IIIT established an editorial board whose effort was to implement the final recommendations of the committees.'

Professor Hamidullah's misgivings about this initiative were reported in the Muslim press. He believed that altering an author's work without permission set a dangerous precedent: 'The right way would have been, in the cases of need, to reproduce the original text and add a footnote to say that the new editor suggests this or that word or opinion.' (*Impact International*, London, 18:22, 25 November 1988 - 8 December 1988).

The Meaning of The Holy Qur'an, 'New edition with revised Translation and Commentary', Maryland: Amana Corporation, 1992. The publisher's note is signed by Fakhri Al-Barzinji, President, Amana Corporation. A postscript, dated February 1991, includes the following clarification: 'We thank those readers of our 1409 AH/1989 AC edition who expressed concern over the use of the expression "New Revised Edition". In this edition we have removed the words "New Revised Edition" to avoid any misconceptions by our non-Muslim readers. This is therefore a new edition of the English *Meaning of the Holy Qur'an*, with revised translation and commentary.'

Both of the Amana/IIIT editions (1989, 1992) include a biographical note on Yusuf Ali with several errors. He is described as 'Dean of the Islamic College', presumably a reference to his principalship of Islamia College, Lahore. Moreover he died in London on 10 December 1953, not in Lahore in 1948.

The Amana/IIIT editions have replaced the Third Edition's use of 'Lord' or 'God' with 'Allah', and 'Apostle' with 'Messenger'. Yusuf Ali's use of the Roman system for numbering chapters of the Qur'an has also been updated. Extra material has been added to commentary notes, e.g. note 4927 refers to the United Nations.

Dar al-Ifta/King Fahd Holy Qur'an Printing Complex edition

The Holy Qur'an: English translation of the meanings and commentary, revised and edited by the Presidency of Islamic Researches, Ifta, Call and Guidance. Medina: King Fahd Holy Qur'an Printing Complex, 1990.

The cover page contains the following declaration: 'The custodian of the two holy mosques, King Fahd ibn Abdul Aziz Al-Saud, King of the Kingdom of Saudi Arabia, has the honour to order the printing of this Holy Qur'an and the translation of its meanings and commentary.'

The only reference to Yusuf Ali in this edition is in the preface note prepared by the Presidency: 'The translation by the late *Ustadh* Abdullah Yusuf Ali was consequently chosen [for a reliable translation] for its distinguishing characteristics, such as highly elegant style, a choice of words close to the meaning of the original text, accompanied by scholarly notes and commentaries.'

The changes are generally similar to those in the Amana Corporation edition though there are variations. The editors – unnamed – have not used any form of notation to indicate changes made. In addition to the appendices absent from the Amana/IIIT editions (Allegorical interpretation of the Story of Joseph; Mystic interpretation of the Verse of Light; The Muslim Heaven), the following are also excluded: Egyptian chronology and Israel; Egyptian religion and its steps towards Islam; Who was Dhu al-Qarnain?; Ancient forms of pagan worship. The Preface and rhythmic commentary of the original have also been removed. There are some oversights – for example the chapters have been re-numbered with the Arabic system but cross-references to them in the commentary notes still use the Roman system. The removal of cross-references to appendices has also left some commentary notes incomprehensible e.g. note 5721. Yusuf Ali's reference to the 'imprudence of *Hadrath* Aisha' in commentary note 5529 has also been removed.

A note on the Amana/IIIT and Ifta/King Fahd Complex editions

In 1980, the World Assembly of Muslim Youth (WAMY) established a committee comprising Professor Muhammad Mustafa Azmi, Dr Jaafer Shaikh Idris and Professor Zafar Ishaq Ansari to select and where necessary revise an appropriate English translation of the Qur'an. The committee's choice was Yusuf Ali, and a revision of the third edition was prepared by them but not published. The Qur'an Centre in Medina (King Fahd Holy Qur'an Printing Complex) and Dar al-Ifta in 1983-1984 called on additional scholars, including Saleem Kayani representing Dar al-Ifta, to continue and complete the committee's work. These cumulative revisions were the starting point for both the Amana Corporation and Dar al-Ifta editions. The former published the material in 1989. Dar al-Ifta however continued with revision work, with the assistance of scholars including Dr Syed Mutawalli ad-Darsh and Suhaib Husain, resulting in the Dar al-Ifta/King Fahd Holy Qur'an Printing Complex edition (1990).

Translation of the Amana (1989) edition

Al-Qur'anu 'l-Karim: Terjemahan dan hurain maksud (Bahasa Malaysia) by Abu Salah Muhammad Uthman El-Muhammady, Dewan Bahasa dan Pustaka, Kementerian Pendidikan Malaysia, Kuala Lumpur, 1992-1993 (publication in instalments).

Translation includes the commentary notes and rhythmic commentary. Though adhering to the Amana edition, the translator regrets the absence of the appendices and other exclusions: 'If the late Allama were still alive, those are the last matters that he would allow to be excluded from his commentary.'

Part 3 - Reviews and Citations relating to Yusuf Ali's Qur'anic scholarship

Asiatic Review, October 1939.

Review by Sir Abdul Qader with the title 'The East interpreted to the West': 'This translation, as Mr Yusuf Ali tells us in his Preface, has been a dream of his for years and is the result of a prolonged study and research. It has taken years to complete, but the writer has the satisfaction of feeling that his labours have received a wide appreciation and that he will be long remembered by his work, which may be regarded as his magnum opus.'

The Muslim World, Vol. 30, 1940, pp. 54-66, 1940.

Review by Arthur Jeffrey who notes: 'the translator is an Indian Muslim from the North [*sic*], English-educated, who has spent a great deal of his active life in the West.'

Times of India, Bombay, 28 June.

Review of *The Message of Islam* (1940) which comprised Yusuf Ali's rhythmic commentary only. The reviewer 'A.A.A.F.' - possibly Fyzee - observes: 'the teaching of the Qur'an has been offered to the layman in language of such distinction and felicity that many a passage keeps ringing in our ears.'

Asiatic Review, July 1940.

Review of *The Message of Islam* by Edward Maclagan.

The Muslim World, Vol. 31, 1941.

Review of *The Message of Islam* by Edward J. Jurji.

A Discussion of the Errors of Yusuf Ali, Majlisul-Ulema of South Africa, Transvaal: Young Men's Muslim Association (undated).

This is a 96-page polemic severely critical of Yusuf Ali's Qur'anic scholarship, particularly references to Paradise and Hell as 'symbolic'.

The Muslim World League Journal, Mecca, February 1985.

Article by A.R. Kidwai, 'Abdullah Yusuf Ali's views on the Qur'an Eschatology'.

Le Saint Coran, Muhammad Hamidullah, Brentwood; Maryland: Amana Corporation, 1985.

A list of translations of the Qur'an refers to Yusuf Ali's translation-cum-commentary and cites some reprints. Professor Hamidullah is in error in specifying his year of death as 1952 (it was 1953).

World bibliography of translations of the meaning of the Holy Qur'an - printed translations 1515-1980, (ed.) I. Binark & H. Eren, Istanbul: Research Centre for Islamic History, Art and Culture, 1986.

Contains a comprehensive list of the various editions and reprints of Yusuf Ali's Qur'anic work.

Muslim World Book Review, Leicester, Vol.12, No.2, 1992.

Review by A. R. Kidwai of the Amana Corporation (1989) and Ifta/King Fahd Complex (1990) editions. While the merits of the original are acknowledged ("a highly readable paraphrase of the Arabic text in chaste, idiomatic English") the reviewer is generally appreciative of the revisions: 'Yusuf Ali's work now stands almost completely free of the author's apologetic, pseudo-rational and too much *tasawwuf*-oriented notes.'

Muslim & Arab Perspectives, Issue No.1, October 1993, Delhi.

Article by S. A. Hasan Rizvi, 'Some errors in Abdullah Yusuf Ali's English translation of the Holy Qur'an'.

Part 4 - Other reviews and citations

The Times Literary Supplement, 22 March 1907.

Review of *Life and Labour of the People of India*.

The Times Literary Supplement, 5 September 1918.

Review of *Traek af Indien Kultur*.

India at the Death of Akbar by W.H. Moreland, London: Macmillan & Co., 1920.

Preface expresses gratitude to Yusuf Ali.

The Times Literary Supplement, 3 December 1925

Review of *The Making of India*.

The Agrarian System of Modern India by W.H. Moreland, Cambridge: W.Heffer, 1929.

Preface states: 'I have drawn freely on some unpublished notes written in consultation with Mr A. Yusuf Ali when we worked together some years ago on the authorities for the reign of Akbar.'

The Statesman, Calcutta, 13 October 1940

Review of *A Cultural History of India during the British Period*.

Asiatic Review, January 1941.

Review by C. Colin Davies of *A Cultural History of India during the British Period*.

Historians of India, Pakistan and Ceylon by C.H. Philips, London: Oxford University Press, 1961.

Reference to *The Making of India* (1925). Philips observes that seventy-four books are listed by Yusuf Ali 'for further study' but these include no work by a contemporary Muslim except for Ameer Ali's biography of the Prophet.

The Indian Civil Service by L.S.S. O'Malley, London: Frank Cass, 1965.

Reference to *Life and Labour of the People of India* (1907).

The Sword and the Spectre edited by Riffat Hassan, Lahore: Iqbal Academy, 1977.

A chapter by Sir Abdul Qader on Iqbal contains a reference to Yusuf Ali's paper 'Doctrine of Human Personality in Iqbal's Poetry' (lecture to the Royal Society of Literature in 1938). Abdul Qader also contributed on Iqbal in *Great Men of India*, (undated, but 1985 reprint), editor L.F. Rushbrook-Williams, Delhi: Gian Publishing House, in which there are quotations from this paper.

Islamic Spirituality edited by S.H. Nasr, London: Routledge Kegan Paul, 1987.

Reference to *Personality of Muhammad* (1929).

Part 5 - Obituary notices on Yusuf Ali

The Times, 15 December 1953

The Daily Telegraph, 17 December 1953

Radio Pakistan, Lahore (undated), but reprinted in the Urdu daily *Iqdam*, Lahore, 27 December 1953.

Islamic Literature, Lahore, Vol. VI, No. 1, January 1954. Editorial by Shaikh Muhammad Ashraf, publisher of *The Holy Qur'an – text, translation and commentary*. Shaikh Ashraf included the following observations: 'Literature and art, painting and sculpture, law and constitution, religion and education, philosophy and history, economics and politics, all were included in his many-sided interests and pursuits, and his versatile genius was manifest in everything that sprouted from his powerful pen. Dr. Ali Hassan Abdel Kader, Director of London's Islamic Cultural Centre, who was a close friend and collaborator of Yusuf Ali for many years, said: "This is a great loss for English-speaking Muslims and Islam generally. There is no doubt he was the greatest translator of the Holy Qur'an in modern times. I consider his English version the only authoritative one" '.

Islamic Culture, Hyderabad Deccan, Vol XXVIII, No. 1, January 1954. Poem in memory of Yusuf Ali by Nawab Sir Nizamat Jung. There is also an obituary note by Professor Abdur Rahman Khan, former principal of Osmania College, which includes this reference to Yusuf Ali's Qur'anic scholarship: 'He has won enduring fame through the publication of an excellent translation of the Holy Qur'an which reproduces the sacred text together with valuable notes and commentary (based, it is said, largely on Shah Abdul Qadir Sahib Dehlavi's standard translation and other works of repute). It is the favourite reading of numerous English scholars and the late Sir Dennison Ross, Director of the School of Oriental Studies, London, was of the opinion that "the whole presentation is superior to any that has appeared hitherto"'.

The Islamic Review, Woking, February 1954, pp.35-37.

Extracts from *The Times* obituary, but with the significant additional information that Yusuf Ali had been a trustee of the Shah Jahan Mosque, Woking.

Appendix II

Selected Writings

APPENDIX II

SELECTED WRITINGS

The selection below spans a forty-year literary career and includes previously unpublished material. The aim is to provide source material that is representative of Yusuf Ali's beliefs and interests at various points of his life.

1906

> This contribution at the age of thirty-three was his first in a leading British learned journal and confirmed him as a young man of great promise. Goethe held a fascination for Western-educated Indians of the period, perhaps because his *Western-Eastern Divan* showed an empathy with Hafiz and Saadi. Yusuf Ali presented this as an example of Goethe's 'orientalism'. The extract below shows the idealistic thinking of the young Yusuf Ali, and in particular his knowledge of esoteric orders.

The finest fruit of the genius of the German people is Goethe. This is not a point that anyone will controvert. The German language, German art, German theology. German strategy, German education, German industry, German music and German philosophy will all have their detractors and defenders. But Goethe stands in the serene regions above prejudices and above differences of opinion. He is not the heritage of Germany only. Like our Shakespeare, he is the heritage of the world. And yet in attaining this airy height he used as stepping stones his German language and the stock of ideas which had been accumulating in his fatherland, waiting for the master-genius to weave them into the finished fabric. No man can create unless he also interprets, nor reap a bountiful harvest unless he sows with seed carefully selected and garnered by those who went before him.

Can we trace a note of Orientalism in the German echoes and ideas which led up to the Goethe harmony?

Yes; in two ways. First, the spirit of the German race has ever moved in an expanding, all-embracing dream of universality. Secondly, that spirit was already taking shape in diverse forms in the age which led up to Goethe, the age whose zeitgeist Goethe partly resisted, partly tamed to his own ideals. When we have considered these, we shall be in a position to consider the spirit of Orientalism in Goethe as an individual.

...Should Charlemagne be regarded as a German or a French hero? His spirit haunts both Aachen and Ingelheim, that spacious Rhineland which concealed for centuries the Rhine-gold, and gave birth to Goethe. His sway extended from the Ebro to the Elbe, and under his aegis met peoples of many tongues and nationalities. He exchanged salutations with the ambassadors of the far-famed Harun al-Rashid in 798. Thus the first German 'Western-Eastern Divan' was not suggested by Goethe's reading of Von Hammer on his visit to the Rhine in 1815. Its seeds were sown in German history by another hero of the Rhineland more than a thousand years earlier!

The Holy Roman Empire of the German Nation was nothing but an attempt to maintain politics on a basis of universality and idealism, the twin rocks on which the medieval Orient, not less than medieval Germany, shattered its politics to atoms - the twin anchors on which German thought, like Eastern thought in its best days, sought safety against the seething billows of narrow interests, selfish aims and barren, bigoted sectarianism. The apparent failure in politics led to greater freedom for the soul, maturer development for the higher faculties of man. Action can only be effective in proportion as it recognises the unity of human hopes with Divine guidance, the merging of the human destiny in the Divine will, the magic transformation of even this world of ours, with its errors and its sorrows, into very Paradise, where the shadows are removed by the beneficent rays that proceed from the countenance of God.

All this is Oriental mysticism, you will say. What if I show it be good German theology, true blue? The 'Theologia Germanica' is a devotional book well known and widely read in Germany. The name of its author is unknown, but it is supposed to have been written by a knight of the

Teutonic Order some time about 1350. No less a judge than Luther valued it next to the Bible and so did St Augustine, and in respect to St Augustine it must be remembered that Luther was an Augustinian monk. It breathes the spirit of German liberty, and the fact that the great leader of the Protestant Reformation stood sponsor to it is sufficient to stamp it as a representative of the innermost spiritual thought of Germany. It says in the 50th Chapter:

> What is Paradise? All things that are; for all are goodly and pleasant, and therefore may fitly be called a Paradise. It is said also that Paradise is an outer court of Heaven. Even so this world is verily an outer court of the Eternal.

A simple argument, and one near akin to that of the Sufis of Persia, though not so elaborately worked out...

It was not France only which was shaken to its foundations by a revolution in the eighteenth century. In Germany there was an equally far-reaching revolution in thought during the whole of the eighteenth century compared to which the so-called re-awakening of Germany in the nineteenth century was a mere episode in the long process of the ploughing of the land, and the sowing, maturing and reaping of the corn. This German revolution took different channels in different directions, but the governing force of it all was the love of the beautiful in art, which may be called Classicism, the yearning after the unknown and the universal which may be called Mysticism, and the detachment from the present and the actual in search of the free and the ideal, which was labelled later on with the name of Romanticism. Now the Mysticism and the Romanticism, looked at from another point of view, may be called Orientalism. What was it that stirred Winckelmann (1717-68) to throw such a passionate, personal and poetical note into his 'History of Ancient Art' (1764), but an intense realisation of the grand emotions of the ancients in modern life, and a glorification of art as the emblem of truth and all that stirs the human soul? This turned him into a Roman Catholic in religion and an Italian in domicile, and if we use these words in a somewhat wide significance, looking merely into the essence and not at the outward and visible forms, we find that the statement applies to the choicest spirits of the age, including even Goethe. Catholic, Italian, pagan, Hellenist, Mystic, Oriental – words connoting widely different ideas and in some cases contradictory views of life – become confounded or unified, as body or spirit, nature and God become confounded or unified in the twilight dreams of Pantheism...The secret orders like the Illuminati, the Rosicrucians and the Freemasons flourished, even as the Ikhwan-us-Safa (the Brethren of Purity) flourished in the city of Basra, the Weimar of Arabian literature, in the tenth century, not for convivial gatherings or political objects, but for the advancement of science, the cultivation of art, the regeneration of society in an earnest, enthusiastic appeal to an intellectual hierarchy. Goethe himself was a Freemason and believed in the spread of culture by means of secret societies, to which admission was to be by strict selection and after a searching probation, and in which the grades and degrees were determined by character and virtue.

Extract from 'Goethe's Orientalism', The Contemporary Review, Vol. XC, August 1906.

1906

> On 13 December, 1906, Yusuf Ali presented an award-winning paper at the Royal Society of Arts, London, on 'The Indian Muhammadans: their Past, Present and Future'. He took great pains to demonstrate that Indian Muslims faced no conflict of loyalty in choosing between Empire and Islam.

It is necessary, even to this day, to clear away the prejudices and inconsistencies that attach to the Muhammedan position in connection with the *Wahhabi* movement in India. The Indian apostle of the movement was Sayyid Ahmed of Bareilly, who proclaimed a *Jihad* on the North-West Frontier in 1830 and was slain in 1831. This Sayyid Ahmed is in no way to be confounded with Sir Sayyid Ahmed Khan of Aligarh: the two men were poles apart. The *Wahhabi* movement, in its earliest phases in India, had two aspects, the religious and the political.

The religious aspect was the more important of the two, and has proved to be the more permanent. In this aspect Wahhabism aimed at going back to the pristine simplicity of Islam and sweeping away the accretions (such as reverence shown to *tazias*, graves of ancestors and saints) which have grown up in India. It also questioned the authority of interpreters of the Sacred Book, and would substitute a plain and simple appeal to the sources of the Law rather than to the network of glosses and analogical systems founded upon it. Put in this abstract way, it could justly be called the extreme Evangelical School in Islam, and has many of the characteristics of evangelical schools and revivals elsewhere. The spirit in which it was preached was that of hostility and an uncompromising attack on the existing order of things, and therefore, the majority of Indian Muhammedans have always rejected it not only with scorn, but with something of the bitter rancour which is always called forth in religious controversies. In orthodox circles the name *Wahhabi* became a term of abuse of even a deeper dye than 'atheist' or 'unbeliever'. The *Wahhabis* as a religious sect in India are now of little importance but their religious fervour has stirred the more orthodox schools to set their own houses in order. A number of new and liberal movements in Muslim theology have sprung up, of which as yet we are only seeing the early beginnings.

The political aspect of *Wahhabism* never appealed to even an appreciable section of the Indian Muhammedans. It arose to a considerable extent from a misappreciation of the lessons to be learned from the twelve centuries of Muhammedan history which had already witnessed the rise and fall of many ideas. These ideas had failed, when translated into facts, to realise the ideal brotherhood of mankind. The further century which has since elapsed has added a more conclusive chapter of warnings against the thoughtless admission of the foul and tainted exhalations of rough-and-tumble politics to what should be the pure and serene atmosphere of religious peace and freedom. The original relation of Church and State at the birth of Islam was so close that the term Erastian [belief in the supremacy of state in ecclesiastical matters] has been applied to the Muslim idea of Church; it would be more correct to say that the Muslim conception of State was theocratic. This conception, unredeemed by the conditions which originally gave it reality, colours the schemes of visionaries who do not learn wisdom from the lessons of history. The *khalifa*, abstract and elective, is the counterpart of the Stoic's perfect man. What a cruel mockery then to dispute, on the religious plane, about the merits of a concrete embodiment which may be a negation of all the virtues postulated! Nor is the spectacle edifying when we see a man claiming to guide events which he does not understand, and hurling anathemas at the heads of other men of similar pretensions. It may be said that the collective conscience of Islam, though it has never formulated the doctrine in plain terms, has come to recognise that it tends to higher nobler spirituality in religion and greater strength in politics to conceive of the *mujtahid* of the age, or several *mujtahids*, – to adopt a term which Akbar sought to apply to himself – as a personality distinct from the king or leader who uses judicial force for the suppression of anti-social force. This lesson has been specially, if unconsciously, brought home to the Indian Muslims. Even the small following which adopted the religious views of *Wahhabism* has practically repudiated its political corollaries. The sect has already split into two. One portion openly and professedly reject the dangerous doctrines of *Jihad*, and the other hedge them round so many qualifications that for practical purposes they may be considered now to hold the same political views as the rest of their co-religionists in India. These sects are principally found in Bengal, and the last census report of the province gives an excellent account of the practical trend of their doctrines. The orthodox schools (*Sunni* and *Shia*) have always opposed the ultra-dogmatic tenets of *Jihad*, by means of numerous *Fatwas* and authoritative opinions.

I have lingered so long on this matter in order to show that there is nothing either in the religion or the history of the Indian Mussalmans to prevent them from taking an honourable place as citizens in a free and progressive Empire. As to their relations with the British Government, they have tended more and more, with recent times, towards cordiality. His Highness the Nizam has always been a faithful ally of the British power but never have his relations with that power been more cordial than they are now. The recent abolition of quarantine at Bombay for the pilgrimage to Mecca has brought solace to many a devout Muslim who had never heard and who never cared about the controversies in a certain portion of North Eastern India. The statesmanlike reply of the Earl of Minto to the

Simla delegation in October, and the speeches of Sir Arthur Lawley, have further helped forward the rapprochement. The way seems now clear for a strong united patriotic party, based not on sectarianism or religious differences, but in a steadfast and manly recognition of all the best interests of India.

For it must be insisted upon that the Muslim position is not grounded upon a blind and implacable hatred of the Hindus or any other class of His Majesty's subjects. A foundation of hatred or hostility can never support an edifice of national life and would be subject to sudden earthquakes when the forces of disorder are let loose. But moral courage, a happy combination of independence and discipline, a directness of aims, and above all, truth, integrity, and loyalty, are the factors which help forward orderly and sustained progress.

Extract from 'The Indian Muhammadans: their past, present and future', Journal of the Royal Society of Arts, No. 2824, Vol. LV, January 1907.

1915

> Throughout the First World War, Yusuf Ali tried hard to make Britain more aware of Indian efforts and sacrifices for the Empire. To a large extent the British press underplayed India's contribution. This extract is from an article entitled 'India's Services in the War', which Yusuf Ali wrote for *The Contemporary Review* of London. It has been selected firstly for the graphic description of the Indian military contribution in the crucial opening months of the War, and secondly for portraying the expectations of political reform in India in recognition of her sacrifices.

Great Britain declared war on Germany on August 4th, 1914, and on September 26th, or little more than seven weeks after the declaration, the first batch of the Indian Expeditionary Force had landed in France. The journey from the military centres in Upper India to the coast and thence to France in troopships would ordinarily take from three to four weeks. The promptness of the response was remarkable, considering the time it must have taken to arrive at a decision about the participation of the Indian troops in the conflict in Europe, the move from the interior to the sea-coast in India, the fitting-out of the transports, the embarkation, the rough weather accompanying the retreat of the monsoons, the long voyage, with German cruisers still at large, and the smooth debarkation without a single casualty among the troops. The feat was only rendered possible by the effective command of the seas by Great Britain. The rapid movements of the *Emden* in the Bay of Bengal in September may possibly have been connected with a mission of destruction (happily baulked) of much more sinister import than the sinking of cargo ships and the shelling of the town of Madras.

The Indian Army is an army of long service men, and is always ready for mobilisation at very short notice. This state of constant preparedness is an asset of the utmost value to the defence of the Empire for in modern warfare time is of the essence of the struggle. It is a trite saying that India saved Natal in the Boer War; her effective assistance was possible on account of her constant preparedness, although Indian troops were not actually permitted to fight in South Africa. The next Colonial troops to arrive in Europe were the Canadians, who landed in England on October 16th. Their magnificent achievements are a source of pride to the whole Empire, but they were a new Army and had to undergo a course of preliminary training in England before they were ready to take their place in the battle line.

The Indian Expeditionary Force landed complete in every detail - ammunition columns, mule, supply and transport, batteries and sappers. After a very short rest they went straight into the firing line. The first month of the war had been characterised by the tremendous impetuosity of the German onrush through Belgium and Northern France, the tide had decidedly turned, and the wave of invasion had been rolled back from the Marne. By the middle of September they had taken up entrenched positions on the Aisne, in which, with few changes, they have practically remained on the defensive ever since. The arrival of the Indian troops synchronised with the German onslaught towards Antwerp and the Belgian coast. The allies gradually lengthened out their line in Northern France. Thereafter the German fury in the West appears chiefly to have been directed towards the Calais objective. In October and November there was heavy fighting in the coastal region on the frontiers of France and

Belgium, as the result of which the hope of the German attempt on Calais was finally wrecked. It was in this critical phase of the fighting that the Indians had their baptism of fire in Europe, and it is in this region that their principal activities have since had scope. Their arrival in the Concentration Area in the middle of October relieved the German pressure south of Lyse and gave much needed rest to their British comrades, who had sustained a gallant fight for weeks against a numerically superior enemy. Ypres, Hollebeke, Festubert, La Bassée and Neuve Chapelle are now classical names in Indian history, and stir the same pride in Indian minds as Blenheim, Ramillies, Oudenarde and Malplaquet stirred in the minds of Englishmen in the reign of Queen Anne.

The camaraderie of the Indian soldiers with their British confrères has been mentioned in the letters of soldiers from the front, both British and Indian. Battalions of British troops from India are brigaded with Indian troops in the Indian Corps, as well as English Territorials. I have met British soldiers, on short leave from the front, returning with quite a collection of watches, electric torches, and trinkets for their 'Indian comrades' in the battle line. More than one British unit can recall instances of Indian soldiers unable to rejoin their own units after confused night-fighting, enjoying the hospitality of their comrades and living and fighting with them for a week or more.

The work of the Indian Expeditionary Force divides itself into three periods. First came their heavy exertions when they were new to their surroundings, in October and November, in co-operating to foil finally the German menace to Calais. They bore their part splendidly, winning two Victoria Crosses. The first Victoria Cross won by an Indian soldier went to Sepoy Khudadad Khan, of the 129th (Duke of Connaught's Own) Baluchis, a Punjabi Mussalman from Jhelum District, who was the sole survivor of a machine section and continued to work his gun till the last possible moment in spite of his severe wounds (Hollebeke, October 31st, 1914). The second Victoria Cross went to Naik Darwan Singh Negi, of the 39th Garhwal Rifles who, wounded in head and arm, continued to face bomb and rifle fire at close range, and did not report himself wounded till after the trenches had been won (Festubert, night of November 23rd-24th, 1914). In the fight of November 2nd Gurkhas had to meet a furious enemy bombardment with enormous shells filled with high explosives. When all their British officers were killed or wounded, the Gurkha officers continued to lead their men with cool courage and determination. Their scouting was particularly good, and the Indian Sappers and Miners skilfully met the enemy's strokes with effective counterstrokes, filling in saps and destroying traverses. Field-Marshal Sir John French thus describes the work of the Indian troops in his Despatch dated November 20th, 1914:

> Since their arrival in this country and their occupation of the line allotted to them, I have been much impressed by the initiative and resource displayed by the Indian troops. Some of the ruses they have employed to deceive the enemy have been attended with the best results, and have doubtless kept superior forces in front of them at bay.

> The Corps of Indian Sappers and Minders have long enjoyed a high reputation for skill and resource. Without going into detail, I can confidently assert that throughout their work in this campaign they have fully justified that reputation.

> The General Officer-Commanding the Indian Army Corps describes the conduct and bearing of these troops in strange and new surroundings to have been highly satisfactory, and I am enabled, from my own observation, to fully corroborate his statement.

The second phase included the extremely trying period of the latter half of December, including the loss of Givenchy on December 20th, its recapture the same day, and the retirement from Givenchy on December 21st. The weather had been getting more and more unfavourable for the Indian troops, but they stood the strain with uncomplaining patience and exemplary constancy. They were inspected on December 1st by the King-Emperor and the Prince of Wales, who saw a heavy battery in action. After two-and-a-half months' hard fighting they needed some rest, which really only meant exercise and preparation out of the trenches, for fresh efforts in relief of other troops when their turn came. Sir John French in his despatch dated February 2nd, 1915, remarks:

The Indian troops have fought with the utmost steadfastness and gallantry whenever they have been called upon.

In the same despatch he writes about the Indian Cavalry Corps:

I saw the whole of the Indian Cavalry Corps, under Lieutenant-General Remington, on a mounted parade soon after their arrival. They are a magnificent body of cavalry, and will, I feel sure, give the best possible account of themselves when called upon. In the meantime, at their own particular request, they have taken their turn in the trenches and performed most useful and valuable service.

The third phase opens with returning spring, and the resumption of activity in a heavy British bombardment with eighteen-pounders. Early in March was fought the engagement of 'Glorious Neuve Chapelle', whose casualties filled the Indian hospitals in this country, but whose echoes still resound wherever the deeds of Indian soldiers are recounted. Neuve Chapelle had already been the site of desperate conflicts between Indians and Germans in October. On March 10th, 1915, Neuve Chapelle was completely captured, and the third Indian Victoria Cross was won by Rifleman Gobar Singh, of the 39th Garhwal Rifles (the second Victoria Cross for the same regiment within four months), who boldly entered enemy trenches with bayonet and bombs, and won them at the cost of his life. Again in April there were many honours won, including a Victoria Cross (the fourth to be won by an Indian), which fell to Jemadar (since promoted Subadar) Mir Dast, of the 55th (Coke's) Rifles, attached to the 57th (Wilde's) Rifles, for conspicuous bravery. Amid a tornado of fire - shrapnel, machine-gun, rifle, and high explosive shells filled with asphyxiating gas - he led his platoon with the greatest gallantry in attack, and subsequently brought in eight wounded British and Indian officers. His calm heroic figure, in a Brighton hospital for wounded, on his way to recovery from wounds and asphyxiating gas, made an impression that makes one proud to be an Indian.

The heroism of the Indian soldiers is matched by that of the Indian camp followers. There is no boast or swagger about them. Some of them even look frail, shrinking individuals, but when in a position of danger their courage has been tested and found to be of the very highest order times out of number. The Kahars and stretcher-bearers attached to field hospitals, the Syces of the Indian Cavalry, the sweepers, Bhishtis (water-carriers), cooks, and mess servants, who lay no claim to valour or glory as they quietly go about their ordinary avocations with shells bursting all about them, have shown unflinching courage in many battle-fields, and saved valuable lives by their plucky resource. No story of Indian troops can be complete without a word of recognition for these humble, but brave, men who in the most matter-of-fact way uphold the name of India.

This war has taught us more geography than we ever learnt at school or college. But it has opened the door of knowledge in a far more important direction. It has brought self-revelation and the inner appreciation of others, which can only come in great crises. Great Britain is no longer spiritually an island. She understands – or ought to understand, herself, her Empire, her Allies, and her friends, in those subtle human relationships which defy outward differences of race, climate, and history. We have probably not heard the last of those who tell us that India is held by the sword, but there should be a keener realisation of Lord Curzon's epigram that the sword is two-thirds forged of Indian metal. In the new vision of a free united Empire, India will claim a place of equality in Council and Camp. Her soldiers are soldiers of the King; they will not be satisfied until the King's Commissions entitle them to lead in war as faithfully and gallantly as they have hitherto followed.

Extract from 'India's Services in the War', The Contemporary Review, Vol. 108, No. 598, pp.446-456.

1917

> India not only contributed to the Great War militarily but also financially. Even less is known about this facet of the colonial experience than the military contribution described in the preceding piece. Yusuf Ali was in his element discussing government financing of the war effort.

In appraising India's financial contribution to the War some very important considerations have to be borne in mind. A rich man's life is worth no more to him than a poor man's life. A man can show no greater love or loyalty than this, that he die for his brother. India has shed freely of the blood of her sons in far-off lands which the Indian countryside had not even heard of before. Indians have given freely their personal services: the grievance is that so many offers were and are rejected. When it comes to hard cash India's levy must be judged, not by absolute figures, but by the standard of her wealth and capital as compared with those of other parts of the Empire. A poor man by the wayside, offering to share his crust of stale bread with one in need, is making a far greater sacrifice than the rich man who writes out a cheque for £100 for the Red Cross Fund, the millionaire who combines patriotism with 5 per cent., or the industrial magnate who battens on excess profits after paying a duty of 60% to the Chancellor of the Exchequer.

The dazzling gifts in cash and kind poured into the War pool of the Allied cause and into the War charities and loans by the Indian Princes and magnates, the Indian provinces, cities, and corporate bodies, must not blind us to the fact – the ever-insistent fact in peace and war – that the mass of the people live in extreme poverty, and have no reserves to tide them over difficult times.

Sir Robert Giffen estimated the income of the larger units of the British Empire for the British Association of 1903 as follows, in millions of pounds sterling:

	£
United Kingdom	1750
India	600
Canada	270
Australia	210
South Africa	100

I know that the figure for India has been challenged, but Sir Robert Giffen's statistical accuracy stands beyond dispute, and he had no political or economic axe to grind. If we divide the figures by the population according to the census of 1901 we get the following figures of average incomes per head in the different countries at the date of Sir Robert Giffen's calculation:

	£
United Kingdom	42
India	2
Canada	50
Australia	41
South Africa	38

The South African average would, of course, be higher if we took into account only the population of European descent. We may roughly say that the per capita income in the United Kingdom and Dominions is about £40 to £50, and the per capita income in India is only about 1/21 of this figure. This proportion also roughly corresponds to the ratio of the wages of an unskilled labourer in the two economic spheres respectively. The capital per head as derived from the same authority's figures works out to £10 for India and £361 for the United Kingdom, and the disparity from that point of view is 1/36.

In any reasonable scheme of taxation according to ability, the principle of graduation is now recognised, so that persons with large incomes do not pay the same rate of taxation, but higher and higher rates as the size of the income increases. There is, moreover, an exemption limit recognised, below which no direct tax is demanded, as the limit is supposed to mark the figure at which the income just barely covers the cost of decent living and leaves no margin of superfluity. If these principles are applied in the comparison of British and of Indian incomes it will at once be perceived that the vast body of the latter will be ruled out for taxation or contribution purposes as below the taxation fringe. The remainder will come under lower rates on a graduated scale than British incomes, and therefore under a single scheme of taxation, Indian incomes would be assessed at much lower average rates than would British incomes.

The Indian income tax is not levied on land, as there is a separate scheme of heavy land taxation, with a long historical past. But making every allowance for this feature, the Indian income tax brings within its net only 332,000 persons out of a population of 244 millions in British India, the exemption limit being as low as £66. Only 13,000 persons have incomes of £666 or over in British India, while in the United Kingdom, with less than one-fifth of the population, the number of persons who paid a super-tax on incomes above £3000 was 28,815 in 1914-15. The Indian incomes have also, in certain cases, to pay a double income tax, one to India where the income accrued, and another to the Imperial Exchequer in Great Britain, the latter in many cases only because it is collected at the source, though it is not legally leviable, in view of the small amount of the income in individual hands...

In estimating India's contribution to the military financing of this War we must not merely look at the figures of the extra expenditure she is now incurring, but also at her military Budget for years past, compared to her local needs and to her own resources, in aid of Imperial defence. If we place side by side the military Budgets of Great Britain, India and the Dominions, and the proportion they bore to their total Budgets, we shall realise at once the enormous contribution which India has been making for years past towards the defence of the Empire, and which alone enabled India to be first in the field, next to Great Britain, with a well-trained veteran army, complete with its equipment, immediately on the outbreak of the War.

	Military Budget 1913-1914 Millions of £	Percentage to Total Budget Revenue
Great Britain	28.2	14.5
India	18.2	22
Australia	2.5	10
Canada	1.5	5
South Africa	1.15	7.7

The figures for India refer to British India only, and do not include the cost of the Imperial Service troops maintained by the Indian States which are also a true contribution from year to year to the military strength of the Empire. If British India had paid for her pre-war army the same percentage of her total revenue as Canada, she would only have paid about £4,000,999 for her army, and saved every year £14,000,000.

In addition to this accumulated 'Spandau treasure' of the British Empire, which has been contributed by India, India pays direct to the central Exchequer all the expenses, direct and indirect, of the troops she has furnished for fighting beyond the Indian frontiers. This contribution amounted to about £11,000,000 from the beginning of the War to the 31st March 1916. For the financial year 1916-17 a sum of £8,000,000 has been budgeted for, but past experience justifies the expectation that it will be much exceeded. The military expenditure for the last completed financial year is nearly £2,000,000 in excess of that provided in the budget, and the estimate for the current financial year increased by half a million between the 1st of March 1916, when the Budget was presented, and the 21st March 1916, when it was discussed. There has been besides a considerable outlay in India which would not have been incurred but for the War. The services and supplies furnished by India are estimated to a value of £48,000,000 for the 2 years and 6 months that the War will have lasted at the close of the present financial year....

India's chief wealth consists at present in her raw produce, and she has placed this freely at the service of the Empire and its Allies, at considerable self-sacrifice. Her foodstuffs have had their influence on the British markets. Her jute has made, and is making, sand-bags for the Allied trenches. Her mineral resources, such as manganese and coal, have been of the utmost value, and Sir Harcourt Butler, the Lieutenant-Governor of Burma, has vigorously brought the mineral resources of that Province into the general allied stock for the purposes of the War and taken effective steps to prevent their reaching the enemy. Such manufacturing facilities as India possesses have been concentrated in the making of munitions and stores of war, and Government and railway workshops, as well as private works and technical schools, have put their quota into the common effort. As Sir James Meston pointed out in his recent address at the Allahabad Durbar, the city of Kanpur alone has sent 1.75 million pairs of socks and 2.5 million pairs of boots to the Front. How many 'well-directed cheques, well loaded, properly primed', will wing their way from India in response to Mr Lloyd George's appeal for the new Loan of Victory we shall not know immediately, but we may be sure that they will represent all that India can spare from her own elementary needs.

To sum up, the fine fighting resources of India have done and are doing untold service throughout our far-flung battle line. Her financial resources, public and private, such as they are, are being thrown into the pool. She is clearing the decks for an unlimited Imperial War Loan. Besides her direct contributions, India has given or released millions in short-term loans, and has helped most substantially, by refraining from borrowing in any available markets at the sacrifice of her own needs and interests. Her Princes and people have shown a loyal determination to subordinate minor issues to the War. Any isolated conspiracies of sedition or disloyalty have been handed up by the people themselves. Constituted political bodies like the Indian National Congress and the Muslim League have shown, no less than official bodies like the Councils, that discretion, moderation, statesmanship, and an earnest desire to uphold the Empire are not foreign to the Indian temperament. If India's man-power has not been utilised to the full, if her men – especially of the class from which officers are drawn in all countries – have had their offers of service rejected over and over again, it is not the fault of the people of India. India's effort in the War, within her opportunities, has been at least as great as that of any other portion of the King's overseas Dominions.

Extract from 'India's effort: is it sufficiently understood?', The Nineteenth Century, Vol. 81, No. 480, February 1917, pp.348-365.

1923

> Yusuf Ali undertook original historical research on Mughal India, assisting W.H. Moreland in studies of Akbar's land revenue system. He was deeply interested in travellers' accounts of Mughal India and published articles on Al-Biruni and Ibn Batuta. In March 1923 he presented a paper on Babar to the United Provinces Historical Society at Lucknow. Yusuf Ali, the historian, offers yet another facet of a most versatile intellect.

In this paper my object is not to narrate the events of Babar's life but to study the psychology and development of a most fascinating personality. The great figures of history are often subjects of wild controversies, and very little of their own thought can be gleaned authoritatively from the voluminous records which other people write about them or contemporary pictures which fix their gaze on particular achievements according to the standpoint of the writers. Even despatches and personal memoranda, written in an atmosphere of power and authority, are apt to be overladen with ponderous matter, and to lack the sincerity and artlessness of notes and reflections jotted down from time to time and reflecting the moods of the moment, which taken collectively constitute life and personality. In Babar's case we have such a simple and private record in his Diary. It is artless in the sense that it comes direct from the heart, proceeds swiftly, and takes the reader into its confidence without any *arrière-pensée*. But in truth these qualities are the very stuff of the highest art. The simplicity, candour, and fullness of the record make it one of the most valuable human documents in history...

When the diary reopens in 1519 he was in Bajaur, on the borders of India. He was then 36 (solar) years old. Now we find frequent mention of drinking parties, quite casually, as if they were an everyday occurrence.

But a more serious habit even than that of drinking wine was the habit of taking intoxicating drugs. He mentions a pleasant but highly intoxicating confection called *kamal*. Although he took in the beginning only the third part of a pill, it affected him so much that he was unable to attend the council meeting of his Begs. After that he went from bad to worse. He drank wine and spirits (*araq*) and took intoxicating drugs, such as opium, daily, and the *maajun* which he took so frequently was probably composed of *bhang*. He was however mindful of the feelings of others. Once, not long afterwards, he was staying at a local *qazi's* house. They made preparations for a jolly party, but the *qazi* came to him and said: 'Such a thing was never yet seen in my house; however, you are emperor and master.' Though all the preparations for a convivial party were ready, they gave up their intention of drinking wine in deference to the feelings of the *qazi*.

Later in life Babar definitely formed a resolve to give up drinking at the age of 40, but he actually carried out this resolution much later. There was a dramatic scene on Monday the 1st Jamad I, 933H, 1527C when Babar was 44 (solar) years of age. At that time he was just about to undertake his most important campaign in India, that against Rana Sanga, for which he had made careful preparations in the spirit of a holy war. He thought of his firm resolve to make an effectual repentance. He wrote some Turki verses, in which he vowed to resist all temptation and never more to drink wine. He sent for the gold and silver goblets and cups, with all the other utensils used for drinking parties, and directed them to be broken. The fragments of the precious metals he divided among dervishes and the poor. His army and courtiers, soldiers and non-officials, to the number of nearly 300 men, made similar vows of reformation. The wine, which was actually there, was poured on the ground, and a stone well and alms house erected on the spot to commemorate the event. Other stocks of wine were converted into vinegar by admixture of salt. An ethical *farman* was issued, in which verses were quoted from the Qur'an, and stress was laid on self-conquest as greater than any victory. 'We have directed' he says, 'this holy warfare to commence with the grand warfare, the war against our passions.' Such was the spirit in which, in spite of the evil prognostications of astrologers, and a feeling of depression in the army, Babar undertook his campaign against Rana Sanaga and carried it through with brilliant success. It were very much to be wished that Babar had at the same time given up the habit of taking drugs and *maajuns*, which greatly affected his health, and in spite of his iron constitution, brought on an early death at the age of 47 (solar) years...

Babar's love of nature is a special feature of his Diary. When he captures Nasukh in 903H/1498C, he records that it was the season when melons were ripe, and describes a special kind of melon called *Ismail Shaikhi*, the skin of which is yellow and puckered like shagreen leather, the seeds of which are about the size of apple pips, and the pulp four fingers thick, while the taste is remarkably delicate and agreeable. One of the things he missed in India was fruit. But he planted vineyards and orchards, and got the best fruit trees from Kabul and Central Asia. Towards the end of his life he was truly delighted with having produced excellent melons and grapes in Hindustan. He takes considerable interest in astronomy and notices the star canopies for the first time from the top of a hill near Kabul. He and his companions are equally delighted...In his account of Samarkand he mentions with pride Ulugh Beg's observatory and adds a note about other observatories in the world. His description of all the important cities makes a point of including an account of their gardens, streams and natural beauties. At Agra he planted several gardens and sank large wells, one of which still exists. He was fond of neatness and order, and especially criticised the haphazard way in which things were planned in India...

His reading had been very wide and had extended to such pure gems of literature as the Qur'an, Firdausi's Epic, the poems of Amir Khusrau, the *masnavi* of Maulana Jalaluddin Rumi, the mysticism of Hafiz and Nizami, the ethics of Saadi, and the allegories of Jami (who was almost his contemporary). Most of his studies and education could only have been possible before the age of eleven. But late in life, only eighteen months before his death, we get a picture of Babar burning the midnight oil. He was marching back from his expedition to Bengal and Bihar towards his capital. It was the month of Ramadhan, and he had finished his night prayers. Shortly before midnight, a great storm arose and blew down his tents. Babar was surprised in his own tent writing, and had scarcely time to gather up his loose sheets of paper before his pavilion came down and nearly killed him. After he escaped he did not sleep, but was busily employed in drying his papers till the morning...

It is not within our province here to discuss the causes of decay that attacked the later Mughal Empire. But Babar's own period is most instructive not only in the history of India but in the general history of the world. Western and Central Europe were then working out a religious revolution, which also meant a political revolution. The Western Turks were still in their prime, and were acting as links between Europe and Asia. Their institutions indirectly supplied the pattern for Persia's reorganisation. Persia's religious revolution under the Safavid dynasty opened the doors of one of the mansions in the House of Islam. The age-long conflict of Persian, Turkish and Mongol civilisations in Central Asia kindled forces whose waves engulfed India in Central Asian politics. If any Indian dreams of an isolated India, history does not support him.

Extract from 'The Self-Revelation of Babar'

1931

> In September 1931 Yusuf Ali completed his most extensive piece of Urdu writing, *Hindustan ki tamaddun ki tarikh*, which was translated (perhaps by Yusuf Ali himself) into English and published with some additions in 1940 as *A Cultural History of India during the British Period*. The book's preface indicates that he saw this work as breaking new ground. The motivation underlying much of his historical scholarship was to demonstrate the importance of the British connection for India.
>
> Three extracts are presented below: the preface; an account of Indian Freemasonry; and the section on the 'Mutiny' of 1857, which illustrates Yusuf Ali's attempt at bridge-building between Britain and India. The Preface to the English edition contains one variation from the Urdu version, indicated in parenthesis.

Preface

An attempt is made in the following pages to trace the cultural evolution of India during the British period. 'Culture' is a difficult word to define, but I have taken it in the broadest sense, to include all those movements which have to do with a people's mind and its social organisation. Manners and morals, journalism and literature, education and public life, the transformation of religious and social ideas, economics, art and industry, and finally, politics in so far as they deal with formative ideas rather than controversial facts, will all claim our attention. But all these matters must be placed in due proportion. Here we are not writing political or literary or religious or social history, or the history of education or journalism, art, economics, or industry. We are taking a bird's-eye view of the forces which are moulding our culture.

The matters I am dealing with are rarely touched on in Indian histories; or touched on so slightly or from such a purely administrative point of view that they lose their human interest. And yet these are the very stuff of history. If we were concerned with a country in Europe or America we should find numerous separate monographs on each of these activities to help us in our synthesis. In dealing with India we have no such help. We must start from the very beginning. We must not only have an architectural plan, but we must seek out our raw materials. We must clear our own sites, make our own bricks and mortar, and perhaps even extract our own metals from the mines direct. Any one who has had experience of research on these lines, through books, newspapers, and manuscripts in various languages, each supplying just the barest hint here and there, will appreciate the enormous amount of labour and time involved in such an undertaking. I have been under the further handicap of writing these pages away from India, in a busy life of travel and devotion to most varied interests. Wherever possible, I have gone direct to the original sources and contemporary documents.

My object has been to interest Indian readers in matters not usually brought to their attention. Many matters unfamiliar to them will be found touched on in these pages. The explanation of unfamiliar matters must necessarily involve the use of unfamiliar words and phrases, for which I must crave the indulgence of readers, especially whose who believe in old traditions and beaten paths. In exploring new territory I have ventured to open up new paths for myself, believing, as I do, that literary style must follow the evolution of new ideas and modes of thought. The evolution of British Indian culture is dominated by British ideas, which lurk even beneath the protests of those who are in revolt against what they term foreign ideas. For my part, I believe, like a character in a famous Latin comedy, that nothing is foreign which is founded on the bed-rock of human nature.

The list of books in the Appendix will show the books to which I have directly referred in the text. The actual amount of reading covered is much wider, and can hardly be indicated in any but a pedantic list. On minor points I have received assistance from many quarters which I have indicated in notes in the appropriate places. I would specially mention the help of competent authorities of the British Museum on points of Oriental typography and the Masonic authorities of Great Britain on the history of Freemasonry in India [Urdu version: About the history of Freemasons in India, I was able to acquire the assistance of many persons who were in the helm of affairs]. In the work of translation, revision, and transcription, my warmest acknowledgements are due to Prof. Saadat Ali Khan, who has devoted the whole of his vacation to this labour of love. I must also acknowledge the friendly assistance of Khan Saheb Maulvi Feroz Din and Mr Waheed Khan. For valuable assistance in translation I am indebted to Chaudhri Ghulam Haidar Khan and Mr Hari Chand Akhtar. If the interest evoked among many personal friends is any indication of the interest to be expected from the public in the work, I may venture to hope that this line of inquiry will be followed by more intensive studies in the future.

Freemasonry

Freemasonry has been a factor in bridging over the racial and social gulf, and was certainly closely identified with the early English education movement in India. Freemasonry established itself in India long before the intercourse of British and Indians as fellow-subjects could be thought of. It would seem that a Masonic Lodge (English Constitution) was opened in Bengal as early as 1728-30, which is remarkable, considering that the early authentic history of Freemasonry from records, in England itself, begins only in 1717. Roger Drake, Governor of Calcutta at the time of the Black Hole, was recorded to have filled the highest local Masonic offices before 1755. The first Lodge in Madras was opened in 1752 and in Bombay in 1758. In 1833, the Calcutta Gazette (31st July) informs us, the Freemasons of Calcutta drank the health of the new Governor-General in these terms:

'That bright Luminary in the Masonic Constellation, the Earl of Moira, whose unremitted (*sic*) exertions for the benefit of Masonry render his name indelibly imprinted on the heart of every Brother of the Craft.' Educational institutions for Indians were actively countenanced by the Fraternity. We saw in the last chapter that the foundation-stone of the new building for the Hindu College in Calcutta was laid in 1824 by the head of Freemasonry in Bengal. Similarly the foundation-stone of the new building for the College in Benares was laid with Masonic honours (2nd November 1847) by His Highness the Raja of Benares and the Deputy Provincial Grand Master of the Masonic body in the North-Western Provinces. Since then Freemasonry has made great progress in India. Though its activities come little before the public, its influence on our cultural and social progress is not inappreciable. Most of the Lodges now have Indian members, men of influence in their society. At least one Lodge (in Hyderabad, Deccan) conducts its ceremonies in Urdu. Under the Grand Lodge of England, there are now about 200 Lodges in India, with an approximate membership of say 50 per Lodge* – and·there are other Lodges, under the Grand Lodges of Scotland and Ireland.

(*For this paragraph I am indebted for some material to Mr G.P.G. Hill, Librarian of the Grand Lodge of England)

Cultural Significance of the Mutiny

Mutiny described in three different ways

The Mutiny of 1857 is a most important, if terrible, event in British Indian history. It has been viewed and described in three different ways: (1) as a military revolt of the Bengal Army, pure and simple; (2) as an insurrection of the people of northern India against the fast-moving tide of British civilisation; and (3) as an unsuccessful War of Indian Independence. Some British writers have even treated it as a mere outbreak of savagery, unreasoning and unreasonable, in which all the Indians who participated were brutes and all the doings of the British, civilians and soldiers, were deeds of heroism, worthy of being commemorated as exhibiting the finest expression of the British character. We are not concerned here, either with the narration of events or with the purely political and military causes and consequences of that dreadful catastrophe. We shall try to see what cultural significance we can deduce from what we know, not only of the events themselves, but of what people thought of them, then and subsequently.

British narratives, but no explanation of motives from the beaten side
The task is not easy. Though a great deal of literature has gathered round the Mutiny, it has chiefly concerned itself with ascertaining concrete facts from the British point of view. From the nature of the case there is no narrative from the other side[1] which could throw light on the objects and motives behind the movement, as viewed from the point of view of the parties which were beaten in the struggle. Sir Sayyid Ahmed Khan wrote a little pamphlet on the causes of the Indian mutiny (*Risala asbab i baghawat i Hindustan*), which was printed in 1859. He had done much during the Mutiny at Bijnaur to assist the British officers and their families and save their lives. He held high judicial office under the Government and received a reward of merit for loyal services. His object in writing the Pamphlet was to inform the Government of the real cultural causes of the Mutiny. And yet it was criticised by Sir Cecil Beadon (Foreign Secretary to the Government of India) as seditious, and apart from the copies which he sent to Government, no copies were then distributed in India.[2] They were merely sent to England for the information of public men. If that was the state of feeling at the time about even a loyalist's discussion of the Mutiny, what chance could there be that a narrative of any merit from the rebel point of view could possibly see the light? The poet Mirza Asadullah Ghalib, who had lived in close touch with Bahadur Shah at Delhi before the Mutiny, and had been commissioned to write a history of the Timur family, was broken in spirit during the Mutiny, and he was reduced to such abject poverty that he could only write laudatory *Qasidas* for the British authorities in order to save himself from starvation...

Racial feeling and hatred
The Lieutenant-Governor of Bengal, in his speech at the Medical College, Calcutta, on the 19th April 1858, deplored among the many lamentable and melancholy results of the Mutiny, 'that heated, embittered, and

exasperated sentiment of antagonism of race, which has sprung up in so many minds'. It was just such a spirit which animated the English papers of the period in attacking Lord Canning's 'clemency' even when he sought to conciliate Indian feeling by rewards for loyal services.[3] Perhaps it is such a spirit which brings out from manuscript obscurity and publishes even at the present time personal narratives full of the passions and prejudices of that dark period.[4] Mr. Edward Thomson has already, as an Englishman, recorded his protests against such books as Sir George Forrest's *History of the Indian Mutiny*, which record the excesses on one side, but not on the other.[5] The better plan is to forget the excesses, except in books of scientific history, where both sides must be represented. If we examine the matter dispassionately, we shall find that very little race feeling found expression on the Indian side during the Mutiny period outside the ranks of the more violent rebels themselves. The papers of Bahadur Shah's government, seized at the capture of Delhi, use the very mild term *Karani* (clerk) in speaking of the District officials of the East India Company. I wish it were possible to make the same claim for Indians at the present day. Our newspapers are full of bitter abuse and hatred, not only on racial, but on cultural and religious grounds, and not only against foreigners, but by sections of our people against each other. This passion of hatred and intolerance, or its more subdued form of suspicion, will have to give place to frank give-and-take and friendly understanding, if we are to have any cultural co-operation between India and England, between East and West, or between different sections of our own people.

The sense in which we must understand the cultural conflict
The cultural significance of the Mutiny lay in a cultural conflict. But that conflict must not be imagined in terms of a hatred between all members of a race culture as against all members of another race culture, or even against different cultures evolved by different races. If that were so, the case would be hopeless. There would be no lesson to be learnt, and no guidance in history for the future. Culture could not assimilate culture, and human evolution would be stopped forever. The cultural conflict should be visualised in this way. The British mental attitude and behaviour towards

the people of India induced in the people of India a certain repugnance against the British, or, if looked at differently, a certain suspicion of motives, a certain feeling that the motives professed were not sincere, and that the real motives were discreditable and could not be professed. This conflict would become personal, but it would be based upon conduct, behaviour, writings speeches, institutions, laws, and the general manifestations of culture. This distinction between two kinds of cultural conflict is important. In the relations between the British and Indians it implied not the conflict of one culture with another, but the conflict of men of one culture with men of a variety of others, who acted together because they believed themselves to be slighted under a common ban. If we bear this distinction in mind, we shall also understand why there was no cultural conflict between Hindus and Muslims in pre-British days though there had been political and military conflicts, and why such Hindu-Muslim conflicts have raged with peculiar fury in our own days. We shall also understand how they became stilled in Delhi and over the country generally during the Mutiny; Bahadur Shah's Special Secretary during the brief days of his 'Restoration' was Mukand Lal, a Hindu; many *walayati* (Afghan) mercenaries fought on the side of the Hindu mutineers, and the rebel Sepoys used British forms in military and judicial procedure, although they were fighting against British supremacy.

Notes

1. *Two Native Narratives of the Mutiny in Delhi*, translated by C.T. Metcalfe, London 1898, is hardly an exception. The first, a short one, was written by Mu'inuddin Hasan Khan, who was afterwards most anxious to keep well in with the British. The second was written by Munshi Jiwan Lal, an actual employee of the British.
2. Altaf Husain Hali, *Hayat i Jawed*, p.71. The pamphlet was reprinted many years afterwards at Agra, in 1903. An English translation was published by Sir Auckland Colvin and General G.F.I. Graham (Sir Sayyid's English biographer) in 1873.
3. The Indian *Punch*, Meerut, 1859, (a British paper) sarcastically observed that he had no time for compensation to Christians in giving gifts to the heathen.
4. For example, see Mrs. Tytler's 'Through the Sepoy Mutiny' in *Chamber's Journal*, London, January 1931 and subsequent numbers. It adds nothing to our historical information, and revives exploded theories, besides expressing racial prejudice and contempt.
5. In his book *The Other Side of the Medal*, London 1925.

A Cultural History of India during the British Period, pp. 132-133; 176-180.

1933

The Religious Polity of Islam has an important place in Yusuf Ali's corpus because it was published at a time when he was deeply immersed in the translation of the Qur'an. The ideas developed in this pamphlet must reflect some of the premises he brought to bear when seeking to interpret the Qur'an. The pamphlet also bears the imprint of his Qur'anic scholarship and captures some of the spirit of Islam's political philosophy. The extract has been selected to reflect both aspects.

The religious polity of Islam is not committed to any particular form for sovereignty, such as Kingship, Aristocracy or Democracy. It defines certain great principles, and lays down certain conditions for a Righteous State. Historically there have been various interesting developments. The cradle of Islam was in Arabia, and Arabian ethnical ideas were apt to come to the surface in the process of historical churning. Before Islam the tribal system was ingrained in the social life of Arabia. Though the Prophet, by his example and his teaching, suppressed sectionalism and pointed the way to a non-tribal, non-racial, non-sacerdotal, non-autocratic State, the tribal revolt after his death showed that the tribal feeling was not extinct. It also showed that Arab obedience in the Prophet's life was purely personal to him. The Arab mind, in its tribal organisation, gives the maximum of freedom to the individual. This is often difficult to reconcile with collective action in a large State. Tribal jealousies were the bane of Muslim politics for many centuries in Arabia, Syria, North Africa, Spain and elsewhere. This extreme impatience of restraint by authority amounted almost to antinomianism [outwardly conforming to the doctrine but in reality doing the opposite – *al-ibahiya*], and is remarked upon by Ibn Khaldun, himself an Arab. In the fortunes of the Islamic peoples in later times and in other countries, when the supremacy passed to other races such as Persians and Turks, it remained as a reproach to the Arabs that, in spite of their intellectual keenness, they had less sense of discipline and cohesive action. It is to be hoped that reproach will be removed in the immediate future, when more than one Arab kingdom will play its part in the family of nations.

With the Ummayad rulers, Byzantine ideas of luxury and despotism were added to tribal exclusiveness. Kingship, which was altogether alien to the Arab mind, was introduced into Islam by them. Ibn Khaldun's dictum is that Kingship may be disapproved but not condemned. And yet the name of King was never very acceptable, and the older nomenclature of *Imam* or *Khalifa* or Commander of the Faithful (*Amir-ul-Muminin*) continued to be employed. When the Turks came to play a prominent role in the politics of Islam, the neutral title of Sultan, which simply means 'authority' in the abstract, began to be used. At first it implied subordinate rank, i.e. subordinate to that of the *Khalifa*. It is said that it was first used by the Buwaihid *Amir* Mu'iss-ud-daula (334/945). But he did not use it on his coins, nor did Mahmud of Ghazna, though the title is commonly used with his name. The title was first used in public prayers by the Saljuq Tughril Bey, who acknowledged his own subordination both to the *Khalifa* and to the Buwaihid power under the *Khalifa* (447/1055). In the Persian mind the attributes of Kingship tended to be approximated to those of the old Persian monarchy, with much pomp and circumstance and something of the halo of divinity that surrounded the Sasanians. The Osmanli Sultan became a powerful Emperor, with the attributes and personal powers of the Great Khan of Turkish tradition. The Osmanli were soldiers, and their Empire became a military Aristocracy. In India, the high-flown adulation of Abu'l-Fazl and others in Akbar's Court, and terms like the Darshan employed in Court ceremonies, recalled the sacred character of Hindu Kingship, and were distasteful to the Orthodox Muslims. When Egypt set up a separate semi-independent line under Muhammad Ali, the Ruler was called Khedive, not king. When Afghanistan became a separate kingdom, the ruler called himself *Amir*, and so did the rulers of Muslim kingdoms of Central Asia.

In our own day the repugnance to the title of Kingship has been overcome. We have a king in Egypt, Iraq, Transjordania, Afghanistan, and even in the *Wahhabi* kingdom of Nejd and the Hejaz. In the last century there was a short-lived kingdom of Oudh in India. In Southern India, in the 18th Century, Tippu remained content with the title of Sultan. Most of the present Muslim kings are on the Constitutional model. Though foreign influences are apparent, there is yet an attempt to link some of these constitutional limitations with the old Islamic formulae, though the Islamic formulae implied much stricter limitations. The present national Turkish State is a Republic, though the extraordinary personal position of the Ghazi Pasha makes him more than the President of a Republic elected for a definite term of years. In calling itself a lay State (*un état laique*), with no established religion, it seems to make a breach with Islamic tradition, though it must be remembered that the breach is less violent than might at first sight appear, because in some aspects Islam is itself a lay religion, having no consecrated or privileged priesthood. In this connection I ought to refer to the work of Ali Abdul Raziq, a former Mufti in Egypt (*Al-Islam-wa-usul-ul-hukm*), published in Cairo in 1925, in which he argues strongly in favour of the separation of Church and State in Islam. Similarly Maulvi Barkatullah of India, in his book on the Khilafat (1925) argues that the Khalifa must be a spiritual leader only, and sketches a scheme of spiritual organisation.

The duty of a Ruler is to take advice and never to act without consultation is one of the cardinal principles of Islamic polity, and is referred to in a Qur'anic injunction (III:158). If, it is argued, the Prophet, who was wiser than anyone else, was commanded and made it his practice to act after consultation, how much more necessary it is for ordinary rulers. Mawardi (in his chapter on the subject in his *Adab ud-Dunya wad-din*) discusses the subject with his usual acumen. Consultation increases social understanding and induces in people the habit of co-operation. Moreover the man who acts in concert makes other people sharers in his action, and has no cause in any event to hold his head down in shame. But the people consulted should have five qualifications. They should be (1) competent, (2) honest, (3) sincerely friendly, (4) independent and free from fear, and (5) disinterested. But it is interesting to read the shrewd remark of Nizam ul-Mulk in his *Siyasat-nama* that every one has more or less wisdom. From the need of consultation is derived the need of a Council, and if our earlier reasoning on representative institutions is valid, the need for legislative assemblies or parliaments. The qualifications specified for those whose counsel is worth having have to be translated from the abstract to the concrete. I do not know where any serious attempt is made to do so completely, but partial attempts are made in most constitutions or parliamentary conventions. For instance, it is reasonable that a man should not vote in any matter in which he is personally interested; that a person should be disqualified for treason to the State; that a vote inffiuenced by corrupt motives or coercion should be discounted; that undischarged bankruptcy should disqualify, and so on. As councillors must reflect the morale of the electorate which they represent, it would be reasonable to prescribe similar but less strict qualifications for electors also. No electorate ought to be allowed to destroy the State, though the tendencies in modern undiluted democracies is to chance everything on a stake of universal suffrage.

I must not leave the subject without referring to Muslim fundamental ideas on finance and taxation, though I cannot here enter into any details. What I want to emphasise is that in Muslim polity (as it should be seen in any polity), finance is the corner-stone of the fabric. It is recognised that, taking as we do a high ideal of the spiritual and ethical value of the State, bad or selfish or inequitable taxation or expenditure may defeat the beneficent purposes of government as much as bad laws or a weak administration. In the early days of Islam an elaborate scheme of finance was worked out. Certain classes of people were exempted on account of poverty, or infirmity, or particular economic conditions. There was no specially privileged class, neither a hereditary aristocracy nor a privileged priesthood. The *Jiziya* was not a penal tax: it was in lieu of military service which was obligatory on every Muslim. The scheme of taxation on *Zimmis* was as fair as was consistent with the ideas of the time. There was always a temptation to raise more revenue by novel forms of taxation, but all virtuous rulers and their Wazirs disapproved of them and tried to conform to the *Shari'a* scheme of taxation. As late as the middle of the 14th Christian century, an Indian ruler, Firoz Tughluq, had qualms of conscience about the legitimacy of levying a water rate on the new canals which he had constructed. A great consultation was held, and after much debate it was decided that the water rate would be lawful even through the State was merely distributing the gifts of nature. The State's service was in the distribution. In the same way, various kinds of expenditure, and certainly all expenditure on the personal whims of the Ruler, were held to be unlawful. The Muslim State never acknowledged that finance was not part of morals - whether it was a question of disproportionate demands, ill-distributed burdens, unreasonable lavishness in proportion to resources, undue partiality in the apportionment of benefits, selfish avarice, or unwise hoarding in the coffers of the State. A minister of Sultan Mahmud is said to have given him this advice: 'Treat gold as your enemy, that men may treat you as your friend.'

Property and Capital, as well as the State's right to control all the resources of the community, are fully recognised. But on the other hand all factors which make for the misuse or selfish abuse of economic power by individuals or corporations are severely regulated. Under this head come the laws against usury. They have been interpreted narrowly, and in my opinion wrongly, to bar commercial interest. The State's duty to provide for the well-being and suitable employment of its citizens is insisted on. As Professor Massignon remarks,[1] 'Islam has the merit of standing for a very equalitarian conception of the contribution of each citizen by the tithe to the resources of the community; it is hostile to unrestricted exchange, to banking capital,[2] to State loans, to indirect taxes on objects of prime necessity, but it holds to the rights of the father and the husband, to private property, and to commercial capital. Here again it occupies an intermediate position between the doctrines of bourgeois capitalism and Bolshevist communism.'

Muslim Polity is an imposing structure, not to be viewed through a narrow aperture. Many wise men have contributed their ideas and ideals to it. Many practical men have staked their reputation in applying them. Many States in history have foundered because they neglected them. Many modern institutions follow logically from them, even though they seem so new. Many races have contributed certain ethnical characteristics to them: the Arabs a passion for freedom; the Turks a habit of disciplined obedience; the Persians a genius for lofty imagination. I wonder if the Indians can contribute a power of synthetic co-ordination. What Professor De Santillana says of Muslim Law may perhaps be applied to the Polity of Islam: 'There is not doubt that the high ethical standard of certain parts of

Arab law acted favourably on the development of our modern concepts; and herein lies its enduring merit.'[3]

Notes

1. *Whither Islam?*, p.378.
2. In my opinion only where its misuse becomes a danger to the Community.
3. *Legacy of Islam*, by Thomas Arnold et al. p.310.

Religious Polity of Islam, Hyderabad-Deccan: Islamic Cultural Office, 1933 (Progressive Islam Pamphlets, No. 8), 21p.

1936

> Yusuf Ali was a prominent participant in the annual conferences of the World Congress of Faiths between 1936 and 1941. His speech 'The Essential Basis of Religion' at the conference held at University College, London, in 1936, contains both biographical references of interest as well as an explanation of the purpose of inter-faith discussion.

Let me relate to you a little experience I had with a Japanese Christian whom I met in climbing up to a Buddhist monastery situated on a high hill. There were many paths going up to the temple at the top. I found different people taking different paths up. I was a little puzzled as to the best way to take for myself. This gentleman of his own accord came up and talked to me in Japanese English, and we became great friends. When I met him he was descending the hill, but when I asked for his guidance, he was not content with merely giving me directions, but actually changed his own course and went up again with me to the temple. We had an interesting talk. When I spoke to him about the multiplicity of paths going up, he said, quite simply: "Is not that the way of Divine things? The goal is one, but the paths to it are many." He asked me if I had come on a special pilgrimage to that temple in my visit to Japan. I told him that I was interested in all religions, but that I was not myself a Buddhist but a Muslim. "Nor am I a Buddhist," said he. "Do you then follow the Shinto way?" I asked. He smiled and said: "I am a Christian, but like you I love to go to Buddhist temples. I should like to go to your Muslim temples if there were any in Japan." I told him something about the Muslim form of worship and Muslim ideas of religion. We remained together for about two hours, but never for one minute in the course of our conversation did either of us feel that the other was an alien.

That is the one great charm of Japan. Their religion like their art is expressed in forms of delicate grace, which it would be difficult to define precisely. The ethnic and national form of their religion is Shinto. But who can define the elusive spirit of Shintoism? The Shinto Scripture Kojiki is, I understand, concerned with rites and ceremonies and beautiful customs which mingle well with almost any religion. They say that Buddhism absorbed Shinto, but I think it is more correct to say that the coalescence of Buddhism and Shinto has produced a national religion which is simple and easy, but not exclusive, except in so far that the Japanese race idea or national idea seems exclusive to foreigners. The complete absorption of a man like Lafcadio Hearn in the Japanese spirit is an experience which has fallen to the lot of very few foreigners.

I now come to Judaism and Christianity, which are sister religions to Islam. There is so much common ground between them that it seems a pity that there should not be more intimate contact between those who bear those labels. It is true that there are certain fundamental doctrines in Trinitarian Christianity which are rejected by Islam. It is also true that the Jews have in the past suffered much persecution in Christian countries and are still suffering persecution in some parts of the world. But I see no reason why, in the freer countries, and in an international atmosphere, these three should not come together in fellowship and establish an understanding without either side giving up beliefs which they consider fundamental. The Jews have lived in Muslim countries from the earliest ages of Islam. They thrived and flourished there and have contributed a great deal to the economic and social life of Muslim countries. In countries like England both orthodox and reformed Jews mix freely in society, in business, and in politics. Since Jewish emancipation they have filled with credit some of the highest posts under the Crown. It is very much to be hoped that the spirit of persecution and misunderstanding which still lingers in some parts of the world will disappear, and in its place a true and sincere fellowship of faiths, such as we all desire, will be substituted. When I advocate contact and understanding between two or three faiths, I must be understood to imply that as a prelude to contact and understanding between all faiths.

I have left to the last the mention of my personal relations with Christians. They have been very intimate through my life. The fellowship of England and India in one United Empire, though it is sometimes overshadowed by racial considerations on both sides, has yet brought about a better understanding of the Christian religion amongst the Indian Muslims, and I also think a better understanding of the religion of Islam amongst the British people. Speaking for myself, I can say that I understand and respect the essential spirit of British Christianity. My guardian, when I came to England at an immature age for study, was a Christian Englishman in the highest sense of the term. I love and revere his memory. I have met other members of his family with whom I have also been on the most friendly terms. I have studied the Christian religion as few Muslims have studied it. Although I am earnestly and sincerely devoted to my own religion and have striven both in writing and in speech to expound it, I have always advocated, and still advocate, the possibility and desirability of a better understanding between Muslims and Christians in all spheres of life. Such an understanding is likely to help us not only in our own Empire, and in international relations generally, but I think it can also become a great guarantee of world peace and international understanding. The Holy Qur'an (V:85) expressly says that the Christians are nearest in faith and friendship to the Muslims. In spite of many wars and misunderstandings, the thirteen centuries and a half that have passed since the birth of Islam have seen a gradual growth of a better understanding between the two faiths.

Again appealing to my personal experience, I can say that many Christian audiences have listened with welcome to my exposition of Islam, and some churches have even invited me to occupy their pulpits. Apart from doctrinal matters, there is so much common ground. The late Archbishop Soderblom of Sweden was a personal friend of mine. He and I had more than one opportunity of discussing some scheme, by which not only the Christian churches, but Islam and other Faiths, could be brought to mutual understanding and harmonious co-operation. In Canada one of the meetings, at which I was expounding Muslim ideas, was presided over by an Archbishop, and he spoke in the most friendly and cordial terms of my exposition. In the development of Christian thought, and especially in Protestantism, many of the points which were raised by Islam by way of protest have been accepted, and Unitarianism is practically Islam. The abolition of a hereditary or privileged priesthood, the right of private judgement, personal responsibility, equality in brotherhood, removal of racial or caste barriers, the selection of rulers by democratic choice, government and corporate action after free consultation – principles like these are the basis of the preaching of Islam, and are now accepted (at least in theory) in all parts of the Muslim world.

I had an extraordinary experience in my early student days when I visited the island of Malta. I visited the Catholic cathedral there. I conducted myself with reverence and attracted the attention of some Italian priests who, afterwards, came up to me and spoke to me in the most friendly terms. In those days I knew no Italian, but I had some knowledge of Latin. When I spoke to them in Latin they were surprised, and their friendliness to me was all the more increased. We could not carry on a very long conversation, as our pronunciations of the classical language were quite different. But the friendly feeling that grew up after that chance meeting induced them to add to their kindness by inviting me afterwards and showing me things which I should never have seen unshepherded. I still carry fragrant memories of that meeting in my heart and remember the words with which we parted. They pointed to the sky and said: 'Let us hope, in Heaven.' (*In coelo, speremus.*)

Thus you will see that, individually, many of us have actually felt and experienced the fellowship of faiths. Why can we not bring it about on a larger scale and in a more organised way? We have seen before our eyes the 'Past's enormous disarray' (Rupert Brooke). Such ills cannot be cured by ordinary means, and certainly not through the instrumentality of politics. We have to look to deep-seated causes within. These are bound up with whole bundles of prejudices, feelings of attraction or repulsion, inherited tendencies and environments, historical and cultural chains of association, varied intellectual responses to common human experiences, and even deliberate misrepresentations or misunderstandings created perhaps for purposes of war or selfish aggrandisement. In so far as history and human experience have cleared our vision, we can put away past conflicts in the limbo of forgotten things. In so far as our actual feelings and sincere beliefs prevent us from seeing things in the same light, we can tolerate and try to understand other points of view. But there is nothing to prevent us, with all our differences, from realising a sense of fellowship and cooperation. The office of Religion is to bind us together in the bonds of a common humanity. Let us go forward, with humble faith and firm resolve, to the achievement of our collective Hope!

Will you allow me to close with a quotation from Dolben's "Shrine"?

> Without, the world is tired and old,
> But once within the enchanted door,
> The mists of time are backward rolled,
> And creeds and ages are no more;
> But all the human-hearted meet
> In one communion vast and sweet.

Extract from 'The Essential Basis of Religion', World Congress of Faiths, London, 1936.

1937

Yusuf Ali is an authoritative source for information on the educational ideals of Sir Sayyid Ahmed Khan, founder of Aligarh. This extract discusses the Aligarh movement's objectives and some ensuing controversies. It is taken from Yusuf Ali's presidential address to the University Section of the 1937 All-India Muslim Educational Conference, held in Aligarh. His fears on the rise of provincial rivalries were to prove well founded, and the comments on science and religion are also significant.

This Conference arose out of the educational ideals of Sir Sayyid Ahmed Khan. While the results of his local efforts are visible in what was the Muhammadan Anglo-Oriental College at Aligarh and is now the Muslim University at Aligarh, with the group of institutions clustering round it, the larger and less localised ideals found expression in this annual Conference, which has met in different centres of India and which aims at reviewing and advancing the cause of Muslim education in all the different Provinces and States in India. The Conference acts as an adjunct and an auxiliary to the numerous Muslim educational efforts which are being carried on in the towns and villages of India. Though it may not be quite accurate to say that it acts as a clearing-house of educational information for the whole of Muslim India, it is I think correct to say that its aim is to bring the search-light of this central organisation to play from time to time upon varied local conditions, to assist local efforts wherever possible, and incidentally to link them together and bring them into touch with Aligarh as the metropolitan centre of Muslim education.

Is it possible to examine Sir Sayyid Ahmed's educational ideals and crystallise them in clear-cut propositions at this distance of time? I had the honour of knowing Sir Sayyid during the later years of his life. I remember some of the conversations I had with him - alas too few - on the subject of Muslim regeneration. I was then on the threshold of my career as a public servant, and I placed my educational ideals with the zeal and assurance of youth before this educational veteran whose life measured the span between the Indian Mutiny and the close of the Victorian epoch. Many of the positions which we younger men then accepted without question had been won after hard struggles by the men of Sir Sayyid Ahmed's generation. Many of the dreams which we then dreamed had not yet suffered under the mellowing influences of time. Many of the disillusions which Sir Sayyid and his co-workers had suffered seemed to us then of little account, but have since become multiplied in the more complex atmosphere of the twentieth century.

Early Aligarh Scheme

No unqualified categorical statements can ever sum up the whole truth about any great man's ideals. But subject to this qualification I think we can say that the Aligarh Movement from its very inception laid stress on the following points in its programme:

1. The lethargy which had crept over the Muslim mind in India owing to its loss of political power could only be cured by modern education.

2. The most effective form of modern education for us is through the medium of the English language and English sciences.

3. The stagnation of religious ideals in the peculiar conditions which prevailed in Muslim India then could only be removed by a re-interpretation or re-examination of many of the fundamental as-sumptions of our religious philosophy.

4. Such re-interpretation and re-examination could not ignore the advances of modern Western science, and should in fact welcome that new light as being the logical result of the labours of our own Muslim scientists and philosophers of the golden age of Islam.

5. Side by side with an increase in knowledge there should be a develop-ment of social life and social institutions on lines that have been tried and found to be successful in the West. In many minds the Aligarh Movement in its beginnings was symbolised by the adoption of English dress, English manners and English ways of life.

If this is a fair statement of early Aligarh ideals, we can see at once that there has been much disillusion since, and many reactions within the body of the Aligarh Movement itself. No healthy movement can grow and fructify without such reactions.

Educated Unemployed
We no longer believe that modern education is the panacea for all the ills from which our society and our people suffer. On the contrary we have come to realise that in our modern system of University Education in India there are many gaps and many defects. Some even go as far as to condemn it as having taken a wholly wrong direction and advocate a new orientation altogether. I am sure that no one who has been in intimate touch with educational institutions and with our youth who receive modern education will support this extreme view. But we do feel that there are many defects – in method, in machinery, in psychological adaptation, and in outlook – which require serious and urgent remedies....The financial depression and the great increase in the number of educated unemployed ...is a country-wide

question and affects all communities. Our Muslim community is specially touched by it because the proportion of men amongst us who follow commercial and industrial occupations is small, and the attempts now being made to increase the scope of industrial and commercial education and to seek out new openings for the products of such education may affect our community to a relatively small extent than it affects our sister communities. In the Muslim Provinces of the Punjab, the Frontier Province, Sind, and Bengal, the Muslim masses mainly live on the land, and in other Provinces except Bombay they have in the past generations mainly made their careers in administrative services. There is no room for unlimited expansion in such services, although we note with some satisfaction that recent Government orders aim at giving a fair deal in such services to the Muslims. How far such orders are carried out will depend upon the vigilance with which our public men study and raise this question with knowledge and tact in the Provincial Assemblies and in the Central Legislature.

Vernacular

Our admiration for English studies has also suffered an eclipse. The question of the vernaculars is very much to the fore. The Muslims are the only section of the Indian population (barring Anglo-Indians, whose numbers are too small for consideration) who have a common language throughout the whole of India and the Indian States. Even this statement will require a little qualification, as we see that with the growth of provincial Autonomy and of a sense of Provincial patriotism, Provincial vernaculars may be pushed up even in the Universities, as is being done in Bengal. I should like to see this question discussed in its many aspects before a definite conclusion can be formed. But I should like to say with emphasis that it would be a mistake on the part of the Muslim community to slacken in their study of English, which is the administrative language of India now and will remain so for as long as we can at present foresee.

Study of Science

As regards the study of western sciences I do not think that we have ever during all this period shown enough enthusiasm or produced any remarkable results. This is a scientific age. Anyone who has lived through this last half century must have realised what a tremendous revolution has taken place in our material life – individual and social – through the new discoveries and inventions of science. The scientist now holds in his hands the key to every kind of future advance in human culture. If there are any amongst us who feel at all disillusioned about the value and utility of the experimental sciences in our education and our life, I would beg of them seriously to examine the question again from a broad and unprejudiced point of view. If they think that modern science is antagonistic to religion, I would point out that modern science is becoming less and less materialistic and mechanistic, and is realising more and more that the highest forces in nature and in human life are invisible forces in the investigation of which we have barely scratched the surface. This is not to say that science and religion are one. But it is to urge that a truly religious mind, open to all the influences of God's material creation, will be stimulated rather than corrupted by traversing the wide and wonderful world of modern science.

Reinterpretation of Religious Philosophy

The re-interpretation and re-examination of many of the dogmas and assumptions of our religious philosophy was undertaken in Sir Sayyid's days with scanty material. It may be that many of the criticisms that were then levelled at what was called the Aligarh school of theology were really aimed at specific deductions or special theories rather than at its methods and outlook as a whole. It may be that some of these criticisms were right, and that with our modern knowledge we can yet meet them and proceed with our tasks of re-interpretation and re-examination in a spirit of reverence and fidelity to the real and original traditions of the best period of our history. In this matter we cannot afford to remain stagnant. The younger generation which is pressing in upon us will demand that our interpretations is consonant with the best knowledge that we possess. The acceptance of the criticism does not necessarily imply the overthrow of the position criticised, but it does require that it should be re-examined and such qualifications as are necessary should be made to bring it into conformity with the completest knowledge that we possess.

Enlightening Public Opinion

How far that is possible in the present state of our public opinion depends very much on the efforts we make to enlighten public opinion. The *odium theologicum* from which Sir Sayyid suffered is not dead. It now shows itself in other forms and sometimes seeks an alliance with the *odium politicum*. If we give a training based on cram work and aiming mainly at examinations we shall not have that forum of independent judgement by which noble efforts are stimulated and their opposites suppressed.

Function of Higher Education

The chief function of higher education, as I understand it, it to equip men for living a higher and fuller life, individually, socially, economically and spiritually, and to provide opportunities of leadership for the people on the part of those who have received that higher education. With the external and material aspects of Western civilisation, the Indian mind has recently shown an increasing amount of disgust. Perhaps the pendulum has swung too far. There is a danger lest in this swing the more important aspects and the essential value of modern scientific and cultural education may be lost sight of.

Golden Jubilee Session, Aligarh, 27 March 1937. Pamphlet of Presidential Address, University Section, All-India Muslim Educational Conference.

1939

Yusuf Ali's *Idea of Salvation in Islam* is an expressive and moving summary of his religious philosophy. The extract below elaborates a number of key Qur'anic terms such as *najaat* (salvation), *jannah* (heaven) and *barzakh* (the period or state from death to the events of Judgement Day). The pamphlet was to be the last piece of extensive writing he undertook on Islamic themes.

The mission of Moses is described (XL: 23-45) in its manifold aspects as expounded in Islam. That mission was not only to save Israel from the bondage of Egypt (which, in a world sense, was a minor point), but to preach the Gospel of Unity to the stiff-necked Israelites, to the arrogant Pharaoh, and to the superstitious Egyptians dazzled by magic. Pharaoh and the Egyptians were seeking to slay Moses, but there was a just man among them who had seen the light, and who boldly addressed them. 'Will ye,' he said, 'slay a man because he says, "My Lord is God"?' (Parenthetically it may be pointed out that Pharaoh claimed godhead himself and exclusive lordship over his people.) This man continued: 'When he has indeed come to you with clear Signs from your Lord? And if he be a liar, on him is the sin of his lie; but if he is telling the Truth, then will fall on you something of the calamity of which he warns you; truly God guides not one who transgresses and lies. O my People! Yours is the dominion this day. Ye have the upper hand in the land; but who will help us from the Punishment of God, should it befall us?' And he goes on arguing for their good and declaring the Faith that is in him, while we may suppose that they are recalling him to the State religion with threats of execution if he renounces it. And so he makes his appeal again: 'O my people! How strange it is for me to call you to *Salvation* while ye call me to the Fire! Ye do call me to blaspheme against God, and to join with Him partners of whom I have no knowledge; and I call you to the Exalted in Power, who forgives again and again!' Salvation here is used in a very comprehensive sense, both for the present and for the future - both in the static meaning of safety from the danger of blasphemy and the dynamic meaning of escape from the future consequences of sin by repentance.

But let us carry the analysis a little more into details. To the subject of Salvation there may be some danger threatening, either now or in the future, and the future may regard either the subsequent course of this life or something to occur in the life to come. Islam postulates all these three kinds of danger. Sin itself is a present danger: it is often spoken of as a stain. But the stain only comes when the evil touches us or we go near it through the perversion of our will. There is no doctrine of 'original sin'. We do not believe in the utter depravity of mankind. The Muslim entirely repudiates the sentiment of the Psalmist: 'Behold, I was shapen in iniquity; and in sin did my mother conceive me' (Ps. LI: 5). On the contrary he is taught that man, as turned out from the creative hand of God, is innocent, pure, true, free, inclined to right and virtue, and endued with true understanding about his own position in the universe and about God's goodness, wisdom and power. 'The pattern according to which God has made mankind'

(XXX: 30) is true and pure. We are exhorted not to spoil this pattern – to make no change in the work wrought by God. We have to establish God's handiwork according to the pattern which He has created, and this is stated to be the true or standard Religion. But there is evil in the world, personified in Satan. He is an enemy to mankind and sets snares. But 'he has no authority over those who believe and put their trust in their Lord: his authority is over those only who take him as patron and who join partners with God' (XVI: 99-100). So it ultimately comes to man's own will. But the danger is there, and the protection from the danger is man's faith and trust in God, and the light which lights him on the way – which gives him Salvation – is the Revelation of God.

But suppose that man has fallen into the snare, as happens with nearly all ordinary men and women. He has succumbed to temptation; he has acquired the taint of sin. The consequences may not be immediately visible, or he may not be immediately conscious of them. Or the time may be delayed before the consequences may be perceptible. Respite is invariably granted for opportunities of repentance. But the consequences operate all the same, and the minor fruits of evil may themselves point the way to repentance and a changed life. Here comes the warning of God's Messengers and of His Revelation. 'Mischief has appeared on land and sea because of the deed that the hands of men have earned, that God may give them a taste of some of their deeds: in order that they may turn back from Evil' (XXX: 41). We are asked to 'travel through the earth and see what was the end of those who went before us' (XXX: 42). In other words we are to learn from history, for travelling may be in time as well as in space, and both the elements of time and of space are involved in the lessons which we learn from other people's examples. In this sense, also, the just Egyptian whom I have already mentioned was calling his people to Salvation. When the peace and mercy of God reach the soul through the purification of the will, the effect is perceptible (not necessarily visible) in this very life. And so in a sense the Salvation already begins to operate in this very life, though the danger of back-sliding remains on this plane of existence.

It is not only for our own salvation that we strive. As stated already, man was created in original purity and innocence, but sin has stained his nature. Sin is not only a stain but a disease (II: 10). As in a disease we lose proper control of the diseased limb, and its function becomes atrophied or even the opposite to that which it was naturally meant to be, so in sin our purity is lost, our motives become corrupted, and our perverted will goes progressively against the pure desires and instincts originally implanted in us. It is the duty of every good man to help in the cure of those suffering from spiritual disease. The best men are in the position of spiritual physicians. By their superior knowledge and experience they are able to cure others. But the humblest of us, if we once understand the nature of sin, can help others to a similar understanding, and thus can help in the effort to prevent a relapse. In this sense we can all bring salvation to our weaker brethren in a greater or less degree. Our effort for salvation, when we once reach a certain stage, regards not only ourselves but all others who come within the range of our influence.

The definite and final Salvation remains for the future world. What is that future world like? That it will certainly come, we are assured again and again. But how can we conceive of it in our present limitations? Our soul is encased in flesh, and our mind can only form material pictures. Our will is being constantly attacked by temptations. There is so much that is evanescent, ugly and false around us. There seems to be so much discord and injustice, pain and suffering, sorrow and disappointment. Man sometimes feels as if he were the Lord of all Creation, but with ever-increasing knowledge, he realises what an infinitesimal dot he is in the stupendous forces around him. He then feels as if he were a helpless, restless, homeless, friendless creature in a universe of infinite dimensions, of which he can barely grasp three! The riddle of the Universe oppresses him and he cries: 'Vanity of vanities! All is vanity!' and includes his own life in the indictment. These several weights are unevenly distributed over the spirit of different men. Some are conscious of one or two or a few of these. Some - a great number - have not even arrived at the stage where the immediate problems of the flesh can give place to the subtle problems of human Destiny. The function of Faith is to help in this awakening. How is it to do it? That process itself is a sort of *aura* of Salvation projected back from the Hereafter to this life.

Such an *aura* must necessarily take its texture or (if the word 'texture' is admissible in this connection) its lights and shades from our daily experiences in this life. Taking mankind as a whole, such experiences have infinite variety and infinite gradations. The most practical way is to take Symbols of universal suggestiveness and build around them ideas which, at least to some extent, reflect the variety and gradations of human longings and human emotions. The Islamic main Symbols in this connection are: *Jannah* (heaven), *Jahannam* (hell), and *Barzakh*. It is a facile step to think by analogy of similar threefold divisions of the Future World in other systems. For example, Dante's Paradiso, Inferno and Purgatorio occur to the mind at once, and the sources of Dante have been connected with Aquinas and (by Asin) with Arabic versions of the Muslim Vision of the Mi'raj. Virgil in his sixth Book of the Aeneid also divides the world after death into Elysium, Tartarus and a neutral region, vaguely and inconsistently suggesting, at the same time, the idea of the transmigration of souls, which he no doubt took from Pythagoras and which we know to be a cornerstone of Hindu conceptions on the subject. The Islamic symbols have a meaning and significance entirely different. Here we can only deal with their bearing on the idea of Salvation.

Whether the three Islamic Symbols are to be understood to represent a state or a place (and orthodoxy in all religions prefers local interpretations), it is clear that the *Barzakh* is not to be co-ordinated with Heaven and Hell. It is a partition, a bar or barrier; the place or state in which people – all human beings – will be after death and before Judgement. It really means the point at which, after the definite rejection of God's healing grace by the unrighteous, the gate of Salvation through repentance is closed. God has sent to mankind the Truth in many ways; but those who have delivered themselves to the bondage of evil live in Falsehood and practice Falsehood. They choose to remain in that state in spite of repeated and continuous warnings. Death opens their eyes. Perhaps then one of such souls desires to be sent back to this life, 'in order' (he may plead) 'that I may work righteousness in the things I neglected' (XXIII: 99-100). But that is not possible. Behind him is the partition or barrier of death, and before him is the partition or barrier of *Barzakh* until Judgement is pronounced. That does not mean there is any long interval of Time. For 'the Decision of the Hour of Judgement is as the twinkling of an eye, or even quicker' (XVI: 77).

What then is the idea of Salvation after Death? Judgement when it occurs is (as we have seen) instantaneous. But the history of man covers a long span of time. Is the Judgement of mankind as a whole simultaneous, or has each person at his death a Judgement or a stage of Judgement for his individual case? There are Qur'anic passages which indicate some kind of Judgement immediately at Death (e.g. LXXV: 26, or VII, 37). Our eschatology calls this the Lesser Judgement and it calls the final Resurrection and the general Judgement the Greater Judgement. But Time as we measure it on this earth has no meaning in the higher or spiritual world: for a Day there, is what may appear to us as 50,000 years as measured by our reckoning here (LXX:4). Therefore the Lesser and the Greater Judgement have significance only with reference to the individual as such and to mankind, and not with reference to Time at all. It will be for some a Day of Wrath, a Day of Terror; for others, a day of rejoicing, of satisfaction, for their 'faces will beam with brightness and beauty, looking towards their Lord' (LXXV: 22-23).

The Salvation, then, will consist not only in their being saved from terror and wrath, but in their being saved from the sight of the terror and wrath. The only refuge, the only place of safety will be in the Presence of God. But as the Righteous will have reached that Presence, they will not even be conscious of the Terror and the Wrath. But that is only the negative side of the question. The positive side is even more important. 'Before thy Lord alone that Day will be the place of rest' (LXXV: 12). They will have attained Life indeed.

In an abstract way we can say that Salvation is the attainment of complete Bliss. But this is explained and illustrated by a series of graded metaphors. The most general metaphor is that of the Garden (*Jannah*), and this word has in Muslim phraseology become practically synonymous with Heaven. But a garden itself suggests different ideas to different souls. Each one forms his own heaven. And so the Garden prepared for the Righteous covers everything that we can severally hold to be typical of good. This is typical in the metaphor that 'its width is that of the whole of the heavens and of the earth' (III: 133). Let us think of some of the many things that a Garden might suggest. To one whose experience has lain in forests inhabited by wild beasts, it suggests a refuge, a place of security, a place of rest. To one who has felt the barrenness and loneliness of a desert it suggests a smiling fruitful place, where all sorts of luscious fruit is available and ready to hand, and there is the companionship and fellowship of beings like ourselves, only glorified as we shall be glorified then. The Garden is associated with streams and rivers flowing, and will at once appeal to one whose longing is to get away from parched and thirsty lands. The Garden means to some minds order, plan and design, and how much the soul thirsts for these, which has experienced chaos, whimsical incongruities, wild unreliable outbreaks of nature or human instability!

Or to look at it in another way, our physical senses will be transformed with the transformation of our whole being. But if personality is to persist, the inner experiences that result from them must persist. And in any case we can only form images of the Future by our experiences of the Present. Our inner response to our sense-perceptions with regard to the Garden may fitly represent some of the highest spiritual truths. As I have written elsewhere (p.1466, Translation of the Qur'an), 'to each of our five senses, in their most refined form, does the Garden minister. For the eye there is the general green, with all the most delicate tints of green in the foliage, and the wonderful colours and shapes in the flowers; the arrangements of paths and parterres; the various gradations of light and shade; the sort of melting beauty of clouds and mists; and the landscape views with cool rivers flowing underneath, or perhaps murmuring brooks. For the ear is the music of birds, the music of waterfalls, and the appropriate moonlight music of the human voice with or without the accompaniment of an instrument like the guitar. For the smell there is not only the perfume of flowers but the more subtle scents of foliage, moisture or morning dew, or even garden soil. For taste and touch the exquisite fruits, and for touch the soft rose petals and the carpet-like lawns, besides the gentle kiss of breezes, all minister to the highest bliss and fulfillment that we can imagine through our senses.'

The social sense is even higher than the delights of our five senses. We can imagine a scene of banquets, full of grace, beauty and social pleasure. 'Reclining on thrones of dignity' (XXXVI: 56), the souls of the blessed share the sense of joy and happiness with associates and companions, among whom will be included those who were nearest and dearest to them on earth, subject only to the condition that these also lived righteous lives.

'And angels shall enter unto them from every gate with the salutation: Peace unto you, for that ye persevered in patience! Now how excellent is the final Home!' (XIII: 23-24). This idea of concord, peace, and the sweetness of Home, is the essential basis of Salvation.

If there is anything in human love and altruism, the idea of Home is enlarged and universalised. For there is not only self-salvation, but the achievement of a universal and beautiful Fellowship (IV: 69). There may be ranks and degrees, differences in tastes and capacities: the Prophets who taught and led mankind; the Devotees, who gave their all; the Martyrs and Witnesses, who suffered and served; and the generality of men and women who led ordinary lives, but with righteous aims. They will all form a united company, living perpetually in the sunshine of God's grace.

But the crown of symbolism goes higher still. Rewards and punishments are often mentioned, as being expressions, in words of ordinary speech, of the Goodness and Justice of God. But as God's grace and bounty transcend all bounds and transcend all our merits, the earthly standards of reward are hardly applicable. And as God's Justice is always tempered with Mercy and His forgiveness and wide-open door of repentance negates a cast-iron belief in *Karma*, the consequences of Sin can only be called Penalties in a very limited sense. Virtue is its own reward. The Qur'an says: 'Is there any reward for Good, other than Good?' (XI:101). There is neither salvation by faith alone nor by good works alone. But faith and good works should combine and the motive behind them should be to seek the 'Good Pleasure of God.' The metaphor used in many places is 'the Face of God.' This metaphor goes much deeper in its mystic meaning than 'the Good Pleasure of God'. It certainly means that. But the divine 'Face' is the divine Self, the divine Nature, the divine Personality. The Miltonic 'human face divine' expresses the idea that in 'Face' is summed up the essence of goodness, beauty, grace, power, and all the attributes which, in another Qur'anic phrase, are called 'the Beautiful Names of God'. Our motive for a good life should therefore be, not reward, not self-salvation, not anything relating to ourselves, but a longing towards something that is the quintessence of Reality, the 'Face' (or countenance) of God – the pure love for a sight of the divine Eyes (XCII:19-20).

The perishable part of us will perish, and is of only momentary consequence. But the 'Face of God' endures for ever (LV: 27). As He poured His spirit into us and we are from Him, it should be part of our nature that we should go back to Him. 'To God we belong, and to Him is our return' (II: 156). Separation from Him should be a cause of pain and restlessness to us. Our object should always be to return to Him. Only there is our rest and satisfaction; only there should be our pleasure. There, is the fulfillment of our nature; there is the achievement of our hope and desire. But as God loves us, it is also His Pleasure, and therefore the achievement of our good is the cause of mutual satisfaction. When we reach that stage of enlightenment and spiritual development, there is no question of Salvation or deliverance from any danger or pain or sorrow. Our heaven is our supreme achievement, the attainment of nearness to Him, or indeed being actually *in* His Presence. That is no longer *our* Heaven: it is God's own Heaven which we have entered.

All this is summed up in the following passage (LXXXIX: 27-30):

O thou soul!
In complete rest and satisfaction!
Come back thou
To thy Lord!
Well-pleased (thyself),
And well-pleasing
Unto Him!
Enter thou, then,
Among my Devotees,
Yea, enter thou
My Heaven!

Progressive Islam Pamphlet No. 14, published by Luzac & Co, 1939. Based on a paper read before the London Society for the Study of Religion, 1 November 1938.

1940

By 1940, Muslims in the sub-continent were reaching a point of no return on the issue of Partition. The Congress Party had not used its success at the 1937 elections, which gave it power in eight provinces, to seek a reconciliation with other Muslim groups. Yusuf Ali made a last-ditch attempt to propose a compromise, very similar to the one of Dr B.R. Ambedkar, leader of the 'Untouchables'. Yusuf Ali outlined his scheme at a meeting of the East India Association held in February at Caxton Hall, London. The speech shows that even for a Muslim with a most enduring faith in Hindu-Muslim cooperation, the attitude of the Congress had become intolerable. A month later, in March, Jinnah addressed the annual session of the Muslim League in Lahore, declaring that the only course open to Muslims was the division of India into autonomous national states.

Apart from local village attacks on Muslim susceptibilities, Congress policy itself often gives rise to difficulties for Muslims in many ways. The shouting of *Bande Mataram* as a national greeting is obnoxious to them because of its idolatrous associations in Bankim Chunder Chatterji's Bengali novel. Muslim endowments are often treated without understanding sympathy where a Congress Government comes into administrative contact with them or where some general legislation seems to affect them adversely. Many of these endowments are partly religious and partly educational. The educational part is often treated with scant courtesy in the matter of grants-in-aid, etc. The recent Shia-Sunni riots in Lucknow are attributed in some Muslim quarters to a clumsy if not provocative handling on the part of the Congress Government in power, which is supposed to incite mutual animosities among the Muslims themselves in order to intervene as arbitrators.

I have referred to educational activities in connection with endowments. Muslim educational grievances are also of a general character. Textbooks are often prescribed in State schools or institutions which are of a character repugnant to Muslim feeling if not actually hostile to Muslim traditions. The location of schools and colleges, and the appointments, promotions and transfers of educational staffs are often made in a manner prejudicial to Muslim interests. The grants-in aid question comes in here

287

also. The Muslims would also like better representation in the educational services.

This point is emphasized by Dr. Waheed in his recently published monograph on *The Evolution of Muslim Education*. He says:

This need for adequate Muslim representation is as important in the educational as in the political world, and it is obviously no mere question of Muslims seeking to obtain a share of the educational loaves and fishes. What Muslims want is to be free at once to make their own contribution to safeguard their own cultural and educational interests. They have a right to insist on being in a position to make this contribution. As a result of their exclusion from this position in the past, the education of India has been standardised on wrong lines so that the stream of education is running in one definite direction, and thousands of young men brought up on this system find themselves unable to fight the battle of life. The attitude of the State should be to foster rather than discourage communal education and to preserve the cultural development of each community.

....At the Round Table Conferences, the British Prime Minister had to make a Communal Award, and a compromise Constitution was adopted, representing the greatest common measure of agreement among the parties. But that Constitution satisfies no one, and for the time being the impasse seems to be complete. There seems to be no outlet of escape. The gulf seems to be unbridgeable.

Unity and Co-operation

But is it unbridgeable? It must be bridged. It is in the interest of the Muslims that it should be bridged. They are not going to remain always in the position of a discontented, impotent, and hopeless minority. Their talent, their past experience, their fitness for survival in many different kinds of environment - physical, moral, and spiritual - require that they should examine their own position and come to some understanding with the forces of unity, which, after all, are the only ones having a survival value. In the field of politics the counting of heads determines the vote value of

288

groups of people. But there are combinations and adjustments possible, by which all intelligent minorities can pull their weight in composite communities.

Mechanical devices can help for a time, but can offer no permanent solutions. Communal electorates have been necessary and useful. But as a permanent wheel in the machinery of politics they will not enable the Muslims to impress their personality and contribute their reasonable share in the development of their country. Schemes of division into mutually exclusive zones – such as those propounded by Sayyid Abdul Latif in *The Muslim Problem in India* – may have some attractive features, but they imply almost impossible exchanges of populations and the abandonment of ground already won instead of moral and political expansion.

The way to unity and co-operation lies in other directions...there is a permanent and radical solution of the minority problem which I should like to present for your consideration. There is no need to accept the dictum that it is the fate of a minority to suffer. All constitutions are made in order to safeguard various interests, and in the complicated business of modern government, the chief test of good government is how far this requirement has been met. Democracy itself is on trial from this point of view. Where it works successfully it does so because people have found by long experience that give-and-take is of the essence of co-operation for common ends, and a citizen's life is a constant round of give-and-take. Even under majority rule the general consent of the whole population must be assumed for smooth working. The minority as well as the majority has to obey the law for the time being; only, the minority hopes some day to become the majority and to make the law more conformable with its views. Not that there should be constant friction, each party changing the law every time it comes to power. That would mean instability and perpetual want of confidence - ultimately confusion and chaos. Each party contributes something of its point of view until an equilibrium is reached, under which all sensible people accept the inevitable while not relinquishing their eternal and inalienable right to grumble.

The Two-Party System

But such an equilibrium can only be reached where there is a two-party system in which individuals can and do change over from one party to another at different times. This is impossible as between Hindus and Muslims as such. But it is not impossible as between the Congress Party as such and a coalition of groups opposed to the Congress. The largest and most important group in such a coalition will be the Muslims, but it is quite possible that some Muslims like Mr Abul Kalam Azad might throw in their political lot with Congress. It is also possible that the various local or social groups – such as Khaksars and Ahrars, or sections of the Jamiat-ul-Ulama, and some groups in the Frontier Province and in Sind – may, in politics, follow their own bents, though in social or religious matters they would be strong supports of unity among the Muslims. On the other hand, among the Hindus, taking the word in its widest generic sense, there are groups that are opposed to the Congress. The most important of such groups, numerically, is that of the Scheduled Castes, who may number anything up to 70 or 80 millions. They are not closely organised, and some of them would undoubtedly be under Congress inffiuence. But the majority could be got into a new and composite political party. Another group, not numerically small but containing men of the highest standing and education, is that of the Liberal Federation. And then there are Congress men who belong to extreme sections at either end. The extreme Socialists (or Communists) think that the Congress is too bourgeois, too much in the hands of the propertied classes. As parties come to power and their labels receive precise definition, this section must part company with the Congress. In Indian conditions it can best work with revolutionary or anarchical groups, which have fortunately no strength among the people that actually count. But the conservative elements in Congress ranks will, when their allegiance is subjected to a practical test, find themselves more at home with the Liberals than with Congressites of the school of Mr Subhas Bose.

Other lines of cleavage which sometimes make a sort of timid appearance in Provincial Legislatures are: Town versus Country, or Agriculturists versus Non-agriculturists, or Capital versus Labour. These lines of cleavage can also be utilised in forming composite parties.

A Composite Party

The upshot of this analysis is that there are many incipient lines of cleavage in Indian politics which can be appealed to for the formation of true political parties, as opposed to purely religious or communal groups. And I look to the Muslims - with their past history, their political experience, and their present insecure position - to take the lead in evolving a composite party which will safeguard legitimate interests and be available - when the need arises - for forming an alternative government. The task is not easy, and may appear impossible to minds wedded to intransigent traditions. But is must be attempted. Each Province will have to deal elastically with it according to its own local conditions. In the Punjab Legislature, for instance, the Sikhs form an element to be considered, and among them, again, the Akalis have a point of view different from their other Sikh brethren. The point would be to examine the purely political issues that arise out of these differences, and attempt a classification and a regrouping that will enable small minorities to pull their weight as political units in large parties rather than fritter away their strength in isolation, which may lead to political extinction.

The formation of federations of parties, each federation being of sufficient cohesion to be a possible alternative government with a definite programme, is the only way that I can see of solving the minority problem in India. Without it there can be no modern constitution, no democratic assemblies, no progressive legislation, no really effective road to self-government. If even the first steps in that direction can be achieved, we can see our way clear to effective provincial autonomy. The way to federal autonomy will be far steeper, and we may have to shed the feature about linking the Indian States with British India in the Central Legislature and Executive before we can envisage smooth working on modern and demo-cratic lines. But that is a large and thorny question that is best left alone at the present stage. The Muslims will have contributed a most vital feature to the working of the Constitution if they help India out of the impasse of fixed communal parties and perpetual impotent minorities.

Paper read before a meeting of the East India Association at the Caxton Hall, Westminster, on 6th February, 1940. Published as 'The Muslims of India, the War, and the Political Field' in 'The Asiatic Review', Vol. 36, 1940, pp. 226-250.

1941

> Lord Meston, a leading member of the Royal Institute of International Affairs, commissioned the compilation of *Modern India and the West* to which Yusuf Ali contributed a chapter. This extract includes his assessment of Iqbal and observations on the changes in Indian Muslim society. It highlights the similarities and differences between Yusuf Ali and Iqbal in the way they responded to the West.

The Punjab literary movement claims Sir Muhammad Iqbal (1876-1938) as its best-known international figure. In the early days of his career he was connected with Punjab education, and his European education, in England and Germany, makes him representative in many ways of the interaction of eastern and western civilizations. His activities were many-sided. He took some interest in current politics, having presided over the All-India Muslim League at Allahabad in 1930 and served a term in the old Legislative Council of the Punjab. But provincial politics afforded too narrow a field for him, and in all-India politics he was more of a philosopher than a practical statesman. His genius lay in the direction of developing a mystical interpretation of Islam as the final form both for the development of human personality and for the working out of a great and eternal State coextensive with the whole of humanity. In the only book which he wrote in English, his chapters on the 'Spirit of Muslim Culture' and on the 'Principle of Movement in the Structure of Islam' have a direct bearing on the subjects we are discussing. While he welcomes the reform in Turkey as 'creating new values' instead of 'mechanically repeating old values', his attitude to reform generally is expressed as follows:

> We heartily welcome the liberal movement in modern Islam; but it must also be admitted that the appearance of liberal ideas in Islam constitutes also the most critical moment in the history of Islam. Liberalism has a tendency to act as a force of disintegration, and the

race-idea, which appears to be working in modern Islam with greater force than ever, may ultimately wipe off the broad human outlook which Muslim people have imbibed from their religion. Further, our religious and political reformers in their zeal for liberalism may overstep the proper limits of reform in the absence of a check on their youthful fervour.[1]

He wholly approves of the spirit of the second *Khalifa* Umar, 'the first critical and independent mind in Islam, who at the last moments of the Prophet had the moral courage to utter these remarkable words:"The Book of God is sufficient for us"'.[2] This implies that Iqbal would prefer an independent and progressive interpretation of the Qur'an itself to the many glosses put upon it by medieval commentators. It does not imply that he would go to the lessons of European experience except as a warning. For to him European civilisation was bad, fraudulent, chaotic, unjust, and greedy. For comments on European civilisation, he would go to such writers as Schopenhauer, Nietzsche, Spengler, or Karl Marx, who take a pessimistic view of it. He looks upon political and economic stability, peace, and justice as essential elements in religions, but he thinks that Europe has deserted them. His criticism of European civilisation is expressed in many scathing lines and passages in his poetry, both Persian and Urdu. The following two couplets will suffice as a specimen:

The glitter of modern civilization dazzles the sight;
But is only a clever piecing together of false gems.

The wisdom or science in which the wise ones of the West took such pride
Is but a warring sword in the bloody hand of greed and ambition.[3]

The boasted power of the West [for Iqbal] is nothing but imperialism to oppress the weak, and the League of Nations is a mere society of robbers to parcel out the graves of those they have killed. The western freedom of women is not real freedom. The unwomanly virgin in the planet Mars in the *Jawid-nama* is an importation from Europe. Woman's true sphere is in a secluded life of love and family. Modern civilization is a godless civilization and can lead to nothing but self-destruction.

Though Iqbal's literary genius and his philosophic interpretation of Islam brought him his immense popularity, he was yet an isolated figure. He founded no school of literary thought, as his principal works were written not in Urdu but in Persian. In public affairs, and in building up the 'new temple' (*naya shiwala*, to use his own words), his influence was negligible. To the conservatives he appeared as a man speaking a new language, and he trod on some of their cherished convictions. To the advanced school with a nationalistic tinge, his attacks on the West seemed to furnish an argument for their patriotism. But in other matters they remained cold...

The irresistible force of example, opportunity, and environment in bringing in western influences is seen every day in such matters as houses, dress, furniture, sports, subjects of conversation, and modes of entertainment. The old-fashioned *haveli* (mansion) with its separate quarters for men and women (*mardana* and *zanana*) is fast becoming *demode*. Even in the houses of the old design there is usually now a room or rooms where guests sit at chairs and tables, and smoke cigars and cigarettes, instead of reclining on carpets on the ground, supported by thick cushions, with a *hookah* (hubble-bubble) to smoke or a *pan-dan* on which to serve betel leaves and betel nut. The modern young Muslim considers a turban a bore and affects a *fez* (or Turkish cap so-called), or, if he is sufficiently advanced, a European hat out of doors and a bare head indoors. It is difficult to get tailors now who can cut and make old-fashioned dresses for men. Women, it is true still adhere to *saris*, but they wear beautiful brooches of western make to keep them in position, and they wear underclothing of western style, though in this matter western fashions are also somewhat approximating to eastern. No one sees a *palki* or *duli* (dooly) in cities nowadays; the motor-car is the rage for those who can afford it, and the plebeian motor buses and lorries crowd urban thoroughfares.

The schools and colleges, though they still support some of the eastern games, are keenest about cricket, football, hockey and tennis. The general run of talk is picked up from newspapers, and the old bazaar gossip is turned into the new journalistic sensationalism. The theatre itself was remoulded a century ago on western models. It has now given place to the cinema. In any large city there are ten or twenty vernacular picture houses, with 'sound' films; and quite a number of people, innocent of English, go to English picture-houses, 'to see English manners and morals'. The wireless, helped and encouraged by official agency, has established a secure position in India. In the towns most well-to-do homes and educational institutions now have wireless sets, and there are community or public receiving sets in the villages. It is true the items which most interest the community are those which relate to their own familiar interests. But the broadcasting stations provide catholic programmes (of music, lectures, speeches etc.) to serve both eastern and western tastes; quite often eastern ears listen to western programmes, and western ears to eastern, and quite a good few sample both impartially. If again you visit a modern Indian fine arts exhibition, you will find that the eastern pictures and exhibits are a mannerism, and the normal exhibits are western in tone, method and subjects.

On the other hand, movements of reaction against western influences are not absent, though they are sporadic and, owing to the logic of facts, not very effective. Journals like *Al-Irshad*, a monthly issued from Amritsar, avowedly aim at waging war against 'westernism' (*maghrabiyat*) among other things. Probably the other aims of such publications have a more direct appeal than the war against westernism, but in any case neither their circulation nor their influuence is to be compared with the force of the rising tide of westernism that is flowing into men's minds and habits, consciously or unconsciously. The periodical meetings at which westernism is denounced from pulpit or platform are attended by way of religious or communal duty, but the very people who do lip service to such propaganda are often found among the foremost of those in the other camp. The literature of anti-westernism is divorced from the actualities of modern life. Perhaps its most caustic verse-exponent is Sayyid Akbar Husain, whose *nom de plume* was Akbar. He attacked modernism from many points of view. Of the 'Young Party's' social reform he said that 'the remedy was worse than the disease'. Their politics he compared to 'an owl teaching the hawk to be a nightingale'. Laughing at science and materialism, he says:

'The days are past when they searched for the light of God in their hearts; now they test what phosphorus there is in the bones.' Modern progress he thinks evil: 'the devil invented a new way to bring down men; he said, "Let us give them a taste for Progress".' Elsewhere he says: 'Not through books or colleges is religion to be attained, but only through those venerable (in faith).'

The old issues debated by Maulvi Chirag Ali, such as *jihad*, slavery, captives of war, the position of Muslims in a non-Muslim State, and of non-Muslims in a Muslim State, and the controversies about the precise meanings to be attached to texts, are now matters of historical or academic interest, discussed by the learned, rather than matters of present concern. Attention is now focused on the practical issues of social and economic problems, e.g. how far exorbitant dowers are permissible in marriage; how far usury (which is forbidden) is to be distinguished from economic interest, which is in the nature of a share in profits; how far *purdah* tends to injure the health of women, to affect mothers in the upbringing of their children, or in the management of their household, and to prejudice the evolution of the larger interests of society; and how far plural marriages, which on principle are condemned, can be prohibited, as they are in Turkey. In all these matters, the actual trend of events is more important than theory or argument, and the trend has decidedly set, in circles that count, in the direction of the usages of the West.

Notes

1. *Six Lectures on the Reconstruction of Religious Thought* (Lahore, 1930), p.227.
2. ibid. p.226.
3. *Nazar ko khira karti hai chamak tahzib hazir ki.*
   Yih sanna'i magar jhute nagon ki reza-kari hai.
   Wuh hikmat naz tha jis par khiradmandan i Maghrib ko.
   Hawas ki panja i khunin men teg i karzari hai.

Extract from 'Muslim Culture and Religious Thought' In: L.S.S.O'Malley (ed.) 'Modern India and the West', Oxford University Press, 1941, pp. 398-414.

1942

During the Second World War, as in the First World War, Yusuf Ali was engaged in propaganda work on behalf of Britain. He wrote numerous short articles for the Ministry of Information and travelled around Britain giving talks on India's support for the war effort. He was now sixty-nine years old. The piece below was entitled 'Oppression in Muslim Countries'.

Nazi allegations refer to 'oppression in Muslim countries'. A sufficient refutation of them is furnished by the actual facts. Nowhere are Nazi oppressions held in more horror than in Muslim countries. Nowhere are Nazi allegations about their 'New Order' appraised at their true value better than in Muslim countries. The whole Nazi doctrine is based on false assumptions and an arrogant claim to race superiority. No scientific ethnological doctrine believes now in the theory of an 'Aryan race'. There are Aryan languages but no Aryan races. The peoples speaking Aryan languages are very mixed races. That great investigator in linguistic studies, Sir George Grierson, came to the conclusion that the English (and by inference the Germans) have no right to call themselves Aryans.

A people rises to power and authority by its character and the work it does in the world. Judged by this standard the English people have no cause to be ashamed of themselves. They have acquired their enormous influence in the world by the law and order they have established wherever they have gone, and by the new horizons of political freedom which they have opened out for peoples in many parts of the world. In the eighteenth century, it is true, many things were done by conquering nations which fell below modern standards. But at the present day public and private conduct and standards are wholly different. We are speaking now of Muslim countries particularly. In Aden the word of an Englishman is taken as his bond. In the bazaars of the East, where the word of a foreigner is generally mistrusted, the word of an Englishman is accepted readily, and his intervention has helped to smooth over many difficulties. The British General Headquarters are in Egypt, from which are controlled the forces in the Western Desert in North Africa as well as those in Syria and Palestine. Both the Italians and the Germans are thoroughly unpopular in North Africa. In Abyssinia the Italians are hated for their large-scale brigandage. The bombing of the seaport of Haifa and the burning of its oil stores by Germany on October 9th is not likely to make the Germans popular in that part of the world. When the effective occupation of Syria by France came to an end through the fall of France and her surrender to Germany, British forces were welcomed there. In 1940 an Arab legion in Syria led by Major John Bagot Glubb, RE, DSO, defeated the Vichy French. In Iraq the dramatic coup attempted by Rashid Ali at the instigation of the Nazis came to an ignominious end, and the people were glad to form a new Government under General Nuri es Said, who established law and order with the goodwill of the British. Turkey, which has consistently guarded her neutrality during this War, is on excellent terms both with the British and the Germans. If any pressure has been put upon her, it has been on the side of Germany, especially in the matter of the supply of chrome.

In Iran the corridor which has been opened from north to south makes it possible for communications to pass from the Indian Ocean to the Caspian Sea and thus on to Russia, and in this way the British Empire is brought into contact with its great ally, Russia. Iran itself has been subject to many disturbances, but the aim of the allies is to help her to regain her feet, and to work out her own life as an independent country. It is to save Iran from oppression that the whole of the efforts of the Allies are directed. Iran on the east touches Afghanistan, and thus what happens in Iran is of great interest to India.

In India itself, the north-west portion, including Punjab and Sind, is predominantly Muslim, but throughout India the cause of the Allies is considered the cause of liberty, and the Muslims particularly are zealous in helping it. This does not look like a protest against oppression, unless it be considered a protest against Nazi oppression in the countries occupied by the Nazis. Sir Sikandar Hayat Khan, Premier of the Punjab, has distinctly stated that the British policy in the Middle East is in the interests of the Muslim States and the Muslims of India. Khwaja Sir Nazimuddin, the Home Minister in Bengal, said in a speech in Calcutta on the 21st October, 1941: 'It is no longer a question of assisting Great Britain; it is in the interest of India's own defence... that we should give support to the War.'

And India is giving support to the War with enthusiastic help in every way. She is carrying out a big ship-building programme; a mine sweeper was launched at Howrah for the Indian Navy towards the end of October, 1941. It was wholly built in India with India labour. India is a large producer of iron and steel, and these essential metals are being thrown into the Allied cause. It may be possible, also, to build up machinery in India, for modern Wars are mainly mechanical. The dockyards in Calcutta and Bombay are busy with all kinds of repair work. In flying, India has made some progress in recent years. There is an energetic Indian Air Force. Then quite recently the Province of Bombay has presented a squadron of twenty machines to that Force, as its contribution to the War effort. Thus India considers the Allied cause as the cause of freedom and progress, and is helping it, in order to defeat the Nazi dreams of expansion and subjection of both east and west."

From the Yusuf Ali Collection

References

Primary Sources

Register of the Proceedings of the General Council of the *Anjuman-Himayat-ul-Islam*, Lahore

Volumes for periods 3/10/1926-22/12/1928, 1/7/1934-28/4/1937

India Office Library and Records, London
  Departmental records
    L/E (Economic)
    L/I (Information)
    L/MIL (Military)
    L/P&J (Public and Judicial)
    L/P&S (Political and Secret)

  Other records
    V/12 (Histories of Services)
    Private Collections:
    MSS Eur F136 Meston Collection
    MSS Eur D523 Montagu Collection
    MSS Eur F197 Younghusband Collection

  Public Record Office
  Foreign Office files
    FO371
    FO372
    FO395

  General Register Office
    Register of Births, Marriages and Deaths
    Probate and Divorce Records.

Yusuf Ali Collection

Yusuf Ali's collection of newspaper cuttings, pamphlets, letters, poems and other papers were retrieved by the author from debris in the library room of Regent's Lodge, London, the old building of the Islamic Cultural Centre. Numerous old books and files were discarded in the evacuation in 1974, when the site was being cleared for the construction of the new mosque. The author was fortunate to spot the scrapbook after one of the last meetings of the London Islamic Circle, which used to be held in the library.

Each entry in the scrapbook was uniquely numbered by Yusuf Ali, and this scheme has been retained in the Notes. The newspaper cuttings are mainly drawn from Lahore's *Civil & Military Gazette* and *Eastern Times*, though there are also extracts from the Urdu press of the sub-continent, as well as British provincial newspapers and *The Times* of London. The scrapbook was meticulously compiled, with a handwritten index in pencil in the front, with 385 numbered entries, for the period 1936-1943. The last entry present in the scrapbook as found by the author was numbered 368, which, according to the index, would make it the penultimate entry for 1941. The missing entries 369-385 are presumably lost, though there are two unindexed entries: a typewritten article with handwritten corrections dated 1942 and a cutting from the October 1944 issue of *Religions*.

The handwriting in the scrapbook is Yusuf Ali's own, indicating that it was very much a personal possession, though the circumstances as to how it came to be lodged in the library are not known. His friendship with Dr Hasan Abdel Kader, director of the Islamic Cultural Centre from 1949-1954, is on record (*Islamic Literature*, Vol.VI, No.1, January 1954, Lahore). Whatever its antecedents, the scrapbook is an invaluable source of biographical material on Yusuf Ali.

Punjab Press Abstract Vol. XXXIX, 1926.

Report on Newspapers and Periodicals in the Punjab, compiled by the Press Branch, Punjab Civil Secretariat. Copy held at the Quaid-e-Azam Library, Bagh-i-Jinnah, Lahore.

Newspapers and journals

Newspaper Library, Colindale.

The Times of London (its indexes have entries for Yusuf Ali under both 'Ali' and 'Yusuf Ali' for the period 1907-1953).

The Bournemouth Observer (1900).

Secondary Sources

Urdu

Muhammad Rafiq Afzal, *Guftar-i-Iqbal*, Lahore: Idara-e-Tahqiq, 1969.

Maftoon Ahmed, *Maulana Shibli Numani - aik mutala*, Karachi: Maktab Usloob, 1986.

Mian Amiruddin, *Yad-i-Ayyam*, Lahore: Kutub Khana Anjuman Himayat-e-Islam, 1983.

Ashiq Husain Batalvi, *Iqbal kay akhri do saal*, Lahore: Sang-e-Meel Publications, 1989.

M.A.Chughtai, *Iqbal kay suhbat mai*, Lahore: Majlis-i-Taraqi-i-Adab, 1977.

S.A. Durrani, *Iqbal Europe mai*, Lahore: Iqbal Academy, 1985.

M.H. Faruqi, *Hayat-i-Iqbal kay chand makhfi goshay*, Lahore: Idara-i-Tahqiqat, 1988.

Baidar Malik, *Yaran-i-Maktab: Tehrik-i-Pakistan aur Islamia College*, Lahore, Lahore: Pakistan Studies Centre, Punjab University, 1986.

Abdussalaam Khurshid, *Way Suratain Ilahi*, Lahore: Qaumi Kutb Khana, 1976.

Nuqush - Makateeb Number, Vol.2, Lahore, 1968.

Qamoos al-mashahir, Vol.2; Compiled by Nizami Badayuni, Badayun,(India):Nizami Press, 1926.

Abul-Laith Siddiqui, *Malfuzat-i-Iqbal*, Lahore: Iqbal Academy, 1977.

Abdul Raoof Urooj, *Rijal-i-Iqbal*, Karachi: Nafees Academy, 1988.

Ghulam Husain Zulfikar, *Tarikh-i-Jam'a-i-Punjab*, Lahore: Punjab University, 1976.

English

Waheed Ahmad, (ed.), *Letters of Mian Fazli-i-Husain*, Lahore: Research Society of Pakistan, 1976.

K.K. Aziz,

   Britain & Muslim India, London: Heinemann, 1963.

   The Indian Khilafat Movement 1915-1933, Karachi: Pak Publishers, 1972.

   The All-India Muslim Conference 1928-1935 - A documentary record, Karachi: National Publishing House, 1972.

   Complete works of Rahmat Ali, Islamabad: National Commission on Historical and Cultural Research, 1978.

   A History of the Idea of Pakistan, Lahore: Vanguard Books, Pakistan, 1987.

Vernon Bartlett, *Behind the Scenes at the Peace Conference*, London: George Allen & Unwin, 1919.

Mihir Bose, *The Aga Khans*, Tadworth, Surrey: World's Work Ltd.,1984.

J.F.Bruce, *A History of the University of the Punjab*, Lahore, 1937.

Peter Clark, *Marmaduke Pickthall, British Muslim*, London: Quartet Books, 1986.

Malcolm Darling, *Apprentice to Power 1904-8*, London: Hogarth Press, 1966.

C. Dobbin, *Urban Leadership in Western India*, Oxford University Press, 1972.

Frances Donaldson, *The Marconi Scandal*, London: Rupert Hart Davis, 1962.

S.R.Dongerkerry, *A History of the University of Bombay 1857-1957*, Bombay: University of Bombay, 1957.

Asghar Ali Engineer, *The Bohras*, New Delhi: Vikas Publishing House, 1980.

M.K. Gandhi, *Gandhi - An Autobiography*, London:Phoenix Press, 1949.

Rajmohan Gandhi, *Eight Lives*, Albany, New York: State University of New York Press, 1986.

G.F.I. Graham, *The Life and Work of Sir Sayyid Ahmed Khan*, London: Hodder & Stoughton, 1909.

Gail Minault, *The Khilafat Movement*, New Delhi:Columbia University Press, 1982.

Harold Nicolson, *King George V*, London: Constable, 1952.

A. C. Niemeijer, *The Khilafat Movement in India 1919-1924*, The Hague: Martinus Nijhoff, 1972.

Pakistan Historical Society, *Mohamed Ali: Life and Work*, Karachi, 1978.

B.N. Pandey, *The Indian Nationalist Movement 1885-1947, Select Documents*, London: Macmillan, 1979.

C.H. Philips,

> *Historians of India, Pakistan and Ceylon*, Oxford University Press, 1961.

> *Select Documents on the History of India & Pakistan*, (ed.), Vol. IV, The Evolution of India & Pakistan 1858-1947, London: Oxford University Press, 1962.

S.S. Pirzada (ed.), *The Collected Works of Quaid-i-Azam Mohammad Ali Jinnah*, Vol.1, 1906-1921, Karachi: East & West Publishing House, 1984.

M.Naeem Qureshi, *Mohamed Ali's Khilafat Delegation to Europe*, Karachi:Pakistan Historical Society Publication No.71, 1981.

Marquess of Reading, *Rufus Isaacs 1914-1935*, London: Hutchinson & Co., 1945.

Sayyid Athar Abbas Rizvi, *A Socio-Intellectual History of the Isna 'Ashari Shi'is in India*, Vol. II, Delhi: Munshiram Manoharlal Publishers, 1986.

P.G. Robb, *The Government of India and Reform*, Oxford University Press, 1976.

M.H.Sayyid, *Mohammad Ali Jinnah – A political study*, Karachi: Elite Publishers, 1962.

Ronald Storrs, *Orientations*, London: Nicholson & Watson, 1945.

A.L. Tibawi, *Arabic and Islamic Themes*, London:Luzac & Co., 1976.

Husain B. Tayabji, *Badruddin Tayabji: a biography*, Bombay: Thacker & Co., 1952.

D.C. Verma, *Sir Chhotu Ram – Life and Times*, Delhi: Sterling Publications, 1981.

Sayyid Razi Wasti, (ed.), *Memoirs and other writings of Sayyid Ameer Ali*, Lahore: People's Publishing House, 1968.

Wilson College, *Thoughts on Indian Education*, Bombay, 1961.

Stanley Wolpert, *Jinnah of Pakistan*, Oxford University Press, 1984.

Zubaida Yazdani, *The Seventh Nizam: The Fallen Empire*, Cambridge University Press, 1985.

Sir Francis Younghusband,

Dawn in India, London: John Murray, London, 1930.

A Venture of Faith, London: Michael Joseph Ltd., 1937.

A.M. Zaidi, *Evolution of Muslim Political thought in India*, Vol.1, Delhi: Indian Institute of Applied Political Research, 1975.

Philip Ziegler, *King Edward VIII*, London:Fontana, 1991.

Index

307